COMPETITION IN THE PROMISED LAND

Robert A. Margo
Wages and Labor Markets in the United States, 1820–1860 (University of Chicago Press, 2000)

Price V. Fishback and Shawn Everett Kantor
A Prelude to the Welfare State: The Origins of Workers' Compensation (University of Chicago Press, 2000)

Gerardo della Paolera and Alan M. Taylor
Straining at the Anchor: The Argentine Currency Board and the Search for Macroeconomic Stability, 1880–1935 (University of Chicago Press, 2001)

Werner Troesken
Water, Race, and Disease (MIT Press, 2004)

B. Zorina Khan
The Democratization of Invention: Patents and Copyrights in American Economic Development, 1790–1920 (Cambridge University Press, 2005)

Dora L. Costa and Matthew E. Kahn
Heroes and Cowards: The Social Face of War (Princeton University Press, 2008)

Roderick Floud, Robert W. Fogel, Bernard Harris, and Sok Chul Hong
The Changing Body: Health, Nutrition, and Human Development in the Western World since 1700 (Cambridge University Press, 2011)

Stanley L. Engerman and Kenneth L. Sokoloff
Economic Development in the Americas since 1500: Endowments and Institutions (Cambridge University Press, 2012)

Robert William Fogel, Enid M. Fogel, Mark Guglielmo, and Nathaniel Grotte
Political Arithmetic: Simon Kuznets and the Empirical Tradition in Economics (University of Chicago Press, 2013)

Price Fishback, Jonathan Rose, and Kenneth Snowden
Well Worth Saving: How the New Deal Safeguarded Home Ownership (University of Chicago Press, 2013)

Howard Bodenhorn
The Color Factor: The Economics of African-American Well-Being in the Nineteenth-Century South (Oxford University Press, 2015)

Leah Platt Boustan
Competition in the Promised Land: Black Migrants in Northern Cities and Labor Markets
(Princeton University Press, 2017)

COMPETITION IN THE PROMISED LAND

BLACK MIGRANTS IN NORTHERN CITIES
AND LABOR MARKETS

Leah Platt Boustan

PRINCETON UNIVERSITY PRESS
PRINCETON AND OXFORD

First paperback printing, 2020

Paperback ISBN 978-0-691-20249-5

The Library of Congress has cataloged the cloth edition as follows:

Names: Boustan, Leah Platt, author.
Title: Competition in the Promised Land : black migrants in northern cities and
labor markets / Leah Platt Boustan.
Description: Princeton, New Jersey : Princeton University Press, 2016. |
Series: NBER series on long-term factors in economic development |
Includes bibliographical references and index.
Identifiers: LCCN 2016013428 | ISBN 9780691150871 (hardback)
Subjects: LCSH: African Americans—Migrations—History—20th century.
| Migration, Internal—United States—History—20th century. | Rural-urban
migration—United States—History—20th century. | African Americans—
Economic conditions—20th century. | African Americans—Social
conditions—20th century. | BISAC: BUSINESS & ECONOMICS / Economic
History. | BUSINESS & ECONOMICS / Labor. | BUSINESS & ECONOMICS /
Development / General. | HISTORY / United States / 20th Century. | HISTORY /
Social History.
Classification: LCC E185.6 .B77 2016 | DDC 305.896/073—dc23 LC record
available at https://lccn.loc.gov/2016013428

British Library Cataloging-in-Publication Data is available

This book has been composed in Palatino LT Std

RELATION OF THE DIRECTORS TO THE WORK
AND PUBLICATIONS OF THE NBER

1. The object of the NBER is to ascertain and present to the economics profession, and to the public more generally, important economic facts and their interpretation in a scientific manner without policy recommendations. The Board of Directors is charged with the responsibility of ensuring that the work of the NBER is carried on in strict conformity with this object.

2. The President shall establish an internal review process to ensure that book manuscripts proposed for publication DO NOT contain policy recommendations. This shall apply both to the proceedings of conferences and to manuscripts by a single author or by one or more co-authors but shall not apply to authors of comments at NBER conferences who are not NBER affiliates.

3. No book manuscript reporting research shall be published by the NBER until the President has sent to each member of the Board a notice that a manuscript is recommended for publication and that in the President's opinion it is suitable for publication in accordance with the above principles of the NBER. Such notification will include a table of contents and an abstract or summary of the manuscript's content, a list of contributors if applicable, and a response form for use by Directors who desire a copy of the manuscript for review. Each manuscript shall contain a summary drawing attention to the nature and treatment of the problem studied and the main conclusions reached.

4. No volume shall be published until forty-five days have elapsed from the above notification of intention to publish it. During this period a copy shall be sent to any Director requesting it, and if any Director objects to publication on the grounds that the manuscript contains policy recommendations, the objection will be presented to the author(s) or editor(s). In case of dispute, all members of the Board shall be notified, and the President shall appoint an ad hoc committee of the Board to decide the matter; thirty days additional shall be granted for this purpose.

5. The President shall present annually to the Board a report describing the internal manuscript review process, any objections made by Directors before publication or by anyone after publication, any disputes about such matters, and how they were handled.

6. Publications of the NBER issued for informational purposes concerning the work of the Bureau, or issued to inform the public of the activities at the Bureau, including but not limited to the NBER Digest and Reporter, shall be consistent with the object stated in paragraph 1. They shall contain a specific disclaimer noting that they have not passed through the review procedures required in this resolution. The Executive Committee of the Board is charged with the review of all such publications from time to time.

7. NBER working papers and manuscripts distributed on the Bureau's web site are not deemed to be publications for the purpose of this resolution, but they shall be consistent with the object stated in paragraph 1. Working papers shall contain a specific disclaimer noting that they have not passed through the review procedures required in this resolution. The NBER's web site shall contain a similar disclaimer. The President shall establish an internal review process to ensure that the working papers and the web site do not contain policy recommendations, and shall report annually to the Board on this process and any concerns raised in connection with it.

8. Unless otherwise determined by the Board or exempted by the terms of paragraphs 6 and 7, a copy of this resolution shall be printed in each NBER publication as described in paragraph 2 above.

Contents

Acknowledgments

THE RESEARCH UNDERLYING this book emerges from my commitment to documenting and interpreting the past as a guide to understanding contemporary social problems. For this view, I am indebted to Claudia Goldin, Lawrence Katz, and Robert Margo, who taught me that economic historians must be careful detectives, seeking out new data sources in unlikely places. Their sleuthing continues to be my main inspiration.

I completed this book while on the faculty of the Economics Department at the University of California, Los Angeles. Among my many excellent colleagues at UCLA, I particularly thank Dora Costa for her steady encouragement to craft my research on black migration into a book. I also appreciate feedback and advice from Sandra Black, Moshe Buchinsky, Walker Hanlon, Naomi Lamoreaux, and Sarah Reber on the manuscript and the articles that preceded it. Quite fitting for this topic, I have the privilege of going to work every day in Ralph Bunche Hall. Bunche, a 1927 UCLA graduate, went on to collaborate with Gunnar Myrdal on his towering study of race relations, *An American Dilemma*, one of the century's most influential and engaged works of social science.

As the book took shape, I had the opportunity to present sections of the manuscript in many venues. I benefited from early book talks at Caltech, UC-Berkeley, the Nelson A. Rockefeller Center at Dartmouth College, and the Stanford Institute for Theoretical Economics summer workshop. I especially value the support that I received from Philip Hoffman, Christina Romer, Jean-Laurent Rosenthal, Andrew Samwick, and Gavin Wright. I am also immensely grateful to Kenneth Chay, Robert Margo, and Paul Rhode, each of whom read an early version of the manuscript and provided comments at a book conference hosted by the Von Gremp Workshop at UCLA in December 2013.

I made substantial progress on the manuscript during a research leave at the Straus Institute at New York University School of Law in the spring of 2014. I thank Ingrid Gould Ellen and Vicki Been for inviting me to participate in this interdisciplinary group and Charles Clot-felter, Desmond King, and Mary Patillo for commenting on sections of the manuscript. During the 2014–15 year, I shared findings from the book at a number of seminars, including at Columbia, Harvard, Vanderbilt, Williams, and Yale. It was particularly special to be able to present in front of Stewart Tolnay at the University of Washington, Jeffrey Williamson at the University of Wisconsin, and my advisors at Harvard, all early sources of encouragement on the project. I thank Jeremy Atack, William Collins, and Steven Nafziger for comments on draft chapters.

Some of the research underlying the manuscript has been previously published in other venues, including the *American Economic Journal: Applied*, *Journal of Economic History*, *Journal of Urban Economics*, and *Quarterly Journal of Economics*. I thank the editors and referees for their insights and suggestions. Chapters 3 and 4 contain elements of my earliest work on the topic of the Great Black Migration, which was completed during my time as a fellow in the Multidisciplinary Program on Inequality and Social Policy at the Kennedy School under the guidance of Christopher Jencks.

The intellectual contributions of my long-term coauthors require special mention. The discussion of immigrant selection and assimilation in chapter 2 is based, in part, on my collaborative work on the Age of Mass Migration with Ran Abramitzky and Katherine Eriksson. The idea of the silver lining to "white flight" in the form of black homeownership in chapter 4 arises from joint research with Robert Margo. Over the years, Bob has shared with me his voluminous knowledge, insight, and passion for African American economic history. My development as an economic historian would not have been complete without the friendship of David Clingingsmith, Carola Frydman, and Eric Hilt (who deigned to hang out with us graduate students during his early years as an assistant professor).

I also acknowledge the thoughtful research assistance of Francisco Haimovich, Owen Hearey, and Gabriela Rubio. Francisco, in particular, worked with me for a number of years to strengthen the empirical analysis underlying the book and the final outcome has benefited from his care.

As with all of my academic work, I reserve my most heartfelt thanks for my family. My parents were my first and remain my most enthusiastic audience. Mom and Dad always encouraged us to ask questions and supported us in finding creative and rewarding careers. I am regularly inspired in my own work by the successes of my sister, Sarah, in film and my brother, Jesse, in medicine.

My husband, Ra'anan Boustan, has been with me in the academic trenches since the day I first enlisted. He is a patient and thoughtful listener whose insights have sharpened my work and eased my worries. I owe an enormous debt to Ra'anan's commitment to true co-parenting. If not for this shared division of labor, I would surely still be writing this book.

No one has motivated me to finish the book more than our sons, Gil and Haskel. With Gil's due date in mind, I worked feverishly during the summer of 2013 to finalize a first draft. I edited the manuscript in the spring of 2015 before Haskel's arrival. As Gil's name, which means "joy" in Hebrew, attests, the birth of our sons has brought us nothing but happiness.

COMPETITION IN THE
PROMISED LAND

INTRODUCTION

In the fall of 1938, Gunnar Myrdal, a Swedish economist and eventual Nobel Prize winner, began his fact-finding tour of the American South. His trip, part of a broader study of race relations in America, was supported by the Carnegie Corporation. At the time, war was threatening in Europe and the United States positioned itself as the champion of freedom against the forces of fascism. Yet Myrdal was struck by the contradiction at the heart of the nation: even as the country adopted the role of defender of democracy, a group of its citizens was disenfranchised and denied basic liberties because of the color of their skin.

As Myrdal embarked on his travels, 75 percent of black Americans lived in the South, the region in which racial restrictions on political and economic freedoms were most severe. However, Myrdal emphasized that the "Negro problem" was not merely a southern failing but, rather, a fully "American dilemma." Northerners often turned a blind eye to the conditions under which many southern blacks worked, raised their families, and struggled to be full participants in the democratic process. This dilemma would only be confronted—and perhaps resolved—when northerners better understood the barriers that blacks faced; Myrdal ([1944] 1962, 48) believed that northerners would "get shocked and shaken in their conscience when they learn the facts."

Northern awareness of the "Negro problem" was hastened by mass migration of poor black southerners to northern and western cities. Seven million black migrants left the South during the twentieth century, with the highest outflow in the 1940s. By 1970, for the first time since the country's founding, the majority of black residents lived outside of the South, the region where their parents and grandparents had toiled in slavery a few generations before. The black share of the population in the typical northern or western city, where black residents were still a rarity at the turn of the twentieth century, increased from 5 percent in 1940 to 22 percent by 1970.[1]

---

[1] Woodson ([1918] 1970, 180), writing a generation earlier, was less sanguine about the role of migration in improving race relations, arguing that "the maltreatment of the

For black migrants, the North held out a promise of social and political equality. In cities like Chicago and Philadelphia, blacks did not need to sit at the back of the bus or drink from water fountains marked "colored only." School buildings were not doubled, one for black children and the other for whites, but instead black and white children could attend school together (even if they rarely did). Black residents expressed themselves at the ballot box and even elected members of their own community as representatives in city councils or in Washington.[2] Just as important, black workers could find a wider array of well-paid industrial jobs in the urban North and often received higher pay even for the stereotypically "Negro" positions that were also available in southern cities (such as cook, porter, and driver). The South was a low-wage region in general and especially so for black workers. The average black worker in the North and West earned nearly 200 percent more than his counterpart in the South in 1940.[3]

As Myrdal ([1944] 1962, 200) predicted, the economic benefits of "migration to the North and West [were] a tremendous force in the general amelioration of the Negro's position." Migration from the low-wage South to the higher-wage North contributed to the national growth of black earnings and the (partial) closure of the black-white earnings gap. During the twentieth century, the ratio of black-to-white earnings for the average male worker increased from less than 40 percent to nearly 70 percent. Much of this change was concentrated in the 1940s and the 1960s, two periods of mass black out-migration from the South. Quantitatively, rising levels of black education (in both quantity and quality) contributed most to improvements in relative black earnings. But migration also played a role. James Smith and Finis Welch (1989) conclude that mass migration from the low-wage South

---

Negroes will be nationalized by this exodus." He believed that discrimination could only be ameliorated by collective action on the part of the black community, including union activity and bloc voting.

[2] By 1980, five of the ten most popular destinations for black migrants in the North had elected a black mayor (Cleveland, Cincinnati, Detroit, Los Angeles, and Oakland), along with two satellite cities (Gary, IN, close to Chicago, and Newark, NJ, near New York City). Nye, Rainer, and Stratmann (2010) document improvements in the economic outcomes of black residents after the election of a black mayor, particularly via increases in municipal employment, with no corresponding decline in white outcomes.

[3] Whites also experienced a sizable regional earnings gap. The mean white worker in the North and West earned 65 percent more than the mean white worker in the South.

can account for 20 percent of the black-white convergence between 1940 and 1980.[4]

Upon arrival in the North, black migrants' earnings quickly caught up with those of their northern-born black counterparts. Some contemporary observers expected that, within a generation, southern black migrants would close the economic gap with northern whites as well. After all, southern blacks were just the latest in a long line of migrants to settle in northern cities, following waves of Irish and German and then Italian, Polish, and Jewish arrivals from Europe. As Oscar Handlin (1959, 120), a prominent early historian of immigration to the United States, reasoned, black migrants would "follo[w] the general outline of the experience of earlier [white] immigrants," who quickly moved up the occupational ladder, using their newfound savings to buy their own homes and provide education for their children.

In hindsight, it is now clear that the optimistic predictions of those who, like Myrdal and Handlin, believed in the transformative power of mass migration did not come to pass. Despite the promise of the North, black migration to industrial cities did not lead to economic parity with whites either for the migrants themselves or for their children.[5] The black-white earnings ratio in the North remained nearly unchanged from 1940 to 1980, despite a period of short-lived improvement in the late 1960s and early 1970s. Moreover, the residential isolation of northern blacks in majority-black neighborhoods increased as the migration got underway, due primarily to the departure of urban white households from central cities. By 1970, 70 percent of black residents in northern and western cities lived in majority-black neighborhoods, many of which were characterized by high rates of poverty and crime. As James Grossman (1989, 265) writes, the "dreams embodied in the Great Migration eventually collapsed" when the frustration borne of stagnant economic opportunities and deteriorating neighborhoods in northern cities culminated in a burst of urban unrest in the mid-1960s.

The standard explanation for slow black economic progress in the North emphasizes two demand-side forces: a weakening of the Ameri-

[4] Maloney (1994) reports a similar figure for the contribution of migration to black-white earnings convergence in the 1940s.

[5] The northern-born children of southern black migrants cannot be directly identified in the Census because, after 1940, the Census does not record parental state of birth. However, the black-white earnings gap in the North has remained relatively unchanged since 1980, despite the entry of many children of southern black migrants into the labor force.

can manufacturing sector after 1960 and racism in northern labor markets.[6] European migrants who settled in U.S. cities circa 1900 enjoyed four or five decades of American manufacturing ascendancy. Black arrivals in the 1940s benefited from only a decade or two of plentiful blue-collar positions before American manufacturing was eclipsed by global competition. Furthermore, although European immigrants faced some discrimination in the labor market, they were able to assimilate into the white majority relatively quickly, a feat that most black migrants, marked by the color of their skin, could not achieve.[7] The racial barriers faced by blacks in the labor market and housing market were both more severe and more persistent.

This book adds a supply-side element to the story. The persistent influx of black migrants to northern labor and housing markets created competition for existing black residents in an economic setting already constrained by weakening labor demand and northern racism. New migrants expanded the supply of black workers competing for the limited set of jobs open to black applicants, keeping black wages in the North low. Black migrants were closer substitutes for existing black workers than for whites with similar observable characteristics (such as years of education). In part, the lack of substitutability by race reflects the fact that some employers restricted black employment to the dirtiest and most unpleasant jobs in northern factories. Furthermore, many black students attended poorly equipped and understaffed schools, especially in the South, and therefore were often less productive than whites who held similar credentials on paper.[8]

In urban housing markets, the often invisible—but all too palpable— barriers dividing white and black neighborhoods initially held firm as new migrants arrived, heightening demand for the already cramped

---

[6] Manufacturing remained a steady 30 percent share of non-farm employment from 1910 to 1960, before declining to 18 percent by 1990 and just under 10 percent by 2006 (Carter and Sobek 2006; International Trade Administration 2010). Calculations from IPUMS data suggest that northern "rust belt" regions of the east north-central and mid-Atlantic experienced a similar percentage decline in manufacturing shares from 1960 to 1990.

[7] Abramitzky, Boustan, and Eriksson (2014) have recently questioned the standard narrative of European immigrant advancement, demonstrating that much of the apparent convergence between immigrants and natives is due to changes in the skills of arrival cohorts over time and selective return migration. In fact, immigrant groups that started out with earnings below those of natives experienced only a minor amount of convergence in a single generation.

[8] Blacks were closer substitutes with foreign-born whites, many of whom were educated in poorly developed prewar school systems in southern and eastern Europe.

and expensive apartments in black enclaves.[9] Seeking relief from high rents, black households were often willing to outbid white households for units on the blocks that stood at the dividing line between black and white areas. As the racial composition of these boundary neighborhoods began to change, some white households intensified their efforts to "defend" their communities, forming neighborhood associations to limit black entry through overt violence and intimidation or more subtle legal or social pressures. Other households chose the less strident but perhaps more effective option of leaving the city altogether for newly built and racially homogeneous neighborhoods in the suburban ring.[10] The possibility of choosing "flight" over "fight" was an outcome of the specific historical moment, following World War II, in which black migration reached its apex. In these years, movement to the suburbs was facilitated by new housing construction on the suburban ring and by state and federal road-building programs that enabled residents of these bedroom communities to quickly and easily commute by car to jobs in the central city.

For some white households, moving to the suburbs was a response to actual or anticipated changes in the racial composition of their local neighborhood. Yet many white households in the central city lived in peripheral neighborhoods far from a black enclave. In 1940, the average white resident lived more than three miles from a majority-black neighborhood, and these outlying neighborhoods remained resoundingly white as late as 1970. Even if white households could successfully isolate themselves from black neighbors while remaining within the city limits, a larger black population in the central city still had the potential to affect urban politics and local public goods. Moving to the suburbs offered white middle-class households political autonomy from an in-

[9] Although the boundaries between white and black neighborhoods were often unmarked, in some cases, white residents erected physical barriers to separate their neighborhoods from adjacent black areas. Famous cases include the Peyton Forest neighborhood of Atlanta (Kruse 2005, 1–3) and the border between Cleveland and Shaker Heights, OH (Martin 1987). Even absent a physical barrier, certain streets or landmarks often became known as the de facto boundary between white and black neighborhoods; one example is Troost Avenue in Kansas City, which became known as the "Troost Wall" (Gotham 2002, 93).

[10] Collective actions to defend a neighborhood, such as protests and firebombings, leave a stronger imprint in the historical record. In contrast, individual household decisions to leave the city leave little trace, save on aggregate population statistics. White flight is an inherently private activity; as Seligman (2005, 6–7) describes the process, many residents "quietly watched the transformations around them, discussed their dismay with family members at the kitchen table, and left without consulting anyone else."

creasingly black and poor urban electorate. Initially, such citywide concerns were fiscal in nature, focused on property tax rates and spending priorities. Race itself became more important in the 1970s after court-ordered desegregation plans challenged the practice of assigning children to neighborhood schools.

Main Themes of the Book

Competition in the Promised Land explores the effect of black in-migration on destination cities and labor markets in the North during the mid-twentieth century. The book's title is a take on *Manchild in the Promised Land*, Claude Brown's (1965) semi-autobiographical tale of growing up in Harlem as the son of southern sharecroppers. To his parents' generation, Brown writes, New York City was "the 'promised land' that Mammy had been singing about in the cotton fields" (1965, 7). But the reality of northern life was less halcyon. Recent arrivals worked hard, replacing "the sore backs of the cotton field for the sore knees of domestic service" (1965, 8). Despite these disappointments, Brown believed that migrants were "better off" in the "frying pan" of New York than in the southern fire. This study provides a new assessment of the benefit of migration to the migrants themselves, alongside a consideration of the effect of these large migrant flows on receiving areas in the North and West. In so doing, the book provides a number of contributions to our understanding of the role of the Great Black Migration in American history.

First, I show that the black migration produced winners and losers in the black community. By competing both with existing black workers and with each other, southern black men who arrived between 1940 and 1970 lowered the wages of black male workers in the North by nearly $4 billion a year overall (in 2010 dollars). This value represented a loss of around $1,000 per worker, or 10 percent of median black earnings in the North in 1940. I show that, if not for the continued migration, black workers would have experienced higher wage growth in the North but still would not have achieved economic parity with whites by 1970.

Competition with in-migrants in the North, while substantial, was smaller than the annual return to migration enjoyed by the migrants themselves, which I estimate to be, in aggregate, $10.2 billion per year (around $5,400 per migrant in 2010 dollars). These new estimates of the economic return to migration from the South are based on a comparison of southern-born brothers, one or more of whom moved to the North. Overall, mass migration from the South was advantageous to the average black worker. But the benefits of migration came, in part, at the expense of black economic advancement in the North and, as a result, can help explain the slow progress in northern cities in the years leading up to the urban unrest of the 1960s.[11] A similar dynamic of in-group competition was present for earlier immigrants from Europe, but these communities benefited (ironically) from the border restrictions of the 1920s.

Second, I offer causal evidence that white households left central cities in response to black in-migration, a phenomenon known as "white flight." The growth of the suburbs can been attributed to a number of factors, including federally subsidized mortgage credit, rising incomes in the decades following World War II, and federal and state road-building projects. In his seminal work on suburban history, Kenneth Jackson (1985, 290) concludes that these "economic causes [were] more important than skin color in the suburbanization of the United States." Even if economic factors were paramount, I show that white flight resulted in substantial outflows from already hemorrhaging cities, with more than two white residents leaving a northern city for every black arrival.[12] My most conservative estimate implies that white flight can account for around one-quarter of total population loss from central cities in the mid-twentieth century. In other words, even absent black in-migration, northern cities would still have lost a substantial amount of population and employment to the burgeoning suburbs.

Third, I argue that the motivations for white flight extended beyond apprehensions about immediate black neighbors to concerns about how the racial and income composition of the city *as a whole* would affect taxes and local public goods. A sizable literature in both economics

[11] A full accounting of the economic effect of migration would also consider the consequences of migrant departure on the southern economy. The fall in black labor supply in the South may have buoyed southern black wages. More speculatively, out-migration may have weakened southern resistance to civil rights legislation; on this point, see Alston and Ferrie 1993. Wright (2013, 18, 34) disagrees, arguing that out-migration from the region "did not disrupt the racial order" in the South and perhaps even "provided the safety valve that kept the southern system running smoothly."

[12] Many southern cities also received black migrants from rural areas and experienced similar patterns of white flight. Kruse (2005, 12) argues that there were "more similarities than differences" in the white response to black arrivals in the North and the South. Kruse reports that, as in northern cities, whites in Atlanta used both collective strategies of defending their neighborhoods against black arrivals and individual strategies of relocation to the suburbs.

and sociology investigates the dynamics of neighborhood change. There is general agreement that white households tend to leave neighborhoods that have a large or growing black population share. Yet many households living in protected white enclaves within the central city also chose to relocate to the suburbs as black households arrived across town.

Regardless of their location, all white households within the city limits had to interact with blacks newcomers, albeit indirectly, through the urban tax base and municipal elections. Desire to avoid such *fiscal/political interactions* with a growing black population provided some households with the impetus to move to the suburbs, a motivation that was intensified by court-ordered desegregation in the 1970s. Stressing the importance of local political economy in the process of white flight accords with work by Robert O. Self (on Oakland) and Kevin Kruse (on Atlanta), among others. These studies maintain that the roots of suburban distinction lie not only in the suburban housing stock and neighborhoods but also in the political autonomy of suburban towns from central cities.

I document the role of fiscal/political interactions using an original data set of housing prices collected along more than one hundred municipal borders. In particular, I find a price penalty for housing units located on the urban side of the city-suburban border and show that this gap widens as the city *as a whole* becomes more racially diverse. Before 1970, the demand for suburban residence at the border can be entirely explained by the correlation between race and median income. Municipalities with poorer residents tended to have higher property tax rates and more spending per capita on non-educational services, two features that the typical homeowner sought to avoid. After 1970, with the advent of court-ordered desegregation in some northern districts, race played an increasingly important role in this form of white flight.

The argument in the book unfolds over five chapters and an epilogue. Chapters 1 and 2 provide new evidence on black migrants themselves: when migrants left the South; who was most likely to make the trip; and where migrants settled in the North. Chapters 3–5 consider the consequences of these migrant flows on the labor and housing markets in the North and West. The epilogue extends the central trends in the book—regional black migration, racial wage convergence, and white flight from central cities—to the present.

Black mobility rose steadily after emancipation as a result of increasing migration flows within the South and new migration streams to the North. Migration to the North increased circa 1915, prompted by the confluence of rising labor demand in northern factories during World War I; a temporary freeze on immigration from Europe, which encouraged northern employers to consider alternative sources of labor supply; and falling labor demand in southern agriculture. Once black migration to the North began, numbers swelled rapidly, with new arrivals assisted by friends and family who themselves had recently settled in the North. Migration flows peaked between 1940 and 1970 and fell thereafter.

Out-migration rates were particularly high from cotton-growing regions of the South and from southern counties that most strongly supported segregation of the races. In leaving the South, migrants tended to head due north, following train lines and established migration routes. The five most popular destinations in the North—New York City, Chicago, Detroit, Philadelphia, and Los Angeles—absorbed around 60 percent of the black migrant flow, but black migrants settled in nearly every large northern and western city during this period.

Previous scholarship emphasized that migrants to the North were more educated than blacks who remained in the South, suggesting that migrants were positively selected from the southern population. Using a novel data set of individuals linked across Census years, I find that the selection of black migrants out of the South was bimodal. Fathers employed in both low- *and* high-skill positions were more likely to have sons who migrated to the North, as compared with fathers in mid-skill occupations. This pattern is more consistent with economic theory, which predicts that unskilled workers would have had the strongest pecuniary incentive to leave the South, where pay for low-skilled work was especially meager. High-skilled black migrants may have been particularly motivated by the political and social freedoms available in the North.

Since 1980, black migration has reversed course, with net black migration now flowing to the South. Black in-migration outpaces national movement toward Sunbelt cities. Even though black in-migration to northern cities has tapered off, relative black wages have not rebounded in the North and white flight has not reversed course (despite media reports of a "return to the city"). The stagnation of relative black earnings in the North from 1970 to 2010 points to the continued role of falling labor demand in American manufacturing, compounded by competition from new migrant arrivals from Mexico and Central America.

METHODOLOGICAL APPROACHES

The new findings in the book emerge from three methodological approaches that are common in economics and economic history but are relatively new to the analysis of the Great Black Migration. First, rather than providing a textured history of black in-migration into one city, I analyze migration flows throughout the North and West. Much of what we know about the consequences of black migration in receiving areas stems from detailed histories of large cities, especially Chicago and Detroit. Although historians have recently expanded their focus to include smaller cities and the West, it is hard to draw wider conclusions from a series of case studies alone. I am able to show, for example, that white flight occurred throughout the Northeast and Midwest (although less so in the West) and was particularly strong in larger cities and cities without a large preexisting black community.

Second, I analyze individual Census records that together aggregate the experience of thousands of northerners, both black and white. Changes in annual earnings provide evidence of competition between southern black migrants and northern workers, while fluctuations in housing prices reveal shifts in the demand for living in central cities. These effects are not discernable from standard historical sources, including oral histories, newspaper reports, and government documents. Furthermore, standard sources may overemphasize the most extreme responses to black in-migration, such as violent protests to defend white neighborhoods. Broader trends in population flows and housing prices provide insight into the response of the more "typical" urban resident.

Third, each stage of my analysis is grounded in an economic framework that considers the relative benefits and costs of individual actions within a set of existing constraints. For example, individual-level models of the migration decision emphasize the relative benefits of remaining in one's current location versus moving elsewhere. This approach generates useful predictions about which black southerners should be most likely to move to the North. I also apply models of the labor and housing markets to predict which workers would be most likely to compete with black newcomers; how many existing residents can be expected to leave the central city as black migrants arrive; and how changes in demand for city residence would be reflected in local housing prices.

Contemporary observers noted the potential for southern black inflows to threaten the economic standing of existing black residents as early as the 1920s, when W.E.B. Du Bois (1923, 539) cautioned that a "great reservoir of [southern black] labor" could reduce black wages in the North and generate tension between blacks and whites over residential space. This sense of rivalry can explain the ambivalence with which blacks in the North greeted subsequent arrivals. Black migrants remember meeting "a chilly reception from many longtime black residents who feared the newly arrived blacks . . . would jeopardize their tenuous position" (Trotter 1985, 115).[13]

Competition between longstanding migrants and recent arrivals in labor and housing markets is not unique to the black experience. Jewish immigrants, many of whom worked in the garment industry, embraced their fellow countrymen but also worried about overcrowding in their occupational niche, even going so far as to support the resettlement of thousands of new arrivals out of New York City via a self-help group called the Industrial Removal Office. In more recent years, swelling numbers of immigrants from Mexico and Central America have generated competition and lowered wages for immigrants who hold a similar set of jobs in gardening, housekeeping, construction, and restaurant work, with little effect on the wages of the native born.

To the extent that immigrants arrive with a similar set of skills and settle in the same neighborhoods, they are more likely to compete for jobs and housing with others from their country of origin. But the stronger the discriminatory barriers that a group faces, the more difficult it is for existing residents to switch occupations or move out of the old neighborhood, and therefore the more concentrated the force of this competition will be. Thus competition was arguably more severe within the black community than among other immigrant groups.

In previous work, two prominent sociologists, Stanley Lieberson (1980) and William Julius Wilson (1987), suggested that continued black in-migration may have had negative consequences for existing black residents of the North. Both scholars were interested in explaining how

[13] On this point, see also Drake and Cayton [1945] 1962, 73–76. Sides (2003, 37) describes this process in Los Angeles: "Some celebrated the influx . . . [because it] brought potential new customers and business opportunities. . . . Others perceived the waves of new migrants as a serious threat to the black community."

blacks failed to get ahead in the same cities that had nurtured white immigrant groups just a generation before. Blacks, they argued, suffered from the inherent openness of the Mason-Dixon Line, while white immigrants benefited from the strict immigration quotas of the 1920s. Wilson (1987, 33) calls "the flow of migrants . . . the most important single contributor to the varying rates of urban racial and ethnic progress in the twentieth-century United States."

Although southern migrants harmed some existing black workers in the northern labor market through job competition, they also served as patrons for black churches, entertainment venues, and businesses, generating a livelihood for black preachers, teachers, politicians, and other professionals (Drake and Cayton [1945] 1962).[14] Members of these professions enjoyed high levels of education and thus were the most likely to express their views in print; fervent editorials in favor of the migration in black newspapers, particularly the *Chicago Defender*, are a case in point. Perhaps as a result, some historians have emphasized the positive consequences of the migration in receiving cities, overlooking the costs borne by black workers in the industrial setting.[15] However, as Isabel Wilkerson (2010, 271) concluded from a series of interviews with participants in the northward migration, "even as the Migration was a bonanza for the colored storekeepers and businessmen, it meant more competition for the already limited kinds of jobs blacks were allotted."

I should emphasize that my focus on competition in labor and housing markets is quite distinct from the (now outmoded) view that migrants harmed existing black residents by importing a maladaptive southern culture to the North, characterized by high rates of male idleness and female household headship. This idea was first voiced by black social reformer Sadie T. Mosell in the 1920s and echoed by E. Franklin Frazier (1939, 295), who bemoaned the fact that "masses of ignorant, uncouth and impoverished migrants . . . changed the whole structure of the Negro community." Gilbert Osofsky picked up this theme in the 1960s. More recently, this view has been advanced rather uncritically by Nicholas Lemann (1991, 31) who, in his sweeping chronicle of the black migration, declared that "black sharecropper society . . .

---

[14] Boyd (1996, 1998a, 1998b) finds that cities with a larger black population had more black entrepreneurship in many realms, including religious institutions, beauty salons, and general business ownership.

[15] Gregory (2005) and Sugrue (2008), for example, have highlighted the role that northern migrants played in black political organizing and the birth of the civil rights movement.

was the equivalent of [and contributed to the rise of] big-city ghetto society today in many ways," spreading out-of-wedlock childbearing, spotty education, and casual violence to the North. Yet the notion that southern migrants spread a culture of poverty to the North is not consistent with the well-documented fact that southern migrants kept pace with northern-born blacks on a number of social outcomes, including marriage rates, earnings, and employment.

A final note on gender: throughout the book, my labor market analyses focus on male workers for two reasons. First, I separate workers into skill groups that faced more or less competition from new black arrivals based, in part, on age. Given that women's labor force participation is often interrupted for childbearing, age is not a reliable indicator of years of labor market experience for female workers. Second, portions of my analysis rely on matching individuals across censuses by first and last name. Because virtually all women changed their name upon marriage at this time, it is difficult to follow women from childhood to adulthood using Census data. Black women in the northern labor force likely experienced a similar (or even greater) degree of competition from new migrant arrivals as did black men. Outside of the South, 44 percent of black women were in the labor force in 1940, with the majority working in domestic service. Over time, black women moved into factory work and eventually into clerical positions. Given the clustering of black women in a limited set of occupations, the extent of competition with new arrivals may have been especially severe.

CHAPTER 1

Black Migration from the South
in Historical Context

IN AN HISTORICAL note to the Pulitzer Prize–winning play *Fences*, August Wilson describes Pittsburgh in the early twentieth century as an industrial machine powered by the sweat of European immigrants. Pittsburgh, a city of a "thousand furnaces and sewing machines, [a] thousand butcher shops and bakers' ovens," was home to "the destitute of Europe," he writes, but "the descendants of African slaves were offered no such welcome" (1991, 103). Indeed, in 1910, the workforce in northern cities was nearly 40 percent foreign born and only 3 percent black. At the time, nearly fifty years after emancipation, 86 percent of African Americans still lived in the South.[1]

The mobility of black southerners began increasing in the birth cohorts born immediately after the Civil War. Many of these moves took place within the South. Despite plentiful industrial jobs in the "thousand furnaces" of nothern cities at the turn of the twentieth century, the potential wage benefits of settling in the North was dampened by the absence of a migrant network that southern blacks could use to secure employment upon arrival. Large flows of northward migration awaited a period of abnormally high economic returns, which arose during World War I. Circa 1915, northern factories supplying the war effort experienced a surge in labor demand, coupled with a temporary freeze in European immigration, which encouraged northern employers to turn to other sources of labor.

Once black migration from the South got underway, the first pioneers facilitated later moves of friends and family. Furthermore, northern employers gained experience with and became more open to hiring

---

[1] The concentration of blacks in the South was disproportionate to the region's size. Only 29 percent of white native born and 5 percent of white foreign born lived in the South in 1910.

black workers. With these conditions in place, black migration to the North accelerated rapidly, doubling from the 1900s to the 1910s and then doubling again by the 1920s. Migration peaked in the 1940s and 1950s; during these two decades alone, 28 percent of the southern black population left the region. By 1970, for the first time in American history, a majority of the country's black residents lived outside the South, with 45 percent living in the Northeast and Midwest and 8 percent in the West.[2]

Black departures from the South were greatest from counties that specialized in cotton agriculture and that were characterized by particularly strong segregationist sentiment (as proxied by support for Strom Thurmond in the 1948 presidential election). Settlement in the North and West was concentrated in the top five destinations: New York City, Chicago, Detroit, Philadelphia, and Los Angeles. Outside of these gateway cities, black migrants were widely distributed throughout northern and western metropolitan areas, underscoring the broad social and economic consequences of black migration throughout the region.

A Long View of Southern Black Mobility: The Birth Cohorts of 1810–1970

The Great Black Migration is usually dated to 1915, the first year of substantial black in-migration to the North. However, the rate of interstate mobility among southern blacks rose steadily, starting with the birth cohort of 1860. Initially, the majority of these moves took place in the South, with some rural blacks moving to urban areas and others seeking agricultural opportunities further west (Gottlieb 1987, 118; Cohen 1991, 248–73; Cobb, 1992, 47–68). In this long-term perspective, the Great Black Migration appears to be a continuation of previous mobility trends, marked by acceleration (rather than a discontinuous jump) in the rate of interstate migration and a gradual shift toward northern destinations. This long-term trend is not consistent with the view that black southerners were uniquely stuck in place through binding credit relationships with landlords and local merchants (Ransom and Sutch 1977, 194; Berlin 2010, 142).

Using multiple waves of Census data, I define migration as living outside of one's state of birth or, alternatively, as living outside of the

---

[2] Despite mass out-migration, blacks were still overrepresented in the South in 1970. In that year, 47 percent of blacks but only 27 percent of native-born whites were southern residents.

South altogether. I mostly follow the Census definition of the South, which includes the eleven states of the former Confederacy, Kentucky, Oklahoma, and West Virginia, but I exclude the District of Columbia and the border states of Maryland and Delaware, which experienced net black in-migration in the twentieth century.[3] For brevity, I often refer to the non-South as the "North," even though this region also includes the western states. Migration figures are calculated for blacks and non-blacks.[4] In this southern context, "non-black" is nearly synonymous with "white," and I use these two terms interchangeably.[5] For the year 2000, when the Census introduced the option to select multiple races, I group all individuals who report being black and some other race into the category "black."[6]

Arranging Census data by birth cohort reveals substantial swings in black (and white) mobility during the nineteenth and twentieth centuries. Figure 1.1a graphs predicted migration for each birth cohort by age thirty, and Figure 1.1b reports the share of these moves occurring within the South. The underlying estimation procedure is described in Appendix Equation 1. Most cohorts are observed at multiple ages, thereby allowing separate identification of the effects of both age and birth cohort on migration. Although migration can occur at any time in the life cycle, individuals are most likely to move in their twenties (Johnson et al. 2005).[7] I therefore interpret the estimated migration activity as taking place around twenty-five years after the cohort's year of birth.

Migration rates were particularly high in the early nineteenth century among southerners of both races. Fifty percent of whites and

[3] I follow Kirby (1983) in classifying border states as northern or southern according to their migration history rather than their official Census region.

[4] Until 1960, the Census enumerator was responsible for categorizing an individual's race. Race is now reported by the household head. In 1990 and 2000, the head is specifically asked to report the race that each individual "considers him/herself to be." For a discussion of changes in the Census racial categories over time, see Foner and Fredrickson 2004.

[5] In 1910, only 0.3 percent of the southern population was neither white nor black; by 2000, this figure had increased to 5.5 percent (1.6 percent Asian and 3.9 percent "other"). The vast majority of residents selecting "other" race were of Hispanic origin.

[6] Only 2.6 percent of southern residents who selected "black" for at least one of their races in the year 2000 also reported being another race. Given the history of sharp racial barriers in the South, it is likely that these multirace individuals would have reported themselves as "black" before the survey change.

[7] Black et al. (2015, Figure 4) estimate the relationship between migration and age for black southern migrants. The vast majority of migration occurs between the ages of eighteen and thirty.

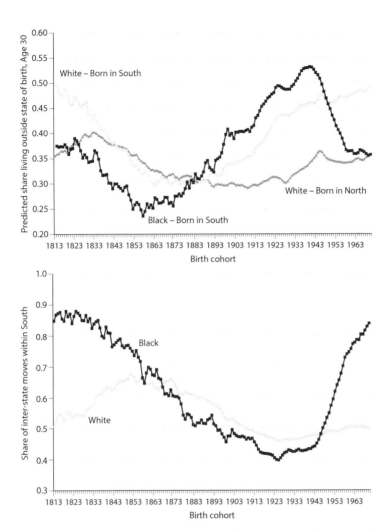

Figures 1.1a and 1.1b. Interstate mobility by birth cohort and race. In Figure 1.1a, samples include whites born in the South or the North and blacks born in the South; the number of blacks born in the North is too small in many years for analysis. Each dot represents a three-year moving average of predicted lifetime migration rate for a thirty-year-old in a given birth cohort; the predictions are derived from Appendix Equation 1. The underlying data on state of birth and state of current residence are calculated by birth cohort from seven Census waves between 1880 and 2000. Figure 1.1b focuses on the southern-born samples. Each dot represents a three-year moving average of the share of predicted lifetime moves that take place within the South (that is, between southern states, rather than to a state outside of the South).

nearly 40 percent of blacks in the birth cohort of 1810 left their birth state by age thirty. For blacks, most of whom were in slavery, nearly 90 percent of these moves took place within the South. High mobility occurred in the context of rising demand for cotton, as planters pushed westward from the older cotton region of the South Atlantic into the fertile land in the Mississippi Delta and Texas.[8] Fogel (1994, 65) reports that 835,000 slaves, nearly one in four, were moved west by their owner or a slave trader from 1820 to 1860.[9]

As the new cotton frontier became settled, the mobility of both white and black southerners declined. By the birth cohorts of the mid-nineteenth century, the share of black southerners living outside of their state of birth had fallen from 40 percent to 25 percent. The low point in black mobility was reached in the birth cohort of 1857, who were "of age" to migrate in the early 1880s. This decline in black mobility followed a wider national trend rather than indicating race-specific barriers to mobility after emancipation. The share of whites, both southern and non-southern born, living outside of their state of birth declined to much the same degree in the mid-nineteenth century.

Although the mobility of southerners of both races moved in tandem, a small racial gap in overall mobility is apparent throughout the nineteenth century. The enforcement of anti-enticement and vagrancy statutes designed to limit black mobility provides one explanation for this racial gap. Anti-enticement laws prevented employers from hiring away workers who already held a job contract, while vagrancy laws made it difficult for workers to leave one job and spend time searching for another (Cohen 1991).[10] Naidu (2010) estimates that doubling the fine for vagrancy decreased the probability of moving in a sample of black sharecroppers by 5 percentage points, the right order of magnitude to explain the observed racial gap in mobility.

---

[8] Wright (1978) estimates that world cotton demand quadrupled from 1830 to 1860. Production increased both through the clearing of new cotton acreage on the western frontier and through innovations like the introduction of new seed varieties that allowed farmers to reap higher yields per acre farmed (Olmstead and Rhode 2008, 107–14).

[9] See Woodson [1918] 1970 on the history of black migration to the North during the nineteenth and early twentieth centuries.

[10] Cohen (1991, 4) argues that such legislation, although symbolically important, was not very effective in preventing black mobility. He writes that "though the laws of labor control undoubtedly helped create an ethos unfriendly to migration, planters were rarely able to use their legal instruments effectively enough to interdict seriously black movement from one state to another. Throughout the period up to World War I, blacks in most parts of the South appear to have moved with relatively little interference when jobs were available." See Blackmon 2008 for an alternative view of the efficacy of such laws.

The birth cohort of 1890 was the first to come of age during the Great Black Migration to the North, which began in 1915. However, black southern mobility started to rise in the birth cohort of 1860 and increased steadily for eighty consecutive birth years, peaking in the cohort of 1940.[11] The pace of black migration accelerated—but did not jump upward—in the birth cohorts of the 1890s, suggesting that the Great Black Migration was part of a longer mobility trend. In contrast, white migration rates remained low for southern whites until the birth cohort of 1890 and for non-southern whites until the birth cohort of 1925, most of whom would have moved after World War II. Indeed, the racial mobility gap had closed completely by the birth cohort of 1880, before the Great Black Migration to the North got under way.[12] The share of black migrants who settled in the North also rose steadily, increasing by around 1 percentage point in every cohort after the Civil War, with no obvious break in trend. Thus the Great Black Migration to the North appears to be an acceleration of existing black mobility rather than a novel form of black movement.[13]

In the late nineteenth century, 70 percent of interstate moves initiated by black southerners took place in the South. Some of these early black migrants moved to southern cities. The share of black southerners living in an urban area increased from 10 percent in 1880 to 22 percent by 1910. But many intra-southern moves occurred between agricultural regions. Steckel (1983) argues that the migration of agricultural workers tended to follow lines of latitude within climatic zones, which allowed farmers to use their accumulated experience in planting particular crops.[14] Migration between rural areas may have contributed to black occupational mobility up the agricultural ladder. Alston and Ferrie (2005) document that 40 percent of blacks working

[11] The birth cohorts of the 1900s, who came of age during the Great Depression, are the one exception to the upward trend in black migration.

[12] This birth cohort analysis is consistent with the work of Rosenbloom and Sundstrom (2004), who examine the mobility of black and white men in their thirties in various Census years. In 1880, black men were 7 percentage points less likely than their white counterparts to leave their state of birth (corresponding to the birth cohorts of 1840–50). The racial mobility gap had already declined to 2 percentage points by 1910, a few years before the Great Black Migration began.

[13] Hall and Ruggles (2004) and Black et al. (2015, Figure 1) document a similar inverted U-shaped pattern for black migration rates from the South to the North, peaking around 1965.

[14] Bazzi et al. (2014) use experimental variation to document that migration between similar climatic zones is associated with higher agricultural productivity in contemporary Indonesia.

as farm laborers or sharecroppers moved into farm tenancy or owner-ship during the 1920s.

BLACK MIGRATION TO THE NORTH IN THE TWENTIETH CENTURY

Few blacks moved North before 1915, despite the higher wages and greater social equality available in the region.[15] The role of migrant networks in facilitating migrant flows to new destinations provides one convincing explanation for low rates of black migration to the North before World War I.[16] High *potential* returns to migration in the North notwithstanding, *actual* returns to migration may have been substantially lower because new arrivals had difficulty finding a well-paid job without the help of an existing migrant community.[17] When networks are important for migration activity, low migration rates can persist indefinitely absent a catalyst that provides the particularly favorable economic conditions necessary for migration to begin. In the case of the black migration, these conditions arose circa 1915 as a result of the combination of heightened labor demand in northern factories during World War I; a sharp decline in immigration from Europe, following a wartime disruption in shipping; and bad harvests and falling labor demand in southern agriculture due to the boll weevil, a cotton pest.[18]

[15] Wages in low-skilled occupations were around 70 percent higher in the North than in the South Atlantic and around 40 percent higher than in the south-central region in the 1870s and 1880s (Margo 2004). Furthermore, in the South, blacks were barred from participating in elections by onerous poll taxes and literacy tests, attended segregated and poorly funded public schools, and were subjected to bouts of arbitrary violence, conditions that were improved (if not fully ameliorated) in the North (Woodward [1955] 1981; Kousser 1974; Tolnay and Beck 1995).

[16] Low levels of black education in the late nineteenth century provide another possible explanation for low black mobility to the North before 1915. Yet Margo (1990, 114–17) shows that expanded literacy can only explain 10 percent of heightened black mobility after 1910. Furthermore, the large increases in black schooling levels began only with the birth cohort of 1905, who came of age around 1930, fifteen years after the Great Black Migration had begun (Aaronson and Mazumder 2011, Figure 1).

[17] For models of chain migration, see Carrington, Detragiache, and Vishwanath 1996 and Hatton and Williamson 1994. The concept of a "migration chain" was first introduced into the sociological literature by Park and Miller (1921) and was further theorized by MacDonald and MacDonald (1964). Munshi (2003) and Beaman (2012) provide empirical evidence of the role of migration networks in the contemporary economy.

[18] Figures 1.1a and 1.1b show that the growing number of black migrants to the North circa 1915 was due to an acceleration of the overall rate of southern black mobility rather than a discontinuous jump in the share of migrants settling in the North.

Labor demand in northern cities was abnormally high during World War I, as military orders kept factories running at full capacity. From 1915 to 1919, the growth in manufacturing employment rose above its already steep trend, leading to the (temporary) creation of two million new positions.[19] Many of these jobs had minimal skill requirements; in 1920, for example, a quarter of men employed in northern manufacturing worked as common laborers. In peacetime, slots in northern factories were often filled by recent foreign arrivals. But as the war disrupted transatlantic shipping lanes, the migration flow from Europe dropped from 1.2 million to only 100,000 annual entrants.[20] The loss of typical labor supply encouraged some industrial firms to send labor recruiters to the South for the first time.[21] Collins (1997) estimates that a decline in labor supply of this magnitude would have encouraged 100,000 southern blacks to move north; this figure can account for half of the uptick in black migration from the 1900s to the 1910s (see Figure 1.2a).[22]

In the early twentieth century, many southern blacks worked in cotton agriculture, which was still planted and harvested by hand. Labor demand in cotton fell in the decade before World War I with the spread of the boll weevil. The weevil arrived in southern Texas in 1892 and slowly moved east, crossing the Mississippi River by 1908. Lange, Olmstead, and Rhode (2009) document that cotton-producing counties experienced a 30 percent decline in population in the years immediately following the weevil infestation, an indication of large out-migration flows.[23] Although black workers displaced by the weevil did not neces-

[19] I estimate this excess demand by plotting annual manufacturing employment from 1900 to 1940, net of a linear time trend (Lebergott 1964). From 1915 to 1919, manufacturing employment cumulatively exceeded its trend by two million jobs, returning to trend by 1921.

[20] In addition, by 1918, over two million American soldiers were drafted into service, further reducing the available labor supply (Yockelson 1998).

[21] Bodnar, Simon, and Weber (1982, 190) report that around one-fifth of black migrants who settled in Pittsburgh in the 1910s were brought North by recruiters. Companies like US Steel, Westinghouse Electric, and the Pennsylvania Railroad all sent labor agents to the South during World War I. However, labor agents may not have been necessary for northward migration. One interview subject, Jasper A., who was brought to Pittsburgh by a labor recruiter, recalls that "I had [moving North] in mind well before that."

[22] See Spear 1967, 130–33 for a good summary of these forces. Vickery (1977, 23–32) disputes the importance of wartime shocks, asserting that the regional wage differential was large enough that migration from the South would have taken off eventually.

[23] The quantitative association between out-migration and the spread of the boll weevil is consistent with references in oral histories to the pest's destruction. Alonzo Parham, a black resident of Chicago, recalls that "the farm situation in the South was pretty rough

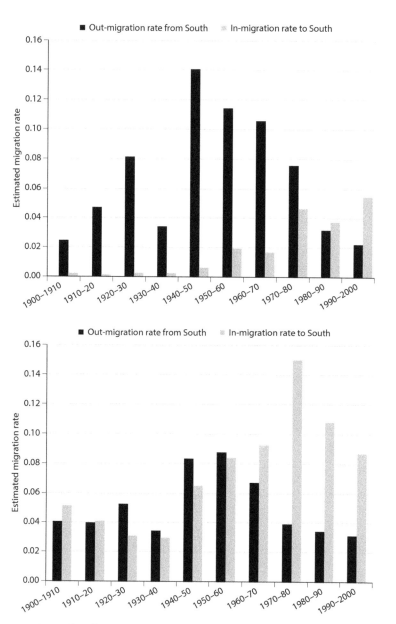

Figures 1.2a and 1.2b. Out- and in-migration rates from the South by decade and race. Figure 1.2a presents migration rates for blacks and Figure 1.2b presents migration rates for whites. Estimates of migration flows between regions are based on Census survival methods with cohorts defined by age, sex, and region of birth, as described by Gregory (2005). Migration rates are calculated

sarily move to the North immediately, they represented a pool of potential migrants ready to move when job opportunities became available in northern factories.[24]

Black out-migration from the South accelerated in the 1920s, peaked in the 1940s, and declined thereafter. Figures 1.2a and 1.2b present new estimates of migration rates out of and into the South by race. Migrant counts are calculated with Census survival methods. Net migration from a location—say, a state—can be approximated by counting members of a sex-race-birth year cohort over two consecutive Census periods (Kuznets and Thomas 1957; Vickery 1977, 140–88).[25] A cohort can only expand or contract over time through mortality or through net migration from that state. Therefore, after estimating the number of deaths during a given Census period, any remaining difference in cohort size can be attributed to net migration. Following Gregory (2005),

---

at that time. Boll weevils were eating practically all the cotton. . . . So my father decided that he would go someplace else" (Black 2003, 117).

[24] Higgs (1976) finds no *state-level* relationship between weevil infestation and black out-migration rates, which suggests that many migrants from weevil-infested counties remained in the South, at least in the short run.

[25] Unlike immigration from abroad, which has been carefully tallied since the nation's founding, there are few records kept—even today—of internal migration between U.S. states. Since 1990, the Internal Revenue Service has released state-to-state and county-to-county migration flows based on the universe of tax filers. Although useful for measuring aggregate migration flows between locations, these data do not contain demographic information to separately identify migrants by race.

---

as the number of out- (or in-) migrants to the South as a share of the population living in the South in the base year by race; population estimates are taken from IPUMS. My approach differs from Gregory's in three ways. First, many observations in 1960 and 1970 are missing information on state of birth. Gregory omits these individuals from the migration counts. I instead impute states of birth based on region of residence, race, and age. Second, Gregory's estimated black mortality rates are higher than the values reported in vital statistics in the 1980s and 1990s; I revise these figures downward. Third, I use unweighted counts for the 1960 and 1970 IPUMS flat samples, which appears to correct an overstatement in the number of southern-born blacks living outside of the South in Gregory's series in 1960. As a result of this overstatement, Gregory's series shows a rebound of migration from the South in the 1970s, while my series shows a steady decline. Falling migration in the 1970s is consistent with contemporary demographic analysis (e.g., Long and Hansen 1975).

I extend this technique to estimate gross migration flows to and from a location by constructing cohorts by sex, race, birth year, *and region of birth* using Census microdata.[26]

In the first decade of the twentieth century, only 200,000 blacks left the South out of a population of nearly eight million, an out-migration rate of 2.5 percent.[27] Migration doubled in the war decade of the 1910s and then nearly doubled again in the 1920s. Although the abnormally strong labor demand that arose during World War I did not persist, migration rates remained high; perhaps once a migration network was in place, early arrivals were able to facilitate the moves of their friends and family. Existing migrants helped newcomers by sending detailed letters describing conditions in the North; distributing northern newspapers with help-wanted ads throughout the South; providing housing and job referrals for new migrants upon first arrival; and contributing to formal institutions like the Urban League that offered job training and employment placement services (Grossman 1989, 66–97; Marks 1989, 24–32; Gottlieb 1987, 40–43).[28] Furthermore, the first black migrants to "get their foot in the door" of northern factories during World War I enabled the hiring of additional black employees in northern industry, both by providing referrals and by dispelling common stereotypes about black workers.[29]

[26] The net migration flow implied by my series is similar to net flows calculated from standard Census survival methods by Ferrie (2006) and Wright (2013). The most notable difference occurs in the 1970s. My series reports a small net out-migration from the South during the 1970s, while Wright's series has a small net in-migration to the region.

[27] Organized migrations from the South, including the "Exoduster" movement to Kansas in 1879 and 1880 and various "back to Africa" expeditions, were quantitatively small. The best estimates suggest that only 2,500 African Americans migrated to Africa in the nineteenth century, while 10,000 joined the Exoduster movement to Kansas (Johnson and Campbell 1981). See also Woodson [1918] 1970, Painter 1976, and Cohen 1991, chapters 6 and 7 on the symbolism of these movements in black history.

[28] Stuart and Taylor (2014) estimate that each black migrant from the South influenced up to four other migrants to settle in the same location in the North. Chay and Munshi (2013) offer additional quantitative evidence consistent with the importance of black migrant networks.

[29] Northern factories relied heavily on ethnic networks to recruit workers (Bodnar, Simon, and Weber 1982). Before World War I, many northern employers believed black workers to be lazy and unproductive. After gaining experience with black workers during the war, some employers changed their views (Whatley 1990). Montgomery (1991) argues that employers value referrals from their existing workforce because current employees have an incentive to provide truthful recommendations to avoid being fired or facing other sanctions. Royster (2003) offers an account of the continued importance of race-based networks in the contemporary labor market.

Black migration from the South slowed in the 1930s, with the out-migration rate falling from 8 percent to 3.5 percent. This temporary shortfall in black migration mirrored a national decline in mobility during the Depression.[30] The disproportionately low rates of black migration in the Depression decade were due, in part, to high black unemployment in northern cities. With only 59 percent of black residents in the North able to find work outside of public relief, there was little incentive for new in-migration.[31]

Black migration resumed as employment conditions in northern cities improved with the outbreak of World War II. Nearly 1.4 million blacks left the South in the 1940s, a migration rate of 14 percent, with many moving in response to strong labor demand in northern factories. Migration continued after the war, in part because of the effect of wartime service on both the skills and the aspirations of southern blacks. Modell, Goulden, and Magnusson (1989, 838–39) argue that "military service influenced the structure of [black] aspirations in a way that contributed to their unwillingness to accept the prewar structure of racial dominance and . . . enhanced the likelihood of interregional migration."[32]

The response to northern employment opportunities in the 1940s was strengthened by the large pool of prospective southern migrants whose economic situation had worsened during the Depression. The Agriculture Adjustment Act (AAA) of 1933, part of a package of New Deal reforms favoring southern landowners, led some tenants to shift into wage labor, causing the southern agricultural wage to fall (Cobb 1992, 186–197).[33] However, despite poor conditions in the South, out-

[30] Figures 1.2a and 1.2b demonstrate that white out-migration from the South in the 1930s was two-thirds as great as that of the previous decade, whereas black out-migration declined to less than half of the 1920s figure.

[31] In the 1940 Census, only 71 percent of black prime-aged men in northern and western metropolitan areas were employed, compared with 81 percent of whites. Furthermore, 17 percent of employed black men (but only 4 percent of employed whites) were recorded as "public emergency" workers, many of whom were working under the auspices of a New Deal program.

[32] Katznelson (2005) points out that the effect of World War II service on black advancement would have been even more profound if black veterans had not been prevented from taking equal advantage of the education and training provisions in the GI Bill.

[33] In response to federal incentives to leave a portion of their land fallow, many southern planters terminated contracts with tenant farmers. In the Mississippi Delta, for example, the share of land harvested by tenant farmers fell from 82 percent to 58 percent during the 1930s (Whatley 1983).

migration was low in the 1930s because opportunities elsewhere were also limited. As Whatley (1983, 928) explains, "displaced labor had not moved out, as previously expected, because of the depressed employment situation in the urban centers during the 1930s." During the wartime recovery, "those laborers who had been displaced from the land but not from the region now . . . left in search of employment in the industrial centers of the North and South."[34]

Black migration from the South remained high in the 1950s and 1960s as the mechanization of the cotton harvest reduced demand for agricultural labor in the South. Cotton was still overwhelmingly picked by hand in 1950. By 1960, 42 percent of the cotton harvest was mechanized; five years later, the share had reached 82 percent (Alston and Ferrie 1993, 862). Mechanization also undermined the prevailing set of "paternalistic" relationships whereby landowners offered tenants a series of services, from credit to housing to protection from violence, in exchange for steady employment. This shift in social relations may have encouraged further out-migration.

Black migration from the South decelerated in the 1970s. By the 1980s, there was a positive net flow of black migrants into the South, following a national pull to rising Sunbelt cities. From 1980 onward, northern cities absorbed a larger number of black migrants from the Caribbean than from southern states (McCabe 2011).[35]

Although a sizable number of white migrants left the South during the twentieth century, Figures 1.2a and 1.2b reveal that the patterns of southern migration differed substantially by race. First, rather than accelerating over time, the white out-migration rate from the South was stable at around 4 percent throughout the century, spiking only in the decades around World War II. Second, the maximum rate of white out-migration from the South was 8 percent, significantly lower than the peak black rate of 14 percent in the 1940s. Third, on net, black migrants left the South for the rest of the country over the century (a loss of 5 million), while white net migration to the South was strongly positive (a gain of 13 million). This comparison holds even before the advent of Sunbelt migration in the 1960s. In fact, only in the 1920s and 1940s did

[34] Fishback, Horrace, and Kantor (2006) document that counties with greater AAA expenditures experienced more out-migration from 1930 to 1940, although these migrants may have moved within the South.

[35] In the 1940s and 1950s, migration from the Caribbean, while notable in some cities (principally New York City), was only 4 percent as large as the southern black migrant flow. By the 1960s, Caribbean migration was 40 percent as large as black southern migration.

substantially more whites leave the South than enter the region. Thus, on balance, the twentieth century was a period of white mobility *to* the South.

LOCAL CONDITIONS AND BLACK OUT-MIGRATION FROM THE SOUTH

The previous section shows that flows of black migration from the South were sensitive to changes in economic circumstances over time, expanding when job opportunities in northern factories were plentiful and contracting when northern unemployment rates were high. A similar responsiveness to economic conditions is apparent across sending locations in the South, with particularly high black out-migration rates from areas reliant on cotton agriculture and relatively low out-migration rates (or even net in-migration) to areas specializing in mining or light industry or home to a growing urban area. Cultural representations of the Great Black Migration depict black departures from the South as a response to pervasive racial violence or to catastrophic events, like the 1927 flood of the Mississippi River. Although violence and flooding did play a role in precipitating black out-migration, I argue that variations in economic conditions across the South were quantitatively more important.[36]

In a simple economic model of migration, prospective migrants compare the expected benefits of remaining in their current location with the value of moving elsewhere (Sjaastad 1962).[37] These models suggest that residents will leave the South if the benefit of doing so is greater than some migration cost. The value of remaining in the South will be lower in areas with low wages or poor opportunities for advancement up the occupational ladder. Furthermore, the utility associated with remaining in the South will be lower in areas with endemic discrimination against black residents, in terms of threats of violence, restrictions on voting, or low expenditures on black schools. The decision to move will also be influenced by the expected benefit of relocat-

---

[36] Vickery (1977) arrived at a similar conclusion in his analysis of state-level migration flows.

[37] Gill (1979, 40–101) applies this model to the case of black migration from the South. More complicated models of migration allow prospective migrants to select between multiple possible destination choices and to make sequential location decisions rather than a once-and-for-all move (e.g., Kennan and Walker 2011). But the central choice in these second-generation models still hinge on a comparison between the expected benefits of remaining in one's current location and moving elsewhere.

ing to the North, which will include the prospect of higher wages in industrial employment, the opportunity to send children to better-resourced schools,[38] and the attractions of living in a big city.[39]

I report the effect of three measures of local economic and social conditions in a southern county on the migration rate: the share of land planted in cotton; per capita federal expenditures on war-related facilities during World War II; and the share of votes cast for Strom Thurmond, the States' Rights (Dixiecrat) nominee, in the presidential election of 1948. The Thurmond vote share is used as a proxy for the local racial climate and the intensity of segregationist preferences, which may be correlated with episodes of racial intimidation and with disparities in public services by race (Cascio et al. 2010). The estimating equation underlying these results is described in Appendix Equation 2 and a full set of regression coefficients is reported in Appendix Table 1.1.

Black out-migration rates were strongly influenced by local conditions, including a county's crop mix and its racial climate. Figure 1.3 reports the implied change in the county-level black migration rate for a one standard deviation change in each economic measure. A county's share of cultivated land planted in cotton predicts black out-migration in both the 1940s and the 1960s, as first the planting and weeding stages of cotton cultivation were automated and then as a viable mechanical cotton harvester diffused throughout the South, replacing hand labor (Grove and Heinicke 2003, 2005).[40] According to the estimates, a one standard deviation change in the cotton share (around 40 percent) is associated with 5 additional black out-migrants from a county per 100 black residents, compared to the mean black out-migration rate of 15

[38] For some families, access to education was an important motivation for migration. Juanita Tucker, for example, who eventually became principal of Wendell Phillips High School on Chicago's South Side, recalls that "our parents put a lot of emphasis on education, and again, I say, that's the reason my people came from the South to Chicago—to get a good education for their children" (Black 2003, 227). However, despite Grossman's (1989, 246) assertion that "education was central to the meaning of the Great Migration," there is no systematic evidence that this is the case. Only seventeen of the few hundred letters written by prospective southern black migrants to the *Chicago Defender* newspaper and collected in Scott 1919a, 1919b mention education as a motivation for migration.

[39] Baldwin (2007, 39) argues that "part of migrants' . . . motivation to move [to the North] included participation in commercialized leisure," which included black-owned clubs, jazz and blues broadcasts on "race radio," and other forms of entertainment, although he emphasizes that similar opportunities existed in southern cities.

[40] The strong relationship between a county's cotton share and black out-migration in the 1940s could also be due, in part, to the role of the AAA in encouraging cotton growers to leave their fields fallow. See Whatley 1983; Fligstein 1981, 137–51; and Wright 1986, 226–38.

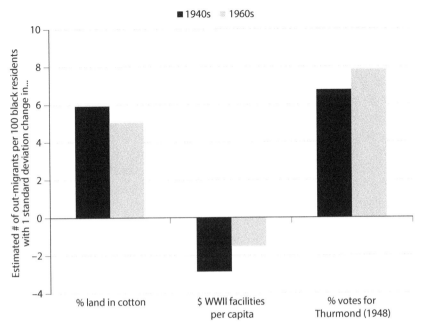

Figure 1.3. County-level conditions and black out-migration rates, 1940s and 1960s. Implied effect of one standard deviation change in county-level variable. Each bar represents the implied number of black migrants predicted to leave or enter a southern county with a one standard deviation change in each county-level characteristic. Magnitudes should be evaluated relative to the mean black out-migration rate of 14.56 in the 1940s (st. dev. = 32.38) and 11.92 in the 1960s (st. dev. = 27.49). Predictions derive from estimating Appendix Equation 2; the resulting coefficients are reported in Appendix Table 1.1.

per 100 in 1940. The Thurmond vote share, an indicator of the condition of local race relations, is also an important predictor of out-migration in both the 1940s and the 1960s. A one standard deviation change in the Thurmond vote share (28 percent) is associated with an additional six black out-migrants per 100 residents in both decades.

Counterbalancing these southern push factors was the pull of emerging southern industry. Schulman (1994) argues that federal contracts during World War II ushered in a sustained era of manufacturing growth in southern states.[41] Around 30 percent of southern counties received at least one federal contract during the war. A county that re-

---

[41] See Jaworski 2014 for more tempered conclusions about the causal effect of federal war spending on the southern manufacturing sector.

ceived an additional standard deviation of federal funds for war-related industry ($550 per resident in 2010 dollars) attracted 2–3 new black migrants in the 1940s and the 1960s. The persistent effect of war contracts on in-migration is consistent with the possibility that initial federal investments spurred subsequent local economic development but could also arise if federal dollars were targeted to areas that were already on a strong industrial trajectory.

One important division within the South is between the cotton belt and the non-cotton-growing counties. Cotton cultivation tended to be associated with poor race relations and higher levels of black-white inequality.[42] To compare the black out-migration rate from the cotton and non-cotton South, I consider increasing both the cotton share and the Thurmond vote share by two standard deviations (that is, from a county with no cotton production to one in which 80 percent of agricultural land is planted in cotton; and from a county with a small [say, 20 percent] core of support for Thurmond to one with an overwhelming majority support [76 percent]). By these estimates, shifting from a non-cotton to a cotton county would lead the black out-migration rate to increase by more than 20 departures per 100 residents in both decades— or roughly two-thirds of a standard deviation. Although this parsimonious model does a reasonably good job predicting variation in out-migration rates across counties, it will, by necessity, leave out many factors that are difficult to measure but may have been decisive for local residents, including proximity to a train line and the availability and quality of schools for black children.[43]

In contrast to this quantitative analysis, cultural representations of the black migration often identify flare-ups of racial violence and catastrophic events, like the periodic flooding of the Mississippi River, as the main triggers for migratory activity. Griffin (1995, 5) argues that violence, especially lynchings, beatings, and rapes, is regularly portrayed in literature and the arts as "a catalyst for leaving the South." One classic representation is Panel 15 in Jacob Lawrence's iconic *Migration of the Negro* paintings, which depicts a huddled black figure sitting

[42] See Cobb's (1992) history of economic and social relations in the Mississippi Delta, the prototypical example of the cotton-growing South.
[43] The R-squared for the county-level model is .20 in both decades. On the empirical relationship between black out-migration and distance to a train line or school availability, see Black et al. 2015 and Aaronson and Mazumder 2011. For earlier work on the role of factors like cotton intensity and farm tenancy on black out-migration, see Lewis [1931] 1968 and Fligstein 1981.

under a noose and is captioned: "It was found that where there had been a lynching, the people who were reluctant to leave at first left immediately after this." Another is Langston Hughes's poem "One Way Ticket," which similarly presents migration as a response to violence: "I am fed up / With Jim Crow laws / People who are cruel / And afraid / Who lynch and run, / Who are scared of me / And me of them. I pick up my life / And take it away / On a one-way ticket— / Gone up North, / Gone West, / Gone!"

Mention of migration in blues lyrics tends to focus on dramatic disasters like the Great Mississippi Flood of 1927. In Bessie Smith's "Homeless Blues" (1927), the protagonist dreams of abandoning the flooded Delta: "Mississippi River, what a fix you left me in / Pot holes of water clear up to my chin . . . Wish I was an eagle, but I'm just a plain old black crow / I'm gonna flap my wings and leave here and never come back no more." Similarly, the protagonist of "When the Levee Breaks," first recorded by Memphis Minnie in 1929, sings of the water levels rising and her plans to "leave my baby and my happy home."[44]

Quantitative work suggests that lynchings and floods, while important determinants of migration, were far from the main cause of black mobility. Tolnay and Beck (1995) find a strong relationship between number of lynching victims in a county and net black out-migration in the 1910s and 1920s.[45] By their estimate, a single lynching event prompted 1 out of every 100 black residents to leave the county.[46] During the 1910s, the typical southern county experienced 0.5 known lynching episodes. Thus, for the 9 million blacks living in the South,

[44] Although both songs refer to out-migration from flooded areas, neither mentions the North as a likely destination. By the time Led Zeppelin covered "When the Levee Breaks" in 1971, the lyrics pointedly mention the North—and, specifically, Chicago—as a destination, ending on the refrain "Going to Chicago . . . Going to Chicago . . . Sorry but I can't take you." This refrain was likely borrowed from the Count Basie and Joe Williams recording "Going to Chicago Blues" (1958), a song that has no relation to the 1927 flood.

[45] The quantitative evidence linking lynchings to out-migration is consistent with migrants' own accounts of their departures from the South. One black resident of Newark, NJ, recalls: "The white folks was so mean to us there. If my boy done something they didn't like, they'd kill him and me too—all of us, you know. They'd blame you because you race bein' black. They'd catch him and hang 'em up on a tree. . . . I didn't come North lookin' for flower beds, but I did come here not wanting my children to be killed like they was bein' killed down there" (Faulkner et al. 1982, 22). See also Wilkerson 2010, 36–46.

[46] Christian (2014, 8) finds a very similar effect of lynchings on migration. He reports that "a standard deviation increase in lynchings is associated with an 8% increase in out-migration." This estimate would imply that one lynching event would increase out-migration by around 10 percent, or by 0.8 migrants per 100 in the population given mean out-migration rates in the 1910s and 1920s.

mob violence alone would have prompted 45,000 departures.[47] If all of these out-migrants settled in the North (an upper-bound estimate), lynchings could explain 10 percent of the black migration flow to the North in the 1910s. Lynchings had dwindled by the 1940s and so were not quantitatively important in the period during and after World War II.[48]

Similarly, the periodic flooding of the Mississippi River was an important—although not pivotal—cause of black migration to the North. Hornbeck and Naidu (2014, Table 2) find that, after the Great Flood of 1927, the black population in flooded counties declined by 16 percent; however, the majority of these out-migrants remained within the South. Their best estimate suggests that around 6 percent of black migration in the 1920s can be attributed to the flood.[49] After the Great Flood, the federal government invested in a series of levees and reservoirs to contain and divert the Mississippi, considerably reducing the role of periodic flooding in subsequent migration activity (Barry 2007).

BLACK MIGRANT DESTINATIONS IN THE NORTH

Upon leaving the South, many southern blacks moved due north, following established train lines or migration chains from southern states to particular northern cities. As a result, the majority of migrants from the South Atlantic states settled in New England and the mid-Atlantic; many migrants from the Mississippi Delta moved to the Midwest; and migrants from Texas and Louisiana tended to relocate to California. Despite this wide regional distribution, black migration was highly concentrated in the top five destinations—New York City, Chicago, Detroit, Philadelphia, and Los Angeles.

Black migration flows out of the South followed lines of longitude from the South to the North. Table 1.1 displays the regional location of

[47] A figure of 45,000 is calculated as 9 million southern blacks × 0.5 lynching victims per county × an increase of 1 percentage point in the out-migration rate per incident.

[48] Forty reported lynchings of black victims, or 1 percent of known events, took place in 1940 or after (http://law2.umkc.edu/faculty/projects/ftrials/shipp/lynchstats .html)/).

[49] In 1920, 1.15 million black residents lived in the 69 counties that Hornbeck and Naidu (2014) identify as having been either flooded or partially flooded in the Great Flood. Sixteen percent of these residents left their home county and, of these, 24 percent moved to the North. These figures imply that, at most, 44,000 flood migrants settled in the North during the 1920s (= 1.15 million residents × 16 percent departure rate × 24 percent to North). Therefore, I calculate that refugees from this dramatic event can account for 6 percent of black migrants from the South during the 1920s (= 44,000/730,000).

southern black migrants in 1950 by state of birth. I focus on southern-born blacks who were between the ages of eighteen and thirty in 1940 and who lived outside of the South by 1950, most of whom would have moved in the 1940s.[50] Overall, 14 percent of the southern black population moved north during the 1940s. Out-migration rates in this core age group ranged from around 20 percent (from Louisiana, North Carolina, and Texas) to more than 40 percent (from Arkansas and Oklahoma).

Many black southern migrants moved due north. More than 85 percent of northward black migrants from the Carolinas and Virginia moved to New England or the mid-Atlantic. Likewise, at least 75 percent of black migrants from the centrally located states of Alabama, Mississippi, Kentucky, and Tennessee settled in the Midwest. Texas, at the western edge of the cotton belt, sent 75 percent of its black migrants to a Pacific or Mountain state.[51] Migrants from Louisiana and Oklahoma were split between the Midwest and the Pacific.

A number of northern cities received sizable inflows of black migrants from 1940 to 1970. Table 1.2 lists the 16 northern and western metropolitan areas that received at least 1 percent of the black migrant in-flow in either the 1940s or 1960s. Black migration was highly concentrated in the top five destinations, which together absorbed around 60 percent of new migrants in both decades.[52] For comparison, consider that these five areas housed only 43 percent of northern-born residents in the same age range in 1950. Eleven other metropolitan areas were home to large concentrations of black migrants; these destinations include seven cities in the Midwest (e.g., Cleveland), three in the mid-Atlantic (e.g., Buffalo), and one in the West (e.g., San Francisco).

In 1950, black migrants were most overrepresented in Detroit and Baltimore, with young southern blacks twice as likely as whites of similar ages to live in these cities. The concentration of black migrants in these cities was a function of their industrial structure and their proximity to train lines or to the South itself. Detroit was home to a large

[50] An alternative approach to identify recent migrants would use the "where did you live five years ago" Census question, which covers the periods 1955–60 or 1965–70. In 1950 the Census only asked about location one year before, thus perhaps capturing many temporary or seasonal migrants.

[51] Migrants from Arkansas, Florida, Georgia, and West Virginia correspond to these regional patterns but are less concentrated in the top destination.

[52] At the time, New York City was the main destination for foreign-born blacks, primarily hailing from the Caribbean. In 1950, 11 percent of the black population in New York City was foreign born, compared with less than 1 percent of the black population in Chicago and Detroit.

Table 1.1: Percentage of southern-born blacks living outside of the South by state of birth, 1950

| | | | | | | *Percentage living in a given region* | | | | | | | | |
| | | | | | | *State of birth* | | | | | | | | |
Region of current residence	AL	AR	FL	GA	KY	LA	MS	NC	OK	SC	TN	TX	VA	WV
New England/Mid-Atlantic	6.2	1.4	18.2	14.8	4.5	1.6	1.4	18.0	2.4	24.5	2.7	1.2	25.5	14.0
North Central	21.4	34.7	6.2	12.7	34.4	7.2	28.5	2.3	21.8	3.9	29.7	3.9	1.7	11.1
Mountain/Pacific	1.3	10.3	1.0	0.9	0.8	12.0	2.5	0.3	22.0	0.2	1.8	15.1	0.1	1.2
Total	28.9	46.4	25.4	28.4	39.7	20.8	32.4	20.6	46.2	28.6	34.2	20.2	27.3	26.3
Share of migrants to top region	0.74	0.75	0.72	0.52	0.87	0.58	0.88	0.87	0.48	0.86	0.87	0.75	0.93	0.53

Note: Regions follow Census definitions. The sample includes southern-born blacks in the IPUMS sample who were between the ages of 18 and 30 in 1940 and who resided in the North by 1950 ($N = 9{,}938$). Individuals in these cohorts likely moved in the 1940s.

Table 1.2: Destinations of southern black migrants in
the North and West, 1950 and 1970

| | Percentage in each metropolitan area | | | |
| | 1950 | | 1970 | |
	Southern black migrants	All northern residents	Southern black migrants	All northern residents
New York City	21.3	18.9	20.6	15.8
Chicago	13.4	8.0	14.0	7.8
Detroit	10.0	4.7	7.9	4.1
Philadelphia	9.5	5.6	5.4	4.6
Los Angeles	5.9	6.2	10.9	9.1
St. Louis	4.4	2.5	3.1	2.0
Baltimore	4.4	2.1	3.5	2.0
San Francisco	4.2	3.7	4.3	3.3
Cleveland	3.6	2.3	3.5	2.1
Pittsburgh	2.4	3.3	–	–
Cincinnati	1.8	1.0	1.0	1.4
Kansas City	1.1	1.3	1.0	1.3
Buffalo	1.1	1.6	1.4	1.3
Milwaukee	–	–	1.3	1.4
Indianapolis	–	–	1.3	1.1
Flint	–	–	1.0	0.5

Note: Columns 1 and 3 report the percentage of southern-born black migrants in the 1950 (1970) IPUMS samples, who were between the ages of 18 and 30 in 1940 (or 1960) and who resided in a given northern metropolitan area in 1950 (or 1970). Results are based on 9,938 cases in 1950 and 8,316 cases in 1970. Individuals in these cohorts likely moved in the 1940s (or 1960s). For comparison, columns 2 and 4 report the percentage of all northern residents in the same age range in each area. In both cases, the sample is restricted to individuals who lived in a metropolitan area outside of the South. The table includes all metropolitan areas that housed at least 1 percent of new black arrivals in each decade. To be consistent with the 1950 metropolitan definitions, New York City is combined with northern New Jersey, the Chicago area includes Gary, IN, and the Los Angeles area includes Orange County.

cluster of manufacturing employment; in 1940, 48 percent of employment in Detroit was in the manufacturing sector, compared with only 33 percent of employment in northern and western metropolitan areas as a whole. Baltimore was the northern city closest to the black populations of Virginia and the Carolinas. In contrast, among large cities, black southern migrants were most underrepresented in Boston, Minneapolis-St. Paul, and Seattle. These cities were characterized by industries with a strong demand for educated workers; their average resident had around one year more in reported schooling than did residents in the typical northern or western metropolitan area.

CONCLUSION

Black migration to the North remained low at the turn of the twentieth century, despite high (potential) returns to migration. Once migration began, prompted by heightened labor demand during World War I, it accelerated quickly as networks of black migrants formed in northern cities. Northern migration peaked in the 1940s and 1950s before declining and eventually reversing by the 1980s. At its height, southern black migration was comparable in magnitude to inflows from European sending countries during the Age of Mass Migration.

A longer-term perspective on black southern mobility suggests that interstate migration began to rise as early as the birth cohort of 1860, many of whom would have moved in the 1880s and 1890s. In this light, the Great Black Migration appears to be the continuation of ongoing increases in black mobility after the Civil War, albeit at an accelerated pace. Areas in the South that were dependent on cotton agriculture, many of which were also characterized by severe racial segregation, tended to have the highest black out-migration rates. Upon arrival in the North, some black migrants clustered in the classic gateway cities of Chicago and Detroit, while others established new black communities in smaller and midsized cities throughout the North and West.

APPENDIX TO CHAPTER 1
Lifetime Migration Rates by Birth Cohort

I define a lifetime migrant as someone living outside his or her state of birth in a Census period. The probability of being a lifetime migrant increases with age because older individuals have had more years in which to potentially leave home. I observe lifetime mobility rates by race for the birth cohorts of 1810 through 1970 using data from seven Census waves (every other Census from 1880 to 2000). Because I observe most birth cohorts in multiple waves, I can separately identify the effects of age and birth cohort on lifetime migration rates. In particular, I estimate:

$$I(outside\ state\ of\ birth) = \alpha + \beta_1(age) + \beta_2(age^2)$$
$$+ \Gamma'(Birth\ cohort\ indicators) + \varepsilon \qquad (1)$$

where $I(outside\ state\ of\ birth)$ is an indicator variable equal to one for individuals who live outside of their state of birth, age and age^2 allow lifetime migration to vary with age according to a quadratic function, and *Birth cohort indicators* is a vector of dummy variables, one for each birth cohort in the sample. In each Census year, the sample includes all southern-born individuals between the ages of 30 and 69. The coefficients of interest (the vector Γ) indicate the age-adjusted lifetime migration rate of each birth cohort in the sample. I plot the predicted lifetime migration rate at age 30 by birth cohort and race in Figure 1.1a. Figure 1.1b presents the share of predicted lifetime moves for the southern born that take place within the South.

Determinants of County-Level Out-migration

I model black out-migration rates from southern counties during a decade (*t* through *t* + 10) as a function of local conditions in the base year *t*. My estimating equation for black migration rates from county *c* in southern state *s* is:

$$mig\_rate_{c,s,t-t+10} = \alpha_s + B' \ (economic \ conditions)_{ct}$$
$$+ \ \gamma(racial \ climate)_c + \delta(WWII \ contracts)_c + \varepsilon_{cst} \qquad (2)$$

where α_s is a vector of state fixed effects. The dependent variable (*mig_rate*) is the number of black out-migrants from a county per 100 black residents during the decade *t* to *t* + 10, estimated using the Census forward survival ratio method described in the text (Gardner and Cohen 1971; Bowles et al. 1990). The black out-migration rate at the county level ranges from 100 to –100, with a mean of –14.5 in the 1940s.[53] *Economic conditions* include the share of tilled land planted in cotton, the share of farmers operating as tenants, and the share of the labor force in agriculture and in mining. *World War II contracts* are defined as per capita federal expenditures on defense contracts from 1940 to 1945. My proxy for the *racial climate* is the share of voters who supported Strom Thurmond's candidacy for president on the States' Rights (Dixiecrat) ticket in the 1948 election.[54] State fixed effects (α_s) control for the fact

[53] Around 30 of the 1,000 southern counties in each year experienced black in-migration rates that were substantially greater than 100, a result of large black inflows into counties with small initial black populations. To prevent these outliers from driving the results, I cap net migration rates at 100, reassigning any in-migration rates greater than 100 to be exactly 100. This restriction leads the results of this analysis to differ slightly from a similar exercise conducted in Boustan 2010.

[54] Data on cotton acreage is collected digitally when possible from the National Agricultural Statistical Service's website and from the Population and Environment in the U.S. Great Plains project (Gutmann 1997). The remainder is collected by hand from the Censuses of Agriculture. Information on vote shares is taken from Electoral Data for Counties in the United States (Clubb, Flanigan, and Zingale 2006). Other southern vari-

Appendix Table 1.1: Net black migration rates
and southern economic conditions

	Mean/SD in 1940	Coefficients, 1940–50	Coefficients, 1960–70
Share land planted in cotton	0.585	−14.568	−14.963
	(0.408)	(3.416)	(3.155)
Share farms operated by tenants	0.501	−5.732	−6.433
	(0.159)	(8.509)	(7.870)
Share LF in agriculture	0.506	−29.512	−8.789
	(0.191)	(6.335)	(7.748)
Share LF in ag × Tobacco state	–	5.714	−28.776
		(13.443)	(14.616)
$ war contracts per capita	$151.66	0.0051	0.0028
(in 1940 dollars)	(546.26)	(0.0017)	(0.0014)
Share LF in mining	0.012	−67.385	−16.502
	(0.041)	(42.700)	(36.665)
Share in mining × (OK or TX)	–	73.393	−39.583
		(52.357)	(37.991)
Share votes for Thurmond 1948	0.252	−23.616	−27.207
	(0.286)	(9.516)	(7.499)
N		943	953
State FE		Y	Y
Mean of DV		−14.56	−11.92
St dev of DV		32.38	27.44

Note: Dependent variable = Net black migration rate. Columns 2 and 3 report coefficient estimates of Appendix Equation 2. Regressions include all southern counties with available data. In addition to the coefficients highlighted in Figure 1.3, the regression includes the share of farms operated by tenants, the share of the labor force working in agriculture, and the share of the labor force working in mining. I also interact the agriculture share with being in a tobacco state to account for slower mechanization in tobacco cultivation relative to other crops and interact the mining share with being in Texas or Oklahoma to account for the boom in oil and natural gas. World War II funding is reported in 1940 dollars; $152 per capita in 1940 is equivalent to $2,350 per capita in 2010.

that Thurmond appeared on the ballot in a different manner in different states.[55] Summary statistics and regression coefficients for the analysis described here are reported in Appendix Table 1.1.

---

ables are drawn from the electronic County and City Data Books (U.S. Bureau of the Census 2012).

[55] Thurmond received more votes in states where he replaced Truman as the Democratic candidate rather than being entered as a third-party candidate.

CHAPTER 2

Who Left the South and
How Did They Fare?

THE BLUES GUITARIST Jimmy Reed migrated to Chicago from Mississippi in 1943. After serving briefly in the U.S. Navy, he returned to the Chicago area and worked in meatpacking. In a series of recordings in the late 1950s and early 1960s, Reed sang about life in the North, which he described as a balance between the toil of hard work and the rewards of material acquisition. In the song "Big Boss Man," he grumbles that his factory job has him "working 'round the clock," but, notably, he does not complain about low pay or poor working conditions. In "Ain't Got You" he bemoans his inability to catch a woman's eye despite his many alluring possessions, including a "charge account at Goldblatt's," a Chicago department store, and an "Eldorado Cadillac / with a spare tire on the back," the most expensive car in the Cadillac line. In perhaps his most famous tune, "Bright Lights, Big City," Reed frets that the affluence of the North has "gone to my baby's head."[1]

By the early 1970s, this tempered, but ultimately positive, view of migration as a route to prosperity had soured. Stevie Wonder, who was raised in Michigan by southern-born parents, penned the 1973 funk-ballad "Living for the City" about a southern migrant with dashed dreams. Wonder sings of a young migrant "born in hard time Mississippi," where his father "worked some days for 14 hours / and you can bet he barely made a dollar." After growing up in this hardscrabble family, moving to the North seemed like a big step up. But immediately upon arriving in New York City, the protagonist of the song is thrown in jail for a crime he did not commit; he ends up homeless and wandering the streets. This despair at northern economic conditions is echoed

---

[1] For general discussions about the influence of the Great Black Migration on the form and content of blues music, see Keil 1966, 50–66; Spencer 1992; and Nall 2001.

in fellow Motown artist and second-generation migrant Marvin Gaye's 1971 lament "Inner City Blues."[2]

Was migration from the South a road to black economic advancement, as Reed claimed in the 1950s, or was it a hollow promise, as Wonder and Gaye asserted (with the benefit of hindsight) in the 1970s? This chapter sides definitively with Reed's view of migration as a route to economic advancement. Black migrants earned a substantial economic return relative to fellow southerners who remained in the South. Even after adjusting for the fact that migrants may have had higher earnings potential, I find that movers earned twice as much as those who stayed behind. Indeed, almost upon first arrival, black migrants earned on parity with northern-born blacks in the northern economy.

Most of the historical literature likewise describes the northward migration as an economic boon to those who made the journey. Kusmer (1976, 222) summarizes these findings, writing that "solid gains [were] made by most newcomers to the city because the conditions they left in the South were much worse than those in the North." However, this historical work has not accounted for potential selection into migration. Simple comparisons of the earnings of migrants and non-migrants can be misleading if migrants have distinctive attributes. For example, previous research has found that blacks who left the South were more educated than those who remained. In this case, we would expect a direct comparison of the earnings of black migrants and black southerners to overstate the true economic benefit of migration.

I therefore begin by investigating the family background of black migrants leaving the South. I find that young migrants living in the North in 1940 were drawn from households at *both* the top and the bottom of the occupational distribution. Migrants were more likely than non-migrants to have a father who was a white-collar worker, but they were also more likely to have a father who was a common laborer. At the same time, migrants were less likely to hail from households headed

---

[2] Another depiction of the disappointment that some black migrants faced upon arrival in the North can be found in Woodson's recent prose poem, *Brown Girl Dreaming*. Before moving North, Woodson's narrator says: "They say the City is a place where diamonds speckle the sidewalk. Money falls from the sky. They say a colored person can do well going there. All you need is the fare out of Greenville. All you need is somebody on the other side, waiting to cross you over. Like the River Jordan and then you're in Paradise" (2014, 93). After arrival, the diamonds have been replaced by cold rock: "Maybe it's another New York City the southerners talk about," she writes. "Maybe that's where there is money falling from the sky, diamonds speckling the sidewalks. Here there is only gray rock, cold and treeless as a bad dream" (2014, 143).

by a tenant farmer, the middle rung on the agricultural ladder. High migration rates for the sons of common laborers are consistent with the fact that the expected gains for leaving the South were higher for men at the low end of the income distribution. The sons of white-collar workers may have been particularly attracted by the social and political freedoms available in the North. These findings are based on a new matched sample that follows individuals over time from the 1920 to the 1940 Census, allowing migrants and non-migrants to be observed in their childhood homes.

Given that migrants were drawn from both the top and the bottom of the occupational distribution, there is no clear prediction about whether simple estimates of the return to migration would be biased by migrant selection. As it turns out, I find little evidence of selection bias; the estimated return to migration is similar in the full population and among pairs of brothers who share a family background. In both cases, I find that southern blacks could have expected to more than double their earnings by moving to the North as of 1940, while southern whites enjoyed a return to migration of 50 percent. These values are much higher than the 30 percent return to migration implied by Smith and Welch (1989, Table 16) and are closer to Collins and Wanamaker's (2014) estimated 100 percent return to migration in 1930.

I find that, after arriving in their destinations, black migrants did not suffer an earnings penalty in the northern economy, but neither did they out-earn northern-born blacks as some have suggested. Rather, southern migrants earned just as much as northern-born blacks upon arrival in the North and experienced a similar pace of earnings growth over time. These results are based on detailed information from the *Racial Attitudes in Fifteen American Cities* survey, conducted in 1968, coupled with Census data from various years.

WHO LEFT THE SOUTH?

Northern cities offered many southern blacks the promise of higher wages. Given the high level of income inequality in the South, blacks at the bottom and in the middle of the income distribution had the most to gain by moving to the North. However, the data show that black migrants were selected from households at both the bottom and the top of the occupational distribution, suggesting that the migration decision was driven by more than just a regional wage comparison. Migrants were more likely than non-migrants to hail from households whose heads held an unskilled occupation, but they were also more likely to have been raised by a household head employed in a skilled blue-collar or white-collar position. Migrants were less likely to be drawn from households whose heads were employed in mid-skill level positions, including farm tenancy and semiskilled blue-collar work. Furthermore, within each skill category, migrants were more likely to have been raised by a household head with relevant urban skills (e.g., skilled blue-collar workers) rather than by heads with agricultural skills (e.g., farm owners).

Theoretical Predictions on Migrant Selection

Simple economic reasoning suggests that prospective migrants will move only if the benefits of leaving their current location outweigh the advantages of staying put (Sjaastad 1962). The potential costs and benefits of migration will vary across individuals on the basis of standard demographic characteristics such as age, gender, and skill level, as well as by harder-to-measure traits like attachment to family and willingness to take risks. Economic models of migrant selection generate systematic predictions about which subgroups are likely to receive the greatest benefits from migration and therefore can be expected to exhibit the highest out-migration rates.

Roy's (1951) classic model of self-selection, which was originally applied to occupational choice, is now a standard tool used to analyze migrant selection. Roy argued that individuals sort themselves into occupations on the basis of "comparative advantage." For example, medical students with high levels of manual dexterity could expect particularly high pay as surgeons and thus might choose to enter a surgical specialty. Equally intelligent students lacking manual skills could not expect such compensation and so might choose a medical specialty. In this way, each student would select the field that maximizes his or her own economic reward.

The same argument has been applied to the decision to migrate between regions. Prospective migrants possessing skills that were particularly valued in northern cities would have expected the highest economic return to migration and thus may have been the most likely to leave the South. This framework implies that if northern cities paid especially high wages for low-skilled work, then the migrant flow out of the South would have been negatively selected on the basis of skill. If, instead, northern cities paid especially high wages for high-skilled work, then the migrant flow would have been positively selected. Of course, migrants were motivated to pick up stakes for many reasons beyond expected wage gains, including the social and political freedoms and higher-quality education available in the North. Vigdor (2002) argues that high-skilled blacks placed a greater premium on these northern benefits, which may have contributed to positive migrant selection.[3]

For southern blacks, the potential wage gains associated with moving to the North were large enough in every skill group that nearly everyone could have expected some pecuniary benefit from migration. Indeed, around half of the southern black population moved north between 1940 and 1970. However, given that migration entails some costs, including living at a distance from family and friends, a portion of the southern black population chose to remain in the region. The Roy model can be used to provide guidance about who among the southern population was most likely to make this move.

Migrant selection in the Roy model is determined by the relative wages of particular skill groups in the destination and source economies (Borjas 1987b). In particular, because low-skilled workers faced a larger relative earnings penalty in the South than in the North, they should have had the highest return to out-migration from the region.[4] Table 2.1 reports measures of the income distribution in 1940 by region for the full male workforce and separately for black workers. The Gini coefficient captures the extent to which an income distribution diverges from perfect equality; higher values of the Gini correspond to greater levels of income divergence between low-skilled and high-skilled workers. The larger income disparities in the South are reflected in a Gini coefficient of 50, compared with a Gini of only 38 in the North. The income distribution was also wider for black workers in the South (Gini = 45) than in the North (Gini = 34).

Income inequality in the South was driven, primarily, by a gap between the highest-paid workers and workers in other parts of the income distribution. Workers at the 90th percentile of the income distri-

---

[3] In addition, educated southern blacks may have moved to avoid being particular targets for racial violence in the South. However, contrary to this hypothesis, Bailey et al. (2011) find that blacks with higher-status occupations were *less* likely to be victims of lynching episodes.

[4] Grogger and Hanson (2011) present a modified version of the Roy model that emphasizes absolute, rather than relative, gaps in earnings between the destination and source economies. In this case, the two models generate similar predictions because the South had larger absolute and relative earnings gaps between high- and low-skilled workers.

Table 2.1: Income distribution by race and region, 1940

	All men		Black men	
	South	North	South	North
Gini	0.50	0.38	0.45	0.34
90/10	14.9	6.6	6.6	6.1
50/10	3.8	3.1	2.1	3.1

Note: The sample includes men between the ages of 18 and 64 who were not enrolled in school, who were not living in group quarters, who were not in active duty military service, and who reported non-zero earnings for the year. I combine wage and salary income for wage workers (using the "incwage" variable from IPUMS) with imputed earnings for the self-employed. Self-employed workers are assigned the median earnings in their occupation-race-region cell from the 1960 IPUMS, adjusted to 1940 dollars using the Consumer Price Index. Cells with fewer than ten entrants in 1960 are assigned the median earnings from their occupation-region cell instead (0.3 percent of all cases, and 2.4 percent of blacks). Occupation categories follow the 1950 occupation classifications available in IPUMS ("occ1950") except in the case of farmers. Farmers who report owning a home are classified as owner-occupier farmers, while those who report renting are classified as tenant farmers. The 90/10 ratio in the second row compares the earnings of men at the 90th percentile of the income distribution to men at the 10th percentile, while the 50/10 ratio in the third row compares men at the 50th and 10th percentiles of the income distribution.

bution in the South earned fifteen times that of workers at the 10th percentile; in the North, this ratio was only seven to one. In contrast, the 50–10 ratio, which measures the disparity between workers in the middle and the bottom of the income distribution, was similar in both regions. Higher levels of income inequality among blacks in the South also seem to be driven by disparities at the top end of the income distribution, as measured by the 90–10 ratio; in fact, for black workers, the 50–10 ratio was actually larger in the North.[5]

A regional comparison suggests that southerners at the low end of the income distribution had the most to gain by moving to the North. The racial pattern of out-migration from the South is strongly consistent with this prediction. Southern blacks earned substantially less than southern whites and were almost twice as likely as their white counterparts to leave the region; compare a black out-migration rate of 14 percent during the 1940s to a white out-migration rate of 8 percent. The Roy model would generate the same prediction for the black popula-

[5] High levels of income inequality in the South, particularly at the top of the distribution, are consistent with evidence of higher returns to skill in the region. In 1940, an additional year of schooling was associated with a 7 percent increase in income in the typical southern state but only a 5 percent increase in income in northern and western states (Collins 2007, 182). Collins (2007) argues that high returns to skill in the South encouraged highly educated workers to move to the South from the rest of the country.

tion—namely, that black migrants should be drawn from the lower and middle rather than the upper segment of the black income distribution, groups that include farm laborers and farm tenants as well as unskilled and semiskilled blue-collar workers.

The simplest version of the Roy model predicts that low-skilled black southerners should be the most likely to leave the region. However, there are a number of extensions that provide a more complex set of predictions. First, applications of the Roy model typically focus on pecuniary benefits to migration rather than potential differences in valuations for the social and political benefits of moving north. If high-skilled workers placed a higher value on the freedoms available in the North, they may have been more likely than other groups to make the move. In addition, poor southern blacks, many of whom were farm laborers in rural areas, may not have been able to save up enough for the trip to the North or may have lacked the relevant information, network of friends and family, or proximity to a train station to facilitate the journey (Margo 1990, 118–20). Therefore, even if the benefits of migration were high for the lowest-skilled blacks, the costs of migration may have been prohibitive.[6]

Existing Literature on the Selection of Black Migrants from the South

In contrast to the simple Roy model, previous work has documented that black migrants from the South were positively selected on the basis of literacy and educational attainment. Black migrants to the North had higher literacy rates than blacks who remained in the South in the early twentieth century (Hamilton 1959; Lieberson 1978; Margo 1988, 1990).[7] In the 1940 Census, the first to include information on educational attainment, black southern migrants had two more years of schooling than non-migrants, even after adjusting for age and gender (Tolnay 1998).[8] Black migrants were also more likely than the average southern

---

[6] Saving up for a trip north may have been difficult for some low-skilled workers. Henri (1975, 66) estimates that train travel from the South to the North cost $.024 per mile in 1918. At this rate, the typical journey of around 1,000 miles would have cost $24. In addition, migrants would have foregone around two weeks of work while traveling and adjusting to the North. At the time, farmhands earned around $1 a day (Trotter 1985, 47). Thus the total cost of migration would have represented around 10 percent of the annual earnings of a farm laborer.

[7] Logan (2009) examines migrant selection using data from the Colored Troops sample of the Union Army data set. He confirms that literate blacks were more likely to leave the South by 1900 but argues that up to one-third of this differential can be attributed to differences in health by literacy status.

[8] See also Margo 1988, Table 2 and 1990, Table 7.2 on the 1940 and 1950 censuses and Bowles 1970 on the 1960 census.

black resident to have lived in an urban area and to have worked out-side of the agricultural sector before moving north.[9] Only 43 percent of black migrants who settled in the North before 1930 had worked in agriculture, compared to 57 percent of the black southern population (Collins and Wanamaker 2014).[10] The Birmingham *Age-Herald* described this pattern in colorful (and outdated) fashion: "It is not the riffraff of the race, the worthless Negroes, who are leaving in such large num-bers. . . . [Many migrants] have property and good positions which they are sacrificing in order to get away at the first opportunity."

Interpreting these patterns as evidence of migrant selection is not without complication. First, Census enumerators in the North (or mi-grants themselves) may have overstated migrants' level of education. In the South, blacks often attended ungraded schools, which may have been hard for northern enumerators to understand and categorize (Margo 1986). Perhaps as a result of this enumeration issue, black mi-grants were 20 percent more likely than non-migrants to report having six or seven years of education, but 200 percent more likely to report exactly eight years of schooling, which may have overinflated their re-corded schooling.[11] Second, rather than being a predetermined charac-teristic, education may be jointly determined with the decision to mi-grate. Some prospective migrants may have opted to remain in school for an extra year as an investment in their hoped-for future in a north-ern city. Furthermore, some black migrants moved as children and re-ceived their schooling in the North. In this case, higher levels of educa-tion would be an outcome of—rather than a precursor to—migration.

New Results on Migrant Selection

Unlike a migrant's own education or urban status, which can be jointly determined with his decision to migrate, a father's occupation is deter-mined before a son's decision to migrate. I compare the occupations of the fathers of migrants and non-migrants as an indicator of migrant

[9] Contemporary observers noted that many migrants had some "experience in lum-bering, railroading, and iron and steel foundries" (Epstein 1918, 35; see also Chicago Commission on Race 1922, 95). These sources were originally cited by Marks (1989, 37).

[10] Data from the Palmer Survey, a retrospective study of men living in six northern cities in 1951, further attests to this pattern: only 12 percent of black migrants in the sam-ple had worked in agriculture in 1940, compared with nearly 50 percent of southern black men at that time (Collins 2000). On this point, see also Alexander 1998.

[11] I thank Bill Collins for pointing out this interesting feature of the data. Evenly redis-tributing the excess mass of migrants who report eight years of schooling between the years six, seven, and eight can account for one (out of the two) years of differential school-ing between migrants and non-migrants.

selection. To do so, I create a matched sample of southern-born men observed in their childhood household in 1920 and linked to their adult records in 1940. Migration status is classified according to region of residence in 1940.

The linked sample of southern-born blacks is matched across Census waves by first and last names, age, race, and state of birth; details on the matching process are included in the appendix to this chapter. This analysis focuses on men owing to the social convention that women change their surname upon marriage. I begin with a sample of southern-born men between the ages of three and fifteen who are observed in their childhood household in the digitized complete-count 1920 Census. I am able to match 37 percent of this sample to the 1940 complete-count data. The resulting data set contains over 200,000 black men. This match rate is slightly higher than in related Census linkage projects using earlier Census years (Collins and Wanamaker 2014, 2015a, 2015b).[12] Appendix Table 2.1 demonstrates that the fathers of black men in the matched sample are similar to a representative group of black southern-born household heads with sons in the same age range in the 1920 IPUMS.

The fathers of migrants and non-migrants are drawn from notably different segments of the occupational distribution. Table 2.2 compares the fathers of men who had moved to the North by 1940 (known migrants) to those who still lived in the South in 1940 (likely non-migrants).[13] I use HISCLASS occupation codes to divide fathers' occupations into seven categories: high-skilled workers (white collar, skilled blue collar, and farm owners); mid-skill workers (semiskilled blue-collar and farm tenants); and low-skilled workers (unskilled and farm laborers) (van Leeuwen and Ineke 2005).[14] As predicted by the Roy model, I find that black migrants are more likely than non-migrants to have been raised by a father working in an unskilled or farm labor position (40 percent versus 35 percent). Yet migrants are also more likely to

[12] Factors that contribute to higher match rates in the 1940 Census include better transcription, a more literate and numerate population able to report their name and age more accurately over time, and improvements in life expectancy.

[13] Given that migration activity is high for men in their twenties, some of the younger men in the sample who eventually migrated to the North may not yet have moved by 1940 and thus would be misclassified as "non-migrants." To address this concern, I conducted a parallel analysis for the subset of men who were at least thirty years old in 1940. Results are similar.

[14] I separate farm owners from farm tenants using information on homeownership. In particular, I code men who report their occupation as "farmer" and who own their own home as farm owners; all other farmers are coded as farm tenants.

Table 2.2: Occupational distribution of the fathers of black migrants and non-migrants, 1920

Occupational categories	Non-migrant sons	At least one migrant son
High-skilled workers		
Farm owner	0.142	0.140
White collar	0.024	0.039
Skilled blue collar	0.034	0.086
Subtotal	*0.200*	*0.265*
Mid-skilled workers		
Farm tenant	0.355	0.226
Semiskilled blue collar	0.095	0.109
Subtotal	*0.450*	*0.335*
Low-skilled workers		
Farm labor	0.145	0.159
Unskilled	0.205	0.241
Subtotal	*0.350*	*0.400*
	1.00	*1.00*

Note: Columns compare the fathers of black southern-born sons who had moved to the North by 1940 (migrants, N = 295) and the fathers of sons who still lived in the South in that year (non-migrants, N = 1,145). HISCLASS occupation codes are used to classify fathers' occupations into five categories: white-collar, skilled blue-collar, farmers, semiskilled blue-collar and unskilled workers (van Leeuwen and Ineke 2005). Farm laborers are broken out from the "unskilled" category using the occupation codes 820–840. Farm tenants and farm owners have the same occupation code (100) but are classified separately using the homeownership variable, with homeowners classified as farm owners and renters classified as tenants.

hail from households headed by a high-skilled worker (27 percent versus 20 percent). This bimodal distribution, in which migrants are drawn from households in both the lower and upper segments of the skill distribution, is not consistent with the simple Roy model. Households with higher levels of skill or education may have placed a higher value on the social climate and political rights afforded by the North (Vigdor 2002).[15]

Within each skill category, migrants also appear to be selected on the basis of the transferability of skills to the northern economy. In particu-

[15] Collins and Wanamaker (2015a) present a set of complementary findings using a Census data set that links migrants and non-migrants to their own pre-migration outcomes (rather than those of their fathers) in 1910. They find little evidence of positive selection on literacy but show that migrants have slightly higher occupation-based earnings than non-migrants.

lar, at each skill level, migrants are more likely to have been raised by a household head with urban skills than by one with agricultural know-how. For example, 47 percent of migrants in the high-skill category were raised by a father in a white-collar or skilled blue-collar profession, as opposed to an owner-occupier farmer, compared to 29 percent of non-migrants.[16] The same pattern holds for migrants in the other skill categories.

DID MIGRANTS OUT-EARN BLACKS WHO REMAINED IN THE SOUTH?

Black migrants were less likely to hail from agricultural households and more likely to be raised by fathers with urban-oriented occupations. If fathers transmitted these skills to their sons, men raised in these households may have been at an advantage in the labor market regardless of their geographic location. This urban-oriented selection may generate bias in the estimates of the economic return to northward migration. The simplest approach to measuring the return to migration is to compare the earnings of black migrants in the North to the earnings of black workers who remained in the South. However, if migrants are selected from the sending population on the basis of skill, this estimate would combine the true benefit of moving to the North with the earnings advantage that workers with this particular skill set would otherwise enjoy.

I present new estimates of the return to migration from the South to the North for both black and white men in 1940. My estimates take migrant selection into account by comparing the earnings of migrants and their non-migrant brothers in the linked sample. Brothers share a family background and some fraction of their genetic material. Of course, brothers differ in their personal attributes and life experiences and so one brother is not a perfect counterfactual for the other. But comparing a migrant with his own brother provides a good estimate of what the migrant himself would likely have earned if he had remained in the South. Abramitzky, Boustan, and Eriksson (2012) used this approach to estimate the return to migration from Europe to the United States during the Age of Mass Migration. Collins and Wanamaker (2014) adapted this method to estimate the return to migration from the

---

[16] I calculate these percentages from Table 2.2 as (0.039 + 0.086)/0.265 for migrant sons compared to (0.024 + 0.034)/0.200 for non-migrant sons.

South in 1930. In my matched sample, I can identify brother pairs by observing children with the same relationship to household head (usually "son") in the 1920 Census. Around 40 percent of the matched sample is a member of a linked brother pair that can be observed in both 1920 and 1940.

Existing Literature on the Earnings of Black Migrants in the North

Scattered wage evidence suggests that black migrants experienced a substantial boost in earnings when moving north circa 1920. Unskilled industrial jobs in Milwaukee and Chicago paid between $3.20 and $4.80 a day (Trotter 1985, 47; Marks 1989, 113). These solid northern wages "contrasted sharply with conditions in the South where, even in urban industrial centers such as Birmingham, unskilled workers earned a maximum of $2.50 for a nine-hour day. Southern farmhands made even less, usually 75 cents to $1.00 a day" (Trotter 1985, 47). Such figures imply that migrants who remained within the industrial sector could have expected a return to migration ranging from 30 to 90 percent (= [$3.20 − $2.50]/$2.50, for example). Southern blacks who were able to move directly from agricultural labor to an industrial occupation in the North may have increased their earnings by as much as 300 percent, akin to the return to migration from Mexico to the United States today (Hanson 2006).

More complete estimates of the wage benefits associated with migration employ Census data to measure earnings for the full distribution of occupations held by black workers in the North and South. Collins and Wanamaker (2014) estimate that black migrants enjoyed a return to migration between 60 and 70 log points (100 percent) in 1930. This value falls between the return to migration within the industrial sector and the return associated with a shift from agriculture into industry in the archival wage data. In contrast, Eichenlaub, Tolnay, and Alexander (2010, 118) question the existence of a positive return to migration between 1940 and 1970, writing that blacks "who left the South during the Great Migration, on average, fared no better than those who stayed behind; in fact, based on some criteria, they may have done worse."

The main cause of these divergent results is the different definitions of "economic gain" used in these two studies.[17] Eichenlaub, Tolnay, and Alexander focus on "relative income," a measure that compares the

---

[17] The studies also differ on a number of other dimensions including time period, income measure, and approach for addressing selection into migration.

earnings of migrants or non-migrants to the average black income in their state of residence. On this measure, migrants appear to fall behind blacks who stay in the South in their relative position in the income distribution. But this pattern is hardly surprising: by leaving low-wage sending areas, migrants sacrificed their position in the local income distribution for an improvement in their absolute standard of living. When instead estimating the absolute income gains associated with migration, Eichenlaub and colleagues find that migrants benefit from their move; their estimates imply a return for long-term migrants of 41 percent in 1950 and 20 percent in 1980.[18] Combining the estimates from these studies, it appears that black migrants enjoyed the highest economic gain from moving North in 1930 and that the return declined somewhat by 1950 and fell further by 1980. A falling return to migration over time is consistent with regional earnings convergence between the North and the South, particularly after 1940.

The estimated effect of migration on nominal earnings may not be an accurate representation of the associated increase in well-being. First, higher wages may have been counterbalanced, in part, by poorer living conditions in northern cities. For example, black migrants to the North ended up in worse health than did blacks who remained in the South, experiencing higher rates of both infant and adult mortality (Black et al. 2015; Eriksson and Niemesh 2015). Second, higher nominal wages in the North may have simply reflected the higher cost of living in northern cities, resulting in equal purchasing power in each region. Collins and Wanamaker (2014) adjust for regional differences in cost of living and demonstrate that migrants enjoy a large increase in real earnings power; I conduct a similar exercise in what follows.

New Evidence on the Return to Migration

I add to recent estimates of the return to migration from the South with new evidence from the 1940 Census. The 1940 Census was the first to include questions about individual income rather than questions about occupation only. The complete manuscripts for the 1940 Census were recently released, allowing me to create a linked sample of brothers,

---

[18] I calculate these returns to migration using Eichenlaub, Tolnay, and Alexander's (2010) coefficients on the effect of migration on absolute income and their reported mean earnings for southern blacks. For example, for long-term arrivals to the North in 1950, the estimated return to migration would be 41 percent (= 503/1237), where 503 is a coefficient estimate from Table 2 and 1237 is the reported income for "sedentary" southern blacks in 1950 from Table A-1.

one or more of whom moved to the North, to control for migrant selection. As a benchmark, I start with a simple comparison of the annual earnings of southern-born men in the North with southern-born men who remained in the South by race. The black bars in Figure 2.1 report the estimated return to migration in the full population; the underlying regression is reported in Appendix Equation 1. By this metric, I find that southern black men could have increased their annual earnings by 82 log points, or around 130 percent, by moving to the North in 1940. White southerners also earned a positive but somewhat lower, return for moving North (45 log points, or nearly 60 percent). For comparison, the gray bars contrast the earnings of migrants and non-migrants in the matched sample. Returns are similar, suggesting that characteristics that increase the likelihood of generating a successful match (e.g., having an uncommon name) are not associated with higher or lower returns to migration.

I then narrow my comparison to brother pairs, with the return to migration identified from pairs in which one brother moved to the North while the other remained in the South. The white bars in Figure 2.1 report estimates from models that add household fixed effects (see Appendix Equation 2). The return to migration in the within-brothers specification is again quite close to the estimate for the full population. If a portion of the estimated return to migration were due to positive migrant selection, we would expect the earnings gap between brothers to be smaller than the gap in the full population. The similarity of the estimates instead suggests that southern migrants were not especially selected, either positively or negatively. The previous section demonstrates that migrant selection on the basis of family background was bimodal: migrants were more likely than non-migrants to be raised by fathers with either a low- or high-skill profession. These two forces appear to cancel out, leaving a migrant flow that, on average, looks representative of the population.

My estimates of the return to migration in the 1940 Census are slightly higher than comparable estimates for 1930 (130 percent versus 100 percent; see Collins and Wanamaker 2014). One difference between these two studies is the state of the economy. The 1940 Census reports on earnings in 1939, at the tail end of the Great Depression. Conditional on finding employment, it may have been slightly more lucrative to live in the North than in the South in this year. Another difference between these two samples is access to individual wage and salary income in 1940. However, estimates for 1940 suggest that, if any-

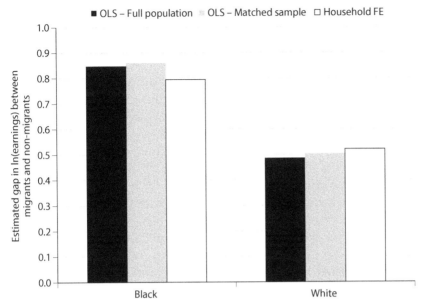

Figure 2.1. Estimated return to migration for southern-born men in the North, 1940. The black bars compare the annual earnings of migrants to the North and men who remained in the South in a 1 percent sample of the complete-count 1940 Census ($N = 12,834$); the underlying regression is reported in Appendix Equation 1. To be consistent with the sample of brother pairs, this analysis is restricted to men between the ages of 18 and 38 in 1940. The gray bars replicate this regression for men in the matched sample linked between the 1920 and 1940 Censuses ($N = 228,425$). The white bars then add a set of household fixed effects, thereby estimating the return to migration within pairs of brothers (see Appendix Equation 2). The notes to Table 2.1 provide additional details on the sample and the construction of the earnings variable.

thing, the return to migration estimated from occupation-based earnings is somewhat *higher* than the return using individual wage and salary income alone (170 percent versus 130 percent). This comparison implies that the economic benefit of migration stemmed from a combination of opportunities to shift into higher-paid industrial occupations and higher average earnings in most occupations in the North. There is no evidence that migrants achieved higher-paid positions within occupational categories.

Black migrants earned substantially more than their counterparts who remained in the South, even within brother pairs. However, a portion of this nominal gain may have been absorbed by higher living costs in the North. A major source of regional variation in cost of living is the price of housing. I use mean rents reported in the 1940 Census by race and state to calculate a cost-of-living adjustment, assuming that housing represented 30 percent of the typical household budget and that non-housing prices were uniform throughout the country. Rents in the typical migrant-receiving state were 200 percent higher than rents in migrant-sending areas, suggesting that the total cost of living was 60 percent higher. As a result, the real return to migration may have been as low as 45 log points for blacks (56 percent) and 24 log points for whites (25 percent). By this measure, half of the nominal return to migration can be attributed to higher living costs, but the other half represents a real increase in purchasing power. However, some of the regional rent gap likely reflected unmeasured differences in housing quality, including electrification and access to running water; in this case, the adjusted estimate would be a lower bound on the real return to migration.

DID SOUTHERN MIGRANTS OUT-EARN NORTHERN-BORN BLACKS?

Thus far, I have shown that black migrants out-earned blacks who remained in the South. I turn now to a comparison between southern migrants and existing black residents in the North. To date, the scholarly consensus holds that, after spending a few years in the North, southern migrants were able to surpass the earnings of northern-born blacks, particularly among men with less than a high school degree (Masters 1972; Long and Heltman 1975; Lieberson and Wilkerson 1976; Lieberson 1978; Margo 1990, 121–27; Gregory 2005, 106–8).[19] This pattern is typically interpreted as indirect evidence that migrants were positively selected on characteristics like aptitude and determination.[20]

Bringing new data to bear on this question, I find, instead, that southern migrants enjoyed earnings equal to those of northern-born blacks upon first arrival in the North and experienced similar earnings

[19] Exceptions include Kain and Persky 1968 and Collins 2000.
[20] Masters (1972, 415), for example, attributes the higher earnings of southern-born blacks in the North to "differences in work effort and in intelligence between migrants and succeeding generations." This form of positive migrant selection is not borne out in the observable measures of family background analyzed earlier in this chapter but could perhaps occur at the individual level within background categories.

growth over time. That is, migrants did not seem to suffer an earnings penalty associated with having been born and educated in the South, but neither did they enjoy the earnings premium that in previous work has been interpreted as a sign of positive selection on the basis of personal attributes.[21]

The earlier literature on the labor market success of black migrants relies on two Census indicators of migration status: among northern residents, recent migrants from the South are men who lived in a southern state five years before the Census date, and long-term migrants are all other men who were born in the South. Long and Heltman (1975, Table 1), for example, report that, in 1970, the earnings of recently arrived blacks from the South were on par with those of northern-born blacks but that southern-born blacks who had been in the North for more than five years earned 11 percent more.[22] Census sources lack detailed information on migrants' year of arrival in the North. Furthermore, even if year of arrival were known, measuring changes in migrants' labor market outcomes using data from a single point in time suffers from a set of well-known biases, including potential changes in the skills of arrival cohorts and the possibility of selective return migration.[23]

I provide new evidence on the earnings growth of black migrants in the northern economy by coupling Census data with information from the *Racial Attitudes in Fifteen American Cities* survey. Combining data from two sources allows me to follow certain arrival cohorts over time as they adapt to the northern economy. The *Racial Attitudes* survey, which was conducted in 1968, is the only data source (to my knowledge) that contains information both on black migrants' year of arrival in the North and on a whole series of economic outcomes (Campbell and Schuman, 1997).[24] The survey collected detailed data on roughly

[21] My findings are consistent with those in Maloney 2001, which uses the World War I service records and the 1920 Census to create a matched sample of black men living in Cincinnati. Maloney (2001, 148) finds that "southern-born blacks experienced rates of upward occupational mobility equal to those of northern-born blacks."

[22] Margo (1990) finds a similar premium for long-term black migrants to the North in 1940.

[23] This point was first made by Douglas (1919) and was developed by Borjas (1985). See also Abramitzky, Boustan, and Eriksson 2014, which addresses these concerns in the context of immigration from Europe to the United States in the early twentieth century.

[24] The goal of the *Racial Attitudes* survey was to understand the rise of race-related civil unrest in the nation's largest cities. To that end, black and white respondents were asked a full complement of Census-style economic questions but were also probed for their attitudes about schools, housing, and police practices.

two thousand black migrants and non-migrants in fifteen large central cities in the North and West with an oversample of black households living in majority-black neighborhoods. Together, these cities contained 56 percent of the black population in the North in 1970.

New Results on the Earnings Growth of Black Migrants in the North

I provide new estimates of the earnings of black migrants in the North, both upon first arrival and after spending more time in the northern economy. The *Racial Attitudes* survey contains detailed measures of time spent in the North and of earnings in one year (1968). Before turning to this new data set, I begin by investigating the representativeness of the fifteen cities covered in the survey in standard Census sources. Long and Heltman (1975) document that black migrants between the ages of twenty-five and thirty-four who had been in the North for more than five years earned 11 percent more than northern-born blacks in the 1970 Census. I find a similar premium (13 percent) when replicating their analysis in microdata, even after controlling for age and education. However, long-term migrants did not enjoy an earnings advantage in the fifteen large metropolitan areas included in the *Racial Attitudes* survey, suggesting that these areas were not representative of the region.[25]

Despite covering only large metropolitan areas, the *Racial Attitudes* survey is useful because it provides detailed information on migrants' time spent in the North. Figure 2.2 classifies migrants into seven categories according to years spent in the North: 0–5 years, 6–10 years, and so on. I compare the hourly wages of migrants to those of their northern-born counterparts by education group, splitting the sample into men with and without a high school degree.[26] Each dot in the graph represents the log wage differential (roughly, the percentage difference) between southern migrants who had spent a given number of years in the North and northern-born blacks of the same age and education level; the underlying estimating equation is reported in Appen-

---

[25] For individuals whose metropolitan area of residence is known, the 1970 Census microdata do not differentiate between central cities and suburbs. However, more than 75 percent of the black metropolitan population lived in a central city in 1970, and so this metropolitan sample should be reasonably comparable to the central city sample in the *Racial Attitudes* survey.

[26] The *Racial Attitudes* survey contains detailed information about hourly wages but only reports annual earnings by category. Therefore, all results based on the survey use hourly wages, rather than annual earnings, as a dependent variable. Estimates are similar if I instead convert earnings bins into the midpoints of each interval and use these coarse earnings data instead.

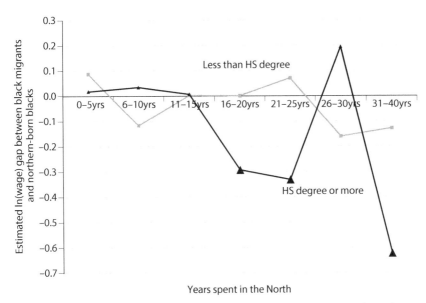

Figure 2.2. Hourly wage gap between southern black migrants and northern-born blacks by years spent in the North. Data drawn from the *Racial Attitudes in Fifteen Cities* survey conducted in 1968. Each dot represents the log wage differential (roughly, the percentage difference) between black southern migrants who had spent a given number of years in the North and northern-born blacks of the same age and education level (*N* = 401 for less than high school degree; *N* = 330 for high school degree or more). The underlying estimating equation is reported in Appendix Equation 3. The size of the marker indicates statistical significance, with the three coefficients that are significantly different from zero marked with a larger triangle.

dix Equation 3. Wage gaps that are significantly different from zero are marked with larger squares or triangles.

I find that migrants with less than a high school degree earned the same amount as similarly educated northern-born blacks, both upon arrival (0–5 years in the North) and after spending time in the northern economy. There is no evidence that lower-skilled black southerners had difficulty adjusting to the northern workforce. Yet there is also no evidence, as is often claimed in the literature, that these low-skilled migrants benefited from either a personal aptitude or a southern cultural advantage that enabled them to out-earn the northern born after a brief adjustment period (at least not in the large metropolitan areas covered by the survey).

Migrants with a high school degree (or beyond) also experienced earnings parity with similar northern-born blacks upon arrival but then appear to *lose ground* after spending fifteen years in the northern labor market. However, what looks like falling behind in the *Racial Attitudes* survey may actually be an indication of changes in the underlying skill level of arrival cohorts over time. In 1968, when the survey took place, recent black migrants were those who moved in the 1960s, while long-standing migrants moved in the 1940s. Educated black migrants who moved during World War II may have had lower earnings potential than educated blacks who moved in the 1960s. In comparing these two arrival cohorts, then, it might appear as if migrants' earnings deterio-rated with time spent in the North; however, this earnings "loss" would simply be picking up underlying skill differences between these two arrival cohorts.

One solution to this problem is to follow members of an arrival co-hort as they spend time in the northern labor market. I do so by cou-pling information from the *Racial Attitudes* survey with data on recent migrant arrivals from various Census years, using the "Where did you live five years ago?" question. In particular, I am able to observe three arrival cohorts of black migrants (1935–40, 1949–50, and 1955–60) in two data sets. Each cohort is observed once in the Census after spend-ing a few years in the North (in the 1940, 1950, and 1960 censuses, re-spectively) and then again in the *Racial Attitudes* survey in 1968.[27] Given the distinctive structure of this sample, there is not enough variation to identify seven separate "years in the North" coefficients. Instead, I col-lapse the migrants into two groups: those who had been in the North for more/less than ten years. Appendix Equation 4 presents this con-densed earnings equation.

Following cohorts over time reveals that what appeared to be earn-ings deterioration for migrants in the cross-sectional data is actually differences in earnings power across arrival cohorts. Table 2.3 reports estimates of the effect of time spent in the North on earnings for high school graduates. Column 1 replicates the cross-sectional results ob-served in Figure 2.2; as before, migrants who had been in the North for less than ten years earned as much as northern-born blacks (see the coefficient for "Born in South"), whereas migrants who had been in the

[27] The sample also includes information on a fourth arrival cohort (1965–70), although these migrants are observed twice in a short period of time (in 1968 and then again in the 1970 Census).

Table 2.3: Hourly wages for southern black migrants and northern-born blacks in the North, high school graduate or above

	(1)	*(2)*
Born in South	0.051 (0.035)	
In North 10+ years	–0.202 (0.062)	–0.056 (0.083)
Arrive 1935–40		0.002 (0.147)
Arrive 1945–50		–0.223 (0.102)
Arrive 1955–60		0.033 (0.050)
Arrive 1965–70		0.069 (0.044)

Note: Dependent variable = Hourly wage. Columns report estimates of Appendix Equation 4. Regressions control for a quadratic in age and a linear measure of highest grade attained. Column 2 replaces the southern-born indicator with a vector of dummy variables for arrival cohort. The data set underlying this table combines observations from the *Racial Attitudes in Fifteen American Cities* survey conducted in 1968 with selected data from the Census ($N = 5,823$). Census data include all northern-born black men living in the North from 1940 to 1970 and the following cohorts of southern black migrants: the arrival cohorts of 1935–40 (from the 1940 Census); 1949–50 (from the 1950 Census); 1955–60 (from the 1960 Census); and 1965–70 (from the 1970 Census). Observations are re-weighted so that the Census and the survey contribute equally to the regression.

North for ten years or more appear to earn 15 percent less than either recent migrants or northern-born blacks (the sum of the coefficients for "Born in South" and "In North 10+ years"). Column 2 replaces the southern-born indicator variable with four dummy variables for year of arrival in the North (1935–40; 1945–50; 1955–60; 1965–70). In this specification, the effect of time spent in the North is identified from variation *within*, rather than between, arrival cohorts. In this case, the apparent earnings divergence between northern-born blacks and long-standing migrants in the North disappears. Instead, educated migrants who arrived circa World War II (1945–50) earn around 20 percent less than northern-born blacks in all years. This pattern may suggest that, at least among men with a high school degree, the migrant flow was negatively selected during the war when factory jobs were plentiful. Changes in school quality do not seem to explain this finding because migrants who arrived in the 1930s would have attended even poorer-quality schools than did migrants who arrived in the 1940s; yet these earlier migrants do not face an earnings penalty.[28]

Measures of earnings growth in this pooled data set may still be biased if there was substantial (and selective) return migration to the South between the Census year and the later *Racial Attitudes* survey.[29] If many black migrants eventually returned to the South, the first observation on each arrival cohort would contain a mixture of temporary and permanent migrants, whereas the second observation would only contain permanent migrants. Furthermore, if return migrants were primarily high skilled, then, as these migrants departed for the South, each cohort's earnings would appear to fall over time. However, few blacks returned to the South during this period.[30] Gregory reports five-year black return migration rates of less than 3 percent (2005, Table A-2), compared with return migration rates to many European countries in the early twentieth century of 25 percent or more (Gould 1980; Bandiera, Rasul, and Viarengo 2013). Given the low return migration rates to the South, the repeated cross-sectional sample will likely provide an accurate estimate of migrants' earnings growth in the North.

CONCLUSION

Leaving the low-wage South for the industrial cities of the North and West provided black migrants with a substantial economic return. Blacks who settled in the North earned at least 100 percent more than men who stayed in the South in 1930 and 1940. I find a similar earnings advantage when comparing migrants and non-migrants in the full population and when narrowing the comparison to pairs of brothers who lived in different regions. The equivalence of the estimated return

[28] I conduct a similar exercise for the lower-skilled sample and find no evidence of changes in the quality of arrival cohorts over time.

[29] This concern was first highlighted by Jasso and Rosenzweig (1988). Lubotksy (2007) investigated return migration bias in contemporary data and Abramitzky, Boustan, and Eriksson (2014) did the same for historical migration from Europe.

[30] Lieberson (1978) argues that black migrants who chose to return to the South between 1965 and 1970 were negatively selected on the basis of earnings. However, Lieberson does not have a measure of pre-return earnings. It could be that many of these men returned to the South to retire and so reported particularly low earnings in the South in 1970.

in these two approaches suggests that black migrants were not particularly positively or negatively selected from the southern population. This pattern is consistent with the bimodal selection of migrants on the basis of father's occupation. Migrants were more likely to hail from households headed by a father at either the top or the bottom of the occupational distribution.

Migrants' earnings kept pace with those of northern-born blacks, both upon first arrival in the North and after spending more time in the northern economy. This pattern could be seen as indirect evidence of migrants' fortitude; migrants managed to quickly find their footing despite having been educated in low-quality southern schools and arriving in a new place where they lacked a strong labor market network. However, this equivalence may instead reflect a lack of opportunities available to northern-born blacks (many of whom were children of the first wave of migration from the South). Despite being educated in northern schools, northern blacks could not pull ahead of recent southern arrivals. The next chapter explores the northern labor market during this period in more detail.

APPENDIX TO CHAPTER 2

Estimating the Return to Migration

The simplest approach to estimating the return to migration is to compare the earnings of southern-born black men living in the North in 1940 (migrants) to southern-born black men remaining in the South (non-migrants):

$$\ln(Earnings_i) = \alpha + \beta_1(Migrant_i) + \beta_2 (Age_i) + \beta_3 (Age_i^2) + \varepsilon_i \qquad (1)$$

where $Earnings_i$ denotes individual i's earnings in 1940 and $Migrant_i$ is a dummy variable equal to one if individual i lives in the North in 1940. The equation also controls for a quadratic function of age. The "return to migration" is captured by β_1, which measures the percentage difference in earnings between migrants and non-migrants, adjusted for differences in the age profile of the two groups.

β_1 would reveal the true return to migration if migrants were selected randomly from the southern population. If, however, migrants were (positively or negatively) selected from the southern population, β_1 will be biased by migrant selection. To eliminate selection across households, I compare the earnings of migrants to those of their non-migrant brothers. I consider the following equation in which the individual error term is decomposed into two components:

$$\ln(Earnings_{ij}) = \beta_1{}' (Migrant_{ij}) + \beta_2{}' (Age_{ij}) + \beta_3{}' (Age_{ij}{}^2) + \alpha_j + v_{ij} \quad \textbf{(2)}$$

where α_j is the component of the error that is shared between brothers in the same household j and v_{ij} is the component that is idiosyncratic to individuals. Running an OLS regression of equation (2) with household fixed effects will absorb the fixed household portion of the error term α_j. Such within-household estimation will eliminate bias due to aspects of family background that are correlated both with the probability of migration and with labor market outcomes later in life. In this case, the coefficient $\beta_1{}'$ measures the return to migration, free from selection across households.

Matching Procedure

Complete Census records (including names) become publicly available seventy-two years after the Census was taken. I use these historical records to create a matched data set of southern-born men linked from their childhood home in 1920 to their adult records in 1940. I use complete-count historical data sets compiled by Ancestry.com and the Minnesota Population Center in both years.

To match records between the two Census years, I use the iterative matching strategy developed by Ferrie (1996) and employed more recently by Abramitzky, Boustan, and Eriksson (2012) and Ferrie and Long (2013). The matching procedure is as follows:

(1) I began by standardizing the first and last names of men in the two samples using the NYSIIS algorithm to address orthographic differences between phonetically equivalent names (Atack, Bateman, and Gregson 1992). I restricted my attention to men who are unique by first and last name, birth year, and state of birth in 1920.

(2) I then attempted to match observations from 1920 to 1940. I started by looking for a match by first name, last name, place of birth (either state or country), and exact birth year. There are three possibilities: (a) if I found a unique match, I stopped and considered the observation "matched"; (b) if I found multiple matches for the same birth year, the observation was thrown out; (c) if I did not find a match at this first step, I tried matching within a one-year band (older and younger) and

Appendix Table 2.1: Comparing fathers in matched
sample to similar men in full population

	Literacy	Own house	Occupation score
Matched Sample = 1	−0.004	0.056	0.510
	(0.111)	(0.099)	(1.450)
Constant	0.656	0.229	14.850
	(0.005)	(0.004)	(0.059)

Note: This sample pools a subset of black fathers of sons in the matched sample (N = 1,576) with black men in the 1920 IPUMS who lived in the South and had at least one son in the relevant age range (N = 9,339). The dependent variables are listed in the column headings and the regression contains an indicator variable equal to one for fathers of sons in the matched sample.

then within a two-year band around the reported birth year. If none of these attempts produced a match, the observation was discarded as unmatched.

The matched sample may not be fully representative of the southern-born men from which they are drawn. In particular, men with uncommon names are more likely to be successfully linked between Censuses, and the commonness of one's name could potentially be correlated with socioeconomic status. I assess this possibility in Appendix Table 2.1 by comparing the socioeconomic characteristics of a subset of fathers of men in the matched sample to the full population of black men in the 1920 IPUMS sample who lived in the South and had at least one son in the relevant age range. I use a 1 percent subset of the matched sample for comparison because I need to collect fathers' characteristics by hand from the 1920 Census manuscripts, given that the complete-count data only digitized certain core variables. Results suggest that the fathers of men in the matched sample are no more likely than the fathers in the full population to be literate and only slightly more likely to own a house, although the differences in homeownership are not statistically significant. Differences in occupation score between the two groups are also statistically indistinguishable and small.

Estimating an Assimilation Profile

Immigrant assimilation profiles estimate how earnings change with time spent in the destination economy. I start with data from the 1968

Racial Attitudes in Fifteen American Cities survey. The survey contains information on black residents of northern and western cities, a portion of whom were born in the South. I estimate the relationship between hourly wages and years spent in the North:

$$\ln(wage_i) = \alpha + \Gamma'[years\ spent\ in\ the\ North_i]$$
$$+ \gamma_1(Age_i) + \gamma_2(Age_i^2) + \varepsilon_i \tag{3}$$

where $wage_i$ is individual i's hourly wage and *years spent in the North$_i$* is a vector of dummy variables in five-year bins (0–5 years in the North, 6–10 years in the North, and so on). These indicator variables all take on a value of zero for the northern born. The vector Γ contains the coefficients of interest, which indicate whether migrants' earnings grow relative to those of the northern born with time spent in the North. This specification is estimated separately for men with more/less than a high school degree.

I combine the *Racial Attitudes* data with selected Census information to obtain repeated observations on a subset of arrival cohorts. In particular, I consider the arrival cohorts of 1935–40, 1949–50, 1955–60, and 1965–70, which can be identified by the "where did you live one/five years ago?" questions in the 1940–70 censuses. I use data on migrants from these arrival cohorts as well as all northern-born black men in the *Racial Attitudes* survey and the relevant Census years. The composite data set is weighted so that survey and Census observations each count equally. With this combined data, I estimate:

$$\ln(wage_i) = \alpha + \delta_1[= 1\ if\ in\ North\ 10+\ years_i]$$
$$+ \Delta'[arrival\ cohort_i] + \delta_2(Age_i) + \delta_3(Age_i^2) + \varepsilon_i \tag{4}$$

I replace the vector of *years in the North* indicators with a single dummy variable equal to one for migrants who have lived in the North for ten years or more. I also control for each five-year arrival cohort with a vector of indicator variables (*arrival cohort$_i$*). The coefficient of interest in this specification is δ_1. A positive value of δ_1 suggests that, within an arrival cohort, migrants experienced earnings convergence with the northern born as they spent time in the North.

CHAPTER 3

Competition in Northern Labor Markets

TWO SHORT DECADES after black migrants hopefully set out from the South in large numbers to fill wartime jobs in northern industry, the streets of Los Angeles erupted in violence during the Watts Riots.[1] Turmoil in Los Angeles was soon followed by similar episodes in Chicago, Detroit, and other large northern cities. The Kerner Commission, established by President Johnson to study this wave of civil unrest, concluded that the riots could be traced to the lack of economic opportunity for black workers in northern cities, compounded by the competition from persistent in-migration from the South. The commission report argued that black frustrations were rooted in northern "employment problems, aggravated by the constant arrival of new unemployed migrants, many of them from depressed rural areas." Black workers were being squeezed from both sides: not only were they contending with "pervasive discrimination and segregation in [northern] employment," but they also faced competition from a steady inflow of black migrants from the South (Kerner Commission 1968, 7).

Southern in-migration doubled the size of the black workforce in the North from 1940 to 1970. As the authors of the Kerner Commission report suspected, the competitive pressure exerted by black migration on northern wages was concentrated among existing black workers. I show in this chapter that northern employers used black migrants more interchangeably with other black workers than with similarly skilled white workers in the North. The lack of substitutability between black and white workers was due both to actual differences in productivity—

---

[1] The unrest in Watts in 1965 was the first in a series of race-related riots spanning the years 1965 to 1968. The Watts riots were preceded by civil unrest in New York City (Harlem) and Philadelphia in the summer of 1964. However, these early incidents were far less destructive, resulting in only a single death (compared with thirty-four fatalities in Los Angeles).

owing to, for example, racial disparities in school quality—and to discrimination in job assignments.

In-group competition has afflicted many migrant communities, including European ethnic groups in the early twentieth century and Mexican Americans today.[2] Although all migrants may compete with their countrymen to some degree, racial barriers can intensify this process. Discrimination prevented northern-born blacks from moving out of traditional "Negro" jobs into other positions, even as the available labor supply for these positions more than doubled with new in-migration. In contrast, groups that face less severe forms of discrimination are able to partially counteract these competitive forces by shifting to other, less-crowded sectors as new migrants arrive.

Evidence from historical case studies illustrates that black workers in the North were concentrated in certain occupational niches and that similarly skilled black and white workers rarely engaged in the same tasks. Using nationally representative Census data, I show that competition with southern blacks generated larger wage losses for black men in the North than for similarly skilled whites.[3] I argue that the migration produced clear economic winners and losers. The southern migrants themselves benefited from the move from the low-wage South, while existing black workers in the North lost ground. In part because of competition from southern in-migrants, black workers experienced little earnings growth in the North relative to whites before 1965.

The racial segmentation of the northern labor market was due to both pre-market and market-based discrimination. Pre-market discrimination includes racial disparities in the education and training necessary to prepare for work opportunities in the North. The most obvious example of pre-market discrimination is the lower average quality of schools attended by black students, particularly in the segregated South. This explanation does not take discrimination "off the hook" but

---

[2] Lieberson (1980) argues that large migrant inflows cause certain niche occupations to become overcrowded. Osofsky ([1966] 1996, 43) agrees, suggesting that both Jews and Italians faced competition from "later arrivals from their countries." Similarly, Borjas (1987a) and Cortes (2008) argue that immigrants today are most likely to compete in the labor force with other immigrants. Peri and Sparber (2009) show that this imperfect substitutability is due, in part, to the fact that natives specialize in communication-intensive occupations.

[3] The analysis in this chapter focuses on men because it is difficult to accurately assign women to skill categories using Census data. Age is not a good proxy for labor market experience for women at midcentury because of time spent out of the labor force for child-rearing, a process that differed along racial lines (Goldin 1992; Boustan and Collins 2014).

rather pushes back the source of discriminatory actions from the northern labor market to southern schools. Market discrimination refers to the hiring practices of employers that prevented some blacks from holding jobs for which they were otherwise qualified, especially in skilled crafts, retail and clerical work, and supervisory positions in manufacturing firms. Much of the existing historical literature focuses on market-based discrimination. Marks (1989, 2), for example, argues that "personal characteristics such as level of skill were less important . . . than institutional barriers in determining migrant assimilation and mobility." In contrast, I find that both modes of discrimination mattered and that, if anything, pre-market discrimination was a larger hurdle for black workers in the North.

Who Competed with Whom? Historical Evidence on Race in the Northern Labor Market

Nearly four million southern blacks moved to the North and West between 1940 and 1970, a period of otherwise limited in-migration.[4] Black arrivals represented only a 4 percent increase in the northern workforce as a whole but resulted in a more than 100 percent increase in the black workforce in the region. If black migrants generated competition for all similarly skilled workers, white and black, these arrivals would have had a small and diffuse effect on a large number of workers. However, if black migrants competed more readily with existing black workers, the migration had potentially large negative effects on a concentrated group. Crucial to estimating the effect of black migration on northern workers, then, is knowing who competed with whom in the northern economy.

I argue that black migrants were most likely to compete with other black workers in the North, both because black and white workers had different levels of educational attainment and because, even within schooling category, black and white workers were assigned to different tasks on the job. First, black migrants' low levels of completed

[4] European immigration was severely curtailed by strict quotas imposed in the 1920s. By 1950, only 3 percent of young men in the North (compared with 28 percent of older men) were foreign born. The Bracero program, active from 1942 to 1964, facilitated some temporary migration from Mexico, primarily for the agricultural sector. However, in 1950, only 1.4 percent of men in the North were born in Mexico, and this number falls to 0.2 percent when excluding the western states. Many southern whites also moved north between 1940 and 1970, but a greater number of northern-born whites relocated to the South, leading to net out-migration from the region.

schooling were closer to those of northern blacks than northern whites. In 1950, for example, 19 percent of young southern black migrants had graduated from high school, compared with 28 percent of young northern-born blacks and 40 percent (or more) of young northern- or foreign-born whites (see Boustan 2009, Figure 1). Only 5 percent of older southern-born blacks had graduated from high school, compared with 10 percent of northern-born blacks and 16 percent of northern-born and foreign-born whites in this age group. Among older workers, the majority of blacks (63 percent) and foreign-born whites (52 percent) had less than an eighth-grade education, compared with only 28 percent of northern-born whites. If anything, older black migrants may have created some competition for older European-born whites.

Moreover, even within narrow educational categories, blacks and whites in the northern economy held very different types of jobs. Figures 3.1a and 3.1b depict the ten most commonly held occupations for northern-born white and black men with exactly an eighth-grade education, the modal grade completed in 1950 (a total of fifteen occupations). Only three types of jobs—truck drivers, mechanics, and clerical workers—employed a sizable share of men of both races, with the remaining occupations being either disproportionately white or black. Black men with eight years of schooling were most likely to work in the stereotypically "Negro" positions of janitor, cook, porter, and service worker, while white men with eight years of schooling held union posts (mine operatives, carpenters, and machinists), supervisory positions (foremen and managers), and occupations that required interaction with the public (salesmen). These jobs were often unattainable for blacks because of discrimination in union membership, promotion opportunities, and customer attitudes.

Detailed historical accounts of the manufacturing sector, particularly in Chicago, Detroit, Pittsburgh, and Milwaukee, corroborate the pattern of nearly complete separation of tasks observed in Census data.[5] Some firms refused to hire blacks in any capacity, while others hired

[5] Only 19 percent of black men in the North were employed in the manufacturing sector in 1940, underscoring the importance of using representative Census data to analyze the degree of racial segmentation in the northern economy more broadly. Before 1915, northern blacks primarily worked in personal and domestic service (see Kusmer 1976, 190–205 on Cleveland and Trotter 1985, 46–52 on Milwaukee). In the 1910s and 1920s, blacks began to enter the industrial sector, typically in unskilled positions. In many cities, employers first began considering blacks for industrial work during the labor shortages of World War I (Phillips 1999, 62, 64; Whatley 1990).

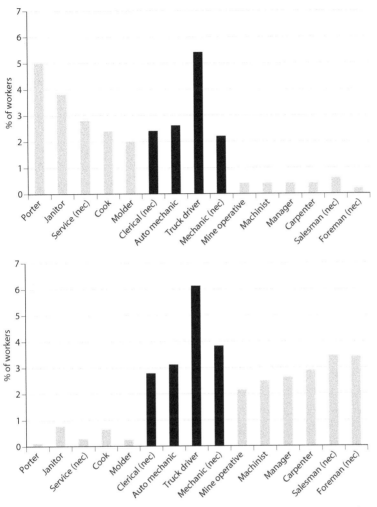

Figures 3.1a and 3.1b. Common occupations for northern-born men with eight years of education, 1950. Graphs report the ten most common occupations held by either white or black men in 1950. Figure 3.1a shows occupational patterns for whites and Figure 3.1b shows occupational patterns for blacks. Together, these 15 categories employ 31 percent of blacks and 35 percent of whites. Occupations that employ at least 2 percent of men of both races are colored as black; the other occupations are shaded as gray. For reasons of scale, I omit two commonly held occupation categories: "laborer and operatives, not elsewhere classified" and "operatives, not elsewhere classified." These categories employ 42 percent of blacks and 29 percent of whites with an eighth-grade education who lived in the North ("nec" stands for "not elsewhere classified").

blacks only for menial positions. For example, for many years, Ford Motor Company was the only automobile manufacturer in Detroit willing to hire black employees. As a result, in the early 1940s, Ford employed 50 percent of black Detroiters and only 14 percent of local whites (Maloney and Whatley 1995). Even by 1960, there was still tremendous variation in the racial composition of the workforce between automobile manufacturing plants in central-city Detroit. For example, within the General Motors Company, the Chevrolet Forge and Gear and Axle plants were majority black, while the Cadillac and Fisher Body plants were less than 25 percent black. Sugrue (1996, 96) attributes this variation in part to the "discretion that company officials exercised at the hiring gate."[6]

Even within "integrated" firms and plants, blacks were often restricted to the hottest, dirtiest, or most dangerous jobs. Historians use evocative language to describe the disagreeable and often unhealthful conditions faced by black workers. To Grossman (1989, 189), working conditions in Chicago's meatpacking plants were akin to one of the circles of hell in Dante's *Inferno*. "Amid hot temperatures and without ventilation," he writes, "[black] men in killing gangs stood on wet, slippery floors, as grease, cold water, and warm blood flowed at their feet. In the beef casing room . . . temperatures reached 115 degrees Fahrenheit." Trotter (1985, 53) describes a similar process in Milwaukee, whereby steel factories confined blacks to "the hottest areas of the plant . . . [feeding] blast furnaces"; tanneries employed blacks only in "the beam house, where dry hides were placed into pits filled with lime to remove hair" and were surrounded by "nearly intolerable fumes"; and packinghouses "relegated Afro-Americans to the worst occupations . . . [in which they] unloaded trucks, slaughtered animals, transported intestines, and generally cleaned the plant."[7] In a more white-collar setting, Jasper M., a black man employed in a department store

---

[6] Trotter (1985, 166–67) likewise reports variation in managers' attitudes toward black workers in Milwaukee in the 1940s; some managers informed black applicants that they "never did and didn't intend to employ Negroes."

[7] Wayman Hancock, the father of famous jazz musician Herbie Hancock and a former meat inspector in Chicago, concurs, remembering that "if you were black, you worked on the killing floor, and that was as far as you could go. Whites had all the other jobs that were done in the processing of meat. They didn't have any blacks in those positions like they have now" (Black 2003, 155). This racial division of labor was present in other cities as well. Gottlieb (1987, 98–99) describes the "emergence of a range of 'black' jobs in Pittsburgh." At the United States Steel Corporation, for example, "black men could advance no higher than first helper in the open hearth department. . . . At A. M. Byers iron mill few southern migrants ever worked at any position other than common labor." Sugrue (1996,

in Pittsburgh, complained that "black people couldn't think about waiting on no customers or things like that. The biggest we could do was porter work and run the elevators, that's all" (Bodnar, Simon, and Weber 1982, 59).[8]

A variety of explanations could account for the racial patterns of job assignment in northern cities. First, black workers may have been less skilled than whites with the same nominal levels of education and work experience because black schools, particularly those in the segregated South, were of lower quality and did not prepare their students for skilled blue-collar work. I call this possibility "pre-market discrimination" because it refers to inequities that occurred before workers entered the labor market. Second, black workers may have been barred from certain types of positions even though they possessed the relevant skills or could have been easily trained to acquire them, a phenomenon I refer to as "market-based discrimination."[9] A third possibility is that pre-market and market-based discrimination interacted, resulting in a form of statistical discrimination (Phelps 1972; Arrow 1971). If northern employers were aware of the poor school quality offered to most black students, they may have assumed that *all* black applicants were less skilled by virtue of their race and therefore may have refused to consider even qualified black workers for certain positions.

Along every measurable dimension, southern black schools were of lower quality than schools in the North; they were chronically underfunded and exhibited shorter school terms, higher pupil-to-teacher ratios, and lower teacher pay. Prime-age workers in 1940 would have been in elementary school around 1910. In that year, the average black student in the South received less than $0.33 of school funding for every dollar spent on a southern white student (Margo 1990, 21). Southern black schools were in session for an average of ninety days, 75 percent

---

99) agrees that, in Detroit, "blacks found themselves placed in the least desirable jobs . . . usually in the dirtiest and most dangerous parts of the plant."

[8] One segment of the northern economy that welcomed black workers was the public sector. Blacks were slightly overrepresented as employees in the federal, state, and local government and the postal service; by 1960, 16 percent of public sector employees in northern and western central cities were black, compared to only 12 percent of the population.

[9] Margo (1990) and Neal and Johnson (1996) present similar division between pre-market and market-based discrimination. Margo (1990, 3–4, 93–95) refers to these two possibilities as the "human capital" and "institutionalist" models of discrimination. Becker (1957) is the classic reference on the economics of discrimination. For recent reviews of the literature on discrimination in the labor market, see Altonji and Blank 1999 and Lang and Lehmann 2012.

of the term length at the average white southern school and only half as long as the average northern school term (Margo 1990, 26). Not only were black school terms shorter but each day of instruction was likely less valuable. Black classrooms had 50 percent more students per teacher; the typical white classroom had twenty-five students, while the typical black classroom had thirty-eight students (Margo 1990, 27). Carruthers and Wanamaker (2014) document that 35 percent of the wage gap between blacks and whites in the South in 1940 can be explained by differences in school quality.

But skill differentials cannot fully account for disparities in job assignments by race in the North; discriminatory attitudes of northern employers also played a role. Contemporary observers noted that black workers who had the skills necessary to move up the ladder were often held back by firms' discriminatory policies or by employer perceptions. Wesley M., who worked in an unskilled position in a steel mill in Pittsburgh, reported that semiskilled operative jobs required only a few weeks of on-the-job training but, despite his job experience, he could not secure one of these higher-paid positions. As he attests, "I worked in that mill and I have learned those white boy [. . .] jobs. [They] would put them on my job, [and I would] learn them their jobs, but still I couldn't get the [better] job" (Gottlieb 1987, 100). Racial barriers also prevented capable black workers from advancing into higher-skilled positions. Chester Himes, an African American writer whose novels chronicled the experience of black migrants in Los Angeles, recalls being blocked from skilled jobs despite his qualifications. "I could read blueprints," he wrote. "I understood, at least partially, most of the necessary skills of building construction—carpentry, plumbing, electric wiring, bricklaying, roofing; I understood the fundamentals of combustion engines; I could operate a number of machine tools—turret lathes, drills, milling machines, etc.; and I was a fairly competent typist" (Sides 2003, 55). Yet despite these many skills, Himes was unable to find skilled work.

Where workers had more control over hiring—as in union settings—blacks were often entirely excluded from the workforce. In crafts unions, blacks "were nearly completely barred from several skilled trades (as blacksmiths, boilermakers, millwrights, and electricians)" (Trotter 1985, 54). Although industrial unions like the American Federation of Labor (AFL) did not impose a blanket exclusion on black members, they often allowed local chapters to determine membership policy; many locals either opted for outright bans on black members or initiated separate (and unequal) black locals (Kusmer 1976, 68).[10] In a few cases, white workers went so far as to strike over the hiring of black workers, although this response was rare.[11] Wilkerson (2010, 316) summarizes the role of worker-based discrimination, reporting that "in the North, companies and unions said that, however much they might want to hire colored people, their white workers just wouldn't stand for it. And, for the sake of morale, the companies and unions weren't going to force the issue."[12]

Pre-market discrimination also interacted with negative attitudes toward black workers, producing a form of statistical discrimination. Employers used race as a proxy for productivity, either refusing to hire any black workers at all or only hiring blacks for menial tasks that did not require high levels of skill. Sugrue (1996, 93) reports that in Detroit, "many employers, basing their decisions on racial stereotypes, assumed that black workers would be unproductive, prone to high absenteeism, and unreliable." Given the potential for statistical discrimination, northern blacks feared that southern migrants would negatively

[10] The Congress of Industrial Organizations (CIO) was more open to black membership than was the AFL (Trotter 1985, 173). However, Sugrue (1996, 101, 106) calls both the United Autoworkers and the United Steelworkers, two of the largest members of the CIO, "inconsistent" in their commitment to racial equality.

[11] Spero and Harris (1931) report that between 1880 and 1900, 60 strikes were organized by white workers who objected to the hiring of blacks. Currie and Ferrie (2000) compiled a data set of nearly 13,000 strikes from 1881 to 1894. If this rate of strike activity continued until 1900, there would have been 18,500 strikes in the United States between 1880 and 1900, suggesting that racial concerns accounted for only 0.3 percent of total strike activity. As for the post-1900 period, Marks (1989, 148) writes that the "East Saint Louis riot [of 1917] was the only riot to result directly from fear by white working men of black economic advances." Other incidents of racial violence during this period were sparked by perceived encroachment across the social "color line"; for example, the Chicago riot of 1919 started when a young black man swam in the "white" section of Lake Michigan.

[12] White workers' objections to working alongside blacks could have many root causes. Goldin's (2014) pollution-based theory of discrimination provides one explanation: If blacks were generally perceived to have lower skills than whites, whites may have feared that sharing a job title with black coworkers would lower the status of their occupation and therefore may have agitated to exclude blacks. Perhaps for the same reason, white workers were loath to report to black managers, limiting the ability of blacks to ascend into supervisory positions (Sundstrom 1994; Fishback 1984). Roediger (1991, 13) makes a similar point, arguing that, in order to enjoy the "status and privileges conferred by race," white workers sought to exclude blacks from their occupations and workplaces. Nelson (2001, xxvi) expands on Roediger's analysis by emphasizing that many white workers were themselves first- or second-generation immigrants who were perceived as "racially 'in between'" and thus were particularly keen on differentiating themselves from their black counterparts.

affect employer perceptions of all black workers. This concern prompted northern black newspapers and self-help organizations like the Urban League to monitor the behavior of southern black newcomers, publishing editorials and "dos and don'ts" lists admonishing migrants to arrive punctually at work and dress appropriately (Grossman 1989, 45–47, 202–3).

THE EFFECT OF BLACK MIGRATION ON THE EARNINGS OF EXISTING WORKERS IN THE NORTH
Theoretical Framework

The historical record provides ample evidence that blacks and whites faced differential treatment in the northern labor market as a result of a combination of pre-market and market-based discrimination. We would expect, then, that the migration of black southerners generated more competitive pressure on existing black workers than on their white counterparts. I provide a simple framework here to test the extent to which similarly skilled blacks and whites were substitutable in production and to calculate the effect of southern migration on the wages of existing black and white workers in the northern economy. The technical details are left for the appendix, but I will describe some of the salient features of the method here. This empirical approach is based on studies of contemporary immigration pioneered by Borjas (2003) and Ottaviano and Peri (2012).[13]

This method begins with a production function that describes how labor is combined with capital to produce output. Labor is divided into skill groups composed of men with similar levels of education and work experience. For example, one skill group might be high school graduates with less than five years of labor market experience, while another might be high school graduates with twenty to twenty-five years of labor market experience. Each skill group is further divided into two subcategories, whites and blacks, to reflect the possible segmentation by race highlighted in the historical case studies (see Appendix Equations 1a–1c).

Although men in different skill cells were not perfectly substitutable for each other in production, neither were they wholly distinct. Some groups were likely used to perform similar tasks, while others were as-

---

[13] Borjas, in turn, builds on Welch (1979), who developed a similar framework to explore the effect of changes in the age distribution on the labor market. See also Card and Lemieux 2001.

signed to quite different activities. Parameters known as "elasticities of substitution" indicate how readily one group was exchanged for another in production. The substitutability between groups is determined by both "technological" and "social" dimensions of the production process. Differences in schooling quality between black and white workers may have imposed technological limits on the substitutability of these two groups; for example, black high school graduates may have learned little of the algebra or chemistry necessary to ascend to upper-level positions in some industries. Yet social conventions also mattered; in a discriminatory environment, employers may have been unwilling to hire similarly skilled black and white workers to perform comparable duties.

Wages in each skill group depend positively on the group's level of productivity and negatively on the available labor supply within the skill cell (Appendix Equation 2).[14] That is, as more workers appear in a given category, wages in that group can be expected to fall because employers can easily find others capable of doing the same set of tasks (Appendix Equation 3). Furthermore, the wages in each group were affected by the availability of labor supply in adjacent groups, a relationship that depends on the substitutability between categories (Appendix Equations 4–5).

Appendix Equation 6 summarizes the effect of black migrant arrivals into a skill cell on the wages of existing white workers in that group, while Appendix Equation 7 allows for the possibility of a stronger effect of migrant arrivals on existing black workers. If blacks and whites were perfect substitutes within skill groups, black migrant arrivals would have had an equal effect on the wages of similarly skilled blacks *and* whites. In this case, wages should only be affected by the *overall* labor supply in a skill cell, not by the racial composition of the workforce within the cell. However, if blacks and whites were used differently in production, black migrants would have had a stronger negative effect on the wages of existing black workers than on those of similarly skilled whites.[15]

[14] The wage equation (Appendix Equation 2) emerges from a model in which labor markets are perfectly competitive and, therefore, workers are paid the value of their marginal product. The model assumes that workers who are paid less than the value of their marginal product should be able to shop around and find another employer willing to offer a higher wage. Labor markets may have been close to competitive within skill-by-race cells, even if discriminatory barriers limited opportunities for blacks relative to whites in the same skill group.

[15] My argument bears some resemblance to that of Lieberson (1980). But Lieberson's

Estimating Equation and Data

The framework outlined in the previous section suggests that the elasticity of substitution by race within a skill cell is the key parameter determining whether black migrants had a diffuse impact on all similarly skilled workers in the North or a more concentrated effect on existing black workers. Empirically, this elasticity of substitution can be estimated by comparing the effect of black migrant arrivals on the earnings of black workers and white workers in the same skill cell in the North. If black arrivals affected the earnings of similarly skilled black and white workers equally, we can conclude that blacks and whites were perfect substitutes in the northern labor market. If, instead, black arrivals had a stronger effect on other black workers, we can conclude that blacks and whites were only imperfectly substitutable in the northern economy, and we can quantify this lack of substitutability.

Appendix Equation 9 reports the estimating equation used to recover the relationship between migrant arrivals and relative black earnings in the North from decadal Census data (1940–70). I divide the non-southern economy into eighty skill cells: five education categories, eight experience levels, and two races.[16] The dependent variable is the ratio of annual earnings for northern-born blacks and whites in an education-experience group. The key independent variable is the ratio of black to white migrants in a skill cell; migrant counts include all men who were born in the South and currently reside in the North. I control for fixed differences in productivity between education-experience cells and for differential trends in productivity over time within education and experience levels.

---

reasoning is based on a "queuing" model, rather than a competitive model, of the labor market. Lieberson supposes that employers offer the best positions to members of preferred racial or ethnic groups. In this case, when a less advantaged group arrives in the North (say, blacks), members are assigned to the least desirable jobs, while other groups (say, Italians) get to move up to the next rung on the job ladder. In Lieberson's framework, it is unclear how more desirable jobs would suddenly appear for Italians without a shift in labor demand. If migration increases labor supply to low-skilled jobs without a corresponding increase in labor demand, the wages of both Italians and existing black workers should fall.

[16] The five education categories are: 0–5 years of schooling, 6–9 years of schooling, 10–11 years of schooling, 12 years of schooling, and 13 or more years of schooling. Work experience is predicted using an individual's age and years of completed schooling and divided into five-year intervals. I allow men to begin accruing labor market experience in the year after they leave school but constrain the earliest age of labor market entry to be 13. Boustan (2009) demonstrates that results are not sensitive to redefining the education categories to account for different divisions between elementary and high school.

Estimates of the Effect of Black Migrants on Northern Workers

Wage estimates suggest that black workers competed more intensively with other blacks in the northern economy. Figure 3.2a reports the estimated effect of southern migrant arrivals on the earnings of existing black and white workers in the North by skill group, with skill group defined by years of schooling and work experience. The darker columns report the implied wage effect (in percentage terms) of a 10 percent increase in labor supply into a skill cell as a result of black in-migration, while the gray columns report similar effects for white in-migration. By this estimate, a 10 percent increase in the number of black southern workers in a skill cell would have reduced the earnings of existing black workers in the North by 1.5 percent while generating a much smaller (but statistically detectable) drop in the earnings of similarly skilled white workers. In contrast, a 10 percent increase in labor supply as a result of white southern migration had a small negative effect on similarly skilled white workers in the North but no discernable effect on existing blacks.

As I argued earlier, the fact that black earnings are sensitive to the ratio of black-to-white workers in their skill cell, rather than simply to the total labor supply, is an indication that black and white workers were not used as perfect substitutes in the northern economy.[17] To be more precise about the degree of substitutability (or lack thereof), note that we can recover the elasticity of substitution between whites and blacks in the same skill cell from the regression estimates.[18] The implied elasticity of substitution between black and white workers in the same skill cell in this period is 8.3.

Is an elasticity of substitution of 8.3 for black and white workers in the same skill cell large or small? Recent work finds an elasticity of substitution between native-born and foreign-born workers in the same

---

[17] Similarly, Sundstrom (2007) finds lower black wages in southern counties that had a larger relative supply of black workers in 1940. He estimates that a 10 percent increase in the black population share is associated with a 2.4 percent reduction in the relative black wage. This value is slightly larger than the estimate presented here, perhaps because blacks and whites were even more segmented in the southern economy.

[18] In particular, comparing Appendix Equations 8 and 9 suggests that the elasticity of substitution between whites and blacks in the same skill cell (σ) is equivalent to $-1/\beta$, or the inverse of the main regression coefficient multiplied by -1. The intuition here is that the smaller the regression coefficient β, the less affected are black wages by the relative supply of black migrants, implying that black and white workers are close substitutes. Thus when the regression coefficient (β) is small, the elasticity of substitution (σ) is large, and vice versa.

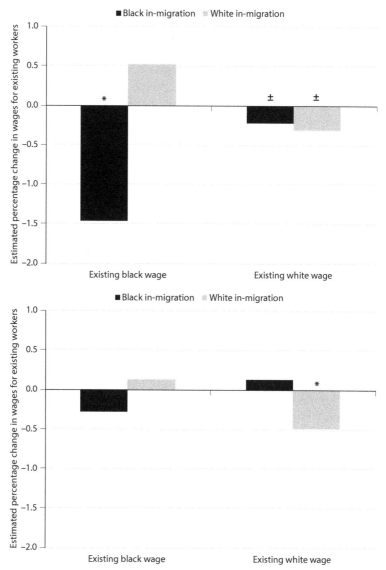

Figures 3.2a and 3.2b. Estimated effects of a 10 percent increase in southern migrant labor supply on the wages of existing workers in the North, 1940–70. Bars report implied effects of increasing the black (or white) labor supply within a skill group by 10 percent on the wages of existing workers in the North. The underlying estimates are derived from Appendix Equation 9 ($N = 156$ skill cells). Skill groups are defined by highest grade completed, years of potential labor market experience, and race. Figure 3.2a classifies men into schooling groups by reported years of education, while Figure 3.2b estimates

skill cell of at least 20 (Ottaviano and Peri 2012; Borjas, Grogger, and Hanson 2008).[19] In contrast, workers with a high school education are imperfect substitutes for workers with at least some college today, with an elasticity of substitution of around 2 (Katz and Murphy 1992; Card 2009). Blacks and whites in the postwar North fell somewhere between these two extremes; they were less substitutable than immigrants and natives in the same skill cell today but were more substitutable than high school– and college-educated workers.

Causes of Imperfect Substitutability by Race: The Role of School Quality

The estimation results corroborate the qualitative evidence that blacks and whites with the same years of schooling and work experience were not used interchangeably in production in the postwar North. This lack of substitutability could have been due to market-based discrimination in job assignment or to pre-market discrimination, perhaps stemming from disparities in school quality. I differentiate between these explanations by revising my measure of a "skill group" in the labor market to take into account differences in school quality between northern and southern schools.

The estimation in Figure 3.2a treats all self-reported years of schooling in the Census identically, regardless of where the schooling was acquired. As a result, a black worker who spent eight years in an overcrowded school in the South with poorly trained teachers and shortened term lengths would be considered educationally equivalent to a white worker who attended eight years of high-quality schooling in the North. Ideally, we could classify skill groups by quality-weighted years

---

[19] Card (2009) partitions the labor market into workers with more than or less than a high school degree. He finds that low-skilled immigrants and natives are perfect substitutes (elasticity of substitution of around 40), while higher-skilled immigrants and natives are imperfect—but close—substitutes (elasticity of substitution of 17).

---

likely days of education by birth cohort, race, and region of birth, accounting for the fact that black schools in the South often had shorter term lengths. The estimation sample includes men who were not enrolled in school, self-employed, or living in group quarters, and who were working full-time. I also omit full-time workers who reported making less than one-half of the prevailing federal minimum wage and replace top-coded incomes with 1.4 times the top-code (Goldin and Margo 1992). Estimates that are statistically significant at the 5 percent level are marked with an *; those that are significant at the 10 percent level are marked with a ±.

of schooling. If black arrivals into this more refined skill group had identical effects on blacks and whites, we could then assume that the imperfect substitutability observed in the main results was driven by pre-market differences in school quality. If, instead, black arrivals continued to affect black wages more than white wages, we could conclude that the lack of substitutability was due to market discrimination in job assignment.

Some measures of school quality—principally, length of the school year, pupil-to-teacher ratios, and expenditures per pupil—are available by race and state for some cohorts (see Margo 1990; Card and Krueger 1992). I focus on differences in the length of the school term because the literature is unequivocal that time spent in school earns a market return but is more mixed on the value added of small class sizes or school expenditures.[20] In particular, I adjust reported years of schooling from the Census for likely days spent in school per year according to an individual's race, birth cohort, and state of birth.[21] I then redefine skill groups by likely days of schooling, rather than reported years of schooling, and reestimate the elasticity of substitution between blacks and whites within these more precisely defined skill groups.[22]

I find that when education is defined using likely days spent in school, a 10 percent increase in the number of black migrants in the cell reduces relative black wages by only 0.4 percent (Figure 3.2b). This estimate implies a much higher elasticity of substitution by race of 25 (rather than 8.3). Although the estimated substitutability between black and white workers in this specification is high—close to the estimates for native- and foreign-born workers today—it can be statistically distinguished from perfect substitution. Consistent with the role of school quality is the fact that black migrants were much more substitutable with foreign-born whites, many of whom attended inferior schools in their home country (estimated elasticity = 16.4) than with native-born whites in the North (elasticity = 7.9).[23]

[20] See Hanushek 1996, 1999 and Krueger and Whitmore 2001 for discussions of the effect of class size and expenditures on student performance.

[21] School term lengths by race and cohort are reported in Card and Krueger 1992. Data were originally drawn from the *Biennial Survey of Education* (1918–58).

[22] Specifically, I replace the year-based education categories with day-based equivalents assuming a standard (northern) school term of 180 days. For example, the lowest education group (0–5 years of schooling) includes men who likely attended school for 900 or fewer days.

[23] These estimates use skill cells based on years (rather than likely days) of reported education. See Ramirez and Boli 1987 on the historical development of primary schooling in Europe.

These findings suggest that at least two-thirds of the imperfect substitutability by race in the northern economy was driven by differences in the quality of black and white schools rather than by discrimination in job assignment for men with otherwise identical skills (= [1.5 − 0.4]/1.5). However, in this simple exercise, I use only one measure to adjust school quality (term length). If better measures of school quality were available, the share of imperfect substitution that could be attributed to pre-market discrimination might rise.[24]

Taken at face value, these results imply that most northern employers were not engaging in market-based discrimination when assigning blacks to manual jobs in steel factories, tanneries, and packinghouses. Rather, the typical black worker—especially southern black migrants—attended systematically lower-quality schools and thus proved to be a less promising candidate for higher-skilled positions. In other words, discrimination originated not at the northern factory gate but in the southern schoolhouse; by the time southern blacks arrived in the North, they were already at a disadvantage.[25]

COUNTERFACTUAL TRENDS IN BLACK EARNINGS

Black migrants generated more competition for existing black workers in the North than for similarly skilled whites, in part because of racial differences in school quality. If black migration to the North had been curtailed after 1940, how much higher would the earnings of northern black workers have been? Would northern black workers have closed the gap with northern whites by 1970 if they had not faced competitive pressure from southern black arrivals?

The nature of these questions requires calculating "counterfactual" wages for whites and blacks in the North for a scenario with limited black migration from the South. Often our task as historians is to assess the causes and consequences of what *did* happen. However, it can be

---

[24] Alternatively, the lower point estimate for β in the regression with skill groups defined by likely days of school may simply be due to measurement error. If term length is *not* closely associated with skill, this procedure would be adding noise to an otherwise reasonable division of skill cells.

[25] In contrast, Margo finds that "much of the employment segregation in the South is not explained by racial differences in the quantity and quality of schooling" (1990, 104). Southern employers appear to have been more discriminatory than their northern counterparts in hiring decisions and job assignments, which is not surprising given the long history of racial animus in the South. On discrimination in southern labor markets, see also Wright 2013, chap. 4.

worth asking how history might have been different if a set of events had not taken place. In this case, how would the history of northern cities have differed if the black migration had been impeded in some way? In thinking through this counterfactual, it is important to keep in mind that even if southern blacks had not moved to northern cities, the labor demand in northern factories would have attracted *some* workers. So perhaps the right question is: what if the immigration restrictions faced by European migrants had been relaxed, leading black in-migrants to be replaced by white ethnic immigrants from 1940 to 1970?

Patterns of Earnings Growth by Race and Region, 1940–2010

Before assessing how in-migration might have changed the course of black earnings in the North, I start by presenting the actual trends in black earnings growth from 1940 to 2010. Figures 3.3a–3.3c illustrate mean annual earnings for prime-age black and white men, both nation-wide and separately by region. Part 1 of each figure depicts white and black annual earnings by year and part 2 of each figure graphs the difference between these two series.[26]

Nationwide, annual earnings of white male workers tripled from 1940 to 1975, while black male income increased over fivefold. Figure 3.3 on page 83 shows that, as a result, the racial earnings gap narrowed during this period.[27] Earnings convergence was driven, in large part, by secular gains in the quantity and quality of black schooling (Smith and Welch 1989; Collins and Margo 2006). Historical events also mattered: relative black wages were buoyed by strong labor demand for low-skilled work during World War II, as well as by President Roosevelt's executive order forbidding government contractors from discriminat-

---

[26] One concern with analyzing trends in mean earnings is differential selection out of the labor market by race over time. In 1940, around 10 percent of black and white men between the ages of eighteen and sixty-four were out of the labor force. By 2010, 31 percent of black men in this age group (but only 18 percent of whites) had left the labor force. The majority of this change occurred after 1970 and so should not affect the primary wage trends under consideration (1940–70). Indeed, results are similar when very low-earning men are included in the sample.

[27] Bailey and Collins (2006, Figure 1) presents a similar wage series for women from 1900 to 1970. The black-to-white earnings ratio for women remained around 45 percent from 1900 to 1940 before increasing markedly, reaching 80 percent by 1970. Before 1940, the share of black women employed in the agricultural sector declined substantially, but most of these agricultural jobs were replaced with equally low-paid service work. Around one-third of the relative black wage gains after 1940 was due to black women shifting out of service jobs, first into operative positions and then into clerical work (Bailey and Collins 2006; Sundstrom 2000).

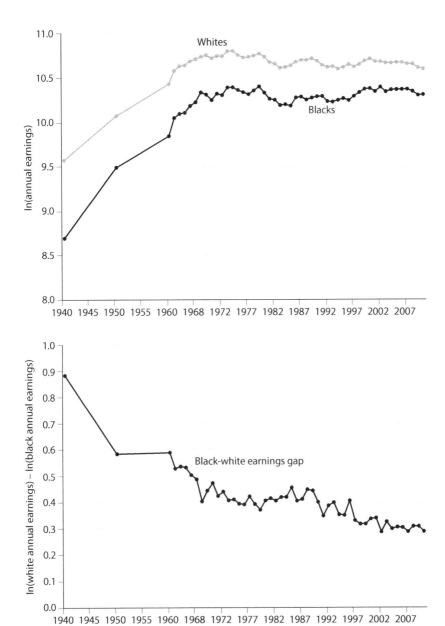

Figure 3.3. Mean annual earnings and the earnings gap between blacks and whites for male workers, by region, 1940–2010. The graphs on page 83 include data from the entire country, while the graphs on page 84 are for the North and the graphs on page 85 are for the South. Mean earnings (in 2010 dollars) for

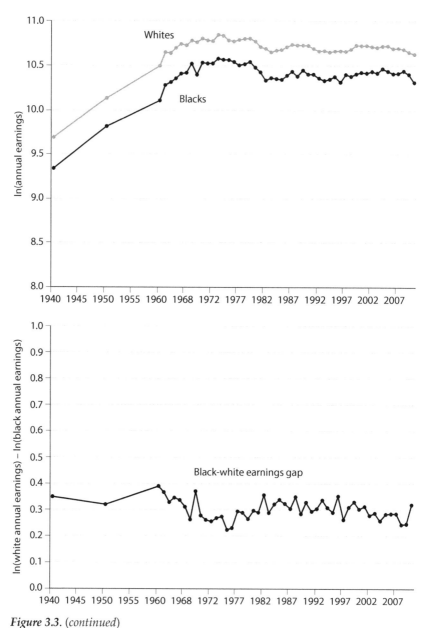

Figure 3.3. (*continued*)

men between the ages of 18 and 64 who were not enrolled in school, who were not living in group quarters, who were not in active duty military service, and who reported annual earnings equal to at least 50 percent of the minimum wage in a given year. Earnings data are from the IPUMS samples of the Census

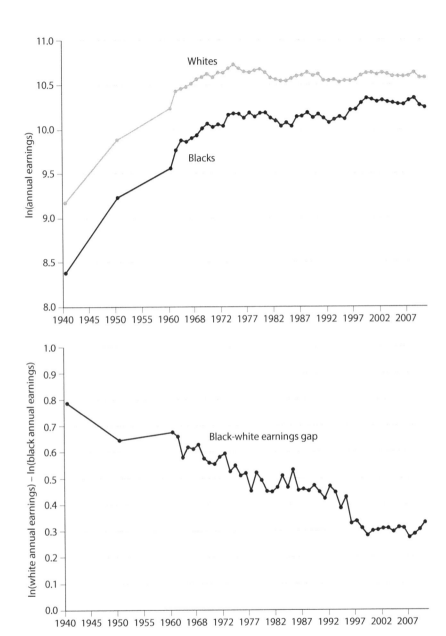

Figure 3.3. (*continued*)
(1940–60) and the Current Population Surveys (1962–2010). From 1950 onward,
annual earnings are based on total income. In 1940, annual earnings are based
on wage and salary income for the non-self-employed and imputed earnings
for the self-employed; see the notes to Table 2.1 for details on this imputation.

ing on the basis of race (Maloney 1994; Margo 1995; Collins 2001). Later, black earnings benefited from legislative efforts to ban racial discrimination in employment, including the Civil Rights Act of 1964 (Donohue and Heckman 1991; Chay 1998). More recently, the pace of black wage growth has slowed to match that of whites, leaving the black-to-white earnings ratio little changed since 1975.[28]

Despite substantial earnings convergence by race nationwide, blacks gained little ground relative to whites in the North since 1940. Instead, most of the national convergence took place in the South, with the remainder (around 20 percent) due to interregional migration (Smith and Welch 1989). From 1940 to 2010, the earnings gap between blacks and whites in the South declined by nearly 60 log points (close to 80 percent) while remaining almost entirely unchanged in the North (Figure 3.3 on pages 84–85). Almost half of the southern earnings convergence from 1940 to 2010 occurred in the 1940s; in this decade, black earnings in the North simply kept pace with white earnings. The 1940s was a period of rising labor demand in wartime industry in the North but also one of considerable black in-migration from the South. Competitive pressure from black migrants may have dampened black earnings growth in the North.[29]

Counterfactual Earnings for Blacks in the North Absent Southern Migration

To assess what black wage growth in the North *might have been* absent in-migration from the South, we can consider a scenario in which all black migration flows are set to zero and the black labor force in each region is only allowed to grow through natural increase. Gaining a complete picture of the effect of in-migration on the earnings of existing black and white workers requires measuring the influence of migrant arrivals not only into a worker's own skill cell (as discussed earlier) but also into all adjacent cells. Plugging these counterfactual labor supply changes into the appendix equations, alongside estimated terms for the relevant elasticities of substitution, reveals the counterfactual changes in black wages; Boustan (2009) describes this method in detail.

---

[28] For more on the slowdown of black-to-white wage convergence after 1975, see Bound and Freeman 1992; Grogger 1996; and Chandra 2003.

[29] Likewise, out-migration may have buoyed the wages of remaining black workers in the South. The effect of black migrant departures on the southern economy is a topic that deserves further study.

According to this calculation, limiting southern black migration would have had a large positive effect on black earnings. If not for the ongoing southern migration, average black earnings in the North would have been around 10 percent higher by 1970, while white earnings would have remained unchanged.[30] This large, concentrated wage effect is due to the fact that migration doubled the number of black workers in the average skill cell in the North during this period. If, instead, black migrants had been replaced with additional European immigration, neither black nor white earnings would have appreciably changed given that flows of this size would have increased labor supply in the average skill cell by only 2 percent.

According to this scenario, in-migration from the South significantly dampened the earnings convergence between blacks and whites in northern cities. In 1940, the black-to-white earnings ratio outside the South was 70 percent. By 1970, this ratio had risen somewhat to 77 percent. These estimates suggest that, if not for the competitive pressure resulting from the ongoing migration, the racial earnings gap in the North would have risen further to 85 percent in 1970. My estimates suggest that the racial earnings gap would have been substantially lower if northern black workers had not faced competition from southern arrivals, but even if the southern migration had been entirely reversed, blacks would not have reached parity with whites in the North.[31]

Closing off southern migration may have benefited existing black workers in the North, but this advantage would have come at some cost to the migrants themselves. The new estimates in chapter 2 suggest that the return to migration was 82 log points (130 percent). Mean black male earnings in the South were $4,300 in 1940 (in 2010 dollars). Therefore, for the 1.9 million black men who left the South after 1940, out-migration increased earnings by $10.2 billion a year (a gain of $5,400 per migrant).[32] On the other hand, there were 1.4 million black men

---

[30] Gardner (2013) does a similar exercise and instead finds that, absent black in-migration from the South, black wages would have been 20 percent higher in the North. The differences between his estimates and mine are primarily driven by time period and treatment of the white foreign born. Gardner considers only the years 1940 through 1960 and excludes the white foreign born from the analysis.

[31] Expressed differently, the earnings gap between blacks and whites was 45 log points in 1940 and fell to around 30 log points by 1970. If not for black in-migration from the South, the racial gap would have fallen to 20 log points by 1970.

[32] These figures differ from aggregate benefits and costs of migration reported in Boustan 2009 in three significant ways. First, Boustan calculates an aggregate return to migration that is too high because it includes all migrants rather than only male migrants.

living in the North in 1940. My analysis implies that the earnings of northern blacks declined by 10 percent as a result of competition with in-migrants. Mean black earnings in the North were $11,500 in 1940 (in 2010 dollars), implying an annual aggregate loss due to in-migration of $1.7 billion for existing black workers in the North (a loss of $1,100 for 1.4 million men). It is also likely that migrants competed with each other in the northern economy. Overall, competition among southern black migrants would lower black earnings in the North by another $1.9 billion a year (a loss of $990 for 1.9 million male migrants), generating a total loss of nearly $4 billion.[33]

This comparison suggests that, in aggregate, the gains for black workers associated with leaving the South were 2.5 times larger than the earnings losses due to competition in the North. Furthermore, migrant departures may have relieved competitive pressure in the southern labor market, thereby increasing the wages of remaining black workers in the South. On net, out-migration from the South increased national black earnings, although the losses experienced by competing workers in the North were sizable.

CONCLUSION

Blacks experienced earnings growth relative to whites at two points in the twentieth century, once in the 1940s and then again from 1965 to 1975. In both cases, racial convergence was slower in the North than in the South. Slow black economic progress in the North was due, in part, to a steady inflow of southern black migrants, who competed with existing black workers in the North, keeping wages low. I estimate that if not for this ongoing migration, northern blacks would have closed a portion of the remaining earnings gap with whites.

To some extent, black migrants were more substitutable with other black workers simply because they had similarly low levels of education. But black migrants were also closer substitutes for northern-born blacks *within* skill cells defined by years of schooling and work experi-

---

Second, she uses base southern black earnings in 1940 that are too high, in part because they are not adjusted for self-employment income. Third, she uses an estimated return to migration that is too low (30 percent, as proposed by Smith and Welch 1989). Overall, these biases cancel out and she finds a similar aggregate benefit of migrant ($7.6 billion).

[33] I assume that southern black migrants earned $9,900 in the North, or a 130 percent return on a southern income of $4,300 (in 2010 dollars).

ence. This racial segmentation in the northern labor market was due both to the pre-market discrimination that blacks experienced in the form of low-quality southern schools and to the market-based discrimination instituted by northern employers. Accounting for the lower quality of black schooling in the South can explain around two-thirds of the weak substitution between otherwise similarly skilled blacks and whites. The remaining racial division suggests that blacks faced additional barriers in the northern labor market.

APPENDIX TO CHAPTER 3

This appendix outlines the framework used to estimate the substitutability of similarly skilled blacks and whites in the northern economy; further details are provided in Boustan 2009. The model is based on a Cobb-Douglas production function in which capital (K) and labor (L) are combined to produce output:

$$Y = A\,L^{\alpha}\,K^{1-\alpha}. \tag{1}$$

Labor is described as a nested composite of education groups (e), experience levels within education groups (x), and racial groups (black and white) within each education-experience cell (r). Total labor supply can be written as an aggregation of the contributions from each education group (L_e):

$$L = [\Sigma_e\ \theta_e L_e^{(\delta-1)/\delta}]^{\delta/(\delta-1)} \tag{1a}$$

where the θ_e terms are technology parameters that shift the relative productivity of education groups (normalized to sum to one). The variable $\delta > 0$ denotes the elasticity of substitution between workers with different levels of educational attainment.

In turn, the labor supply of each education group is a combination of the contributions of workers with different levels of experience:

$$L_e = [\Sigma_x\ \theta_{ex} L_{ex}^{(\eta-1)/\eta}]^{\eta/(\eta-1)} \tag{1b}$$

where η measures the elasticity of substitution across experience levels within an education category. It is likely that workers are closer substitutes within education categories than across them; in this case, we expect $\eta > \delta$.

Finally, I allow black and white workers in the same skill group to be imperfect substitutes, perhaps due to discrimination in the labor market. The labor supply within an education-experience cell combines the contributions of black and white workers:

$$L_{ex} = [\theta_{exw}L_{exw}^{(\sigma-1)/\sigma} + \theta_{exb}L_{exb}^{(\sigma-1)/\sigma}]^{\sigma/(\sigma-1)}. \tag{1c}$$

The θ_{exr} terms ($r = w, b$) are race-specific productivity parameters, and σ is the elasticity of substitution between black and white men in the same skill cell.

In a competitive equilibrium, we can recover the wages of men with education level e, experience x, and race r by differentiating equation 1 with respect to L_{exr}—that is, asking how a small increase in a particular type of labor increases overall productivity. The resulting expression is:

$$\ln w_{exr} = \ln(A^{1/\alpha}\kappa^{(1-\alpha)/\alpha}) + 1/\delta \ln(L) + \ln\theta_e - (1/\delta - 1/\eta) \ln(L_e)$$
$$+ \ln\theta_{ex} - (1/\eta - 1/\sigma)\ln(L_{ex}) + \ln\theta_{exr} - 1/\sigma \ln(L_{exr}). \tag{2}$$

Equation 2 demonstrates that wages depend positively on the own education-, experience-, and race-specific productivity terms (θ) and negatively on own-group labor supply (L_{exr}). The extent to which labor supply in adjacent groups reduces own-group wages is determined by the elasticities of substitution by education (δ), experience (η), and race (σ).

Equation 2 allows us to analyze the effect of black migration on the wages of white and black workers in the North.[34] Let us start with the case of white workers in the education-experience group e-x. A portion of the black migration flows directly into this skill group. Black migration into group e-x has the following effect on the wages of white workers in this cell:

$$\Delta w_{exw}/w_{exw} = [1/\delta + (1/\eta - 1/\delta)(1/s_e)$$
$$+ (1/\sigma - 1/\eta)(1/s_{ex})] \cdot s_{exb} \cdot \Delta L_{exb}/L_{exb}. \tag{3}$$

Other migrants have the same amount of education but different experience levels, while still others are in different education groups. These arrivals influence the wages of white workers in e-x as follows:

$$\Delta w_{exw}/w_{exw} = [1/\delta + (1/\eta - 1/\delta)(1/s_e)] \cdot s_{exb} \cdot \Delta L_{exb}/L_{exb} \tag{4}$$

$$\Delta w_{exw}/w_{exw} = 1/\delta \cdot s_{exb} \cdot \Delta L_{exb}/L_{exb}. \tag{5}$$

[34] A general expression for the effect of an increase in the supply of factor b on the wages of factor a is given by d log w_a/dlogL_b = s_b $Y_{ab}Y/Y_aY_b$, where s_b is the share of income earned by factor b and Y_x denotes the partial derivative of output with respect to a factor x (Hamermesh 1996).

Adding equations (3)–(5) across all skill groups contributing to the migration flow indicates the total effect of the migration on the wages of white workers in group e-x:

$$\Delta w_{exw}/w_{exw} = 1/\delta \; \Sigma_i \Sigma_j \; (s_{ijb}\Delta L_{ijb}/L_{ijb}) + (1/\eta - 1/\delta)(1/s_e)$$
$$\Sigma_j \; (s_{ejb}\Delta L_{ejb}/L_{ejb}) + (1/\sigma - 1/\eta)(1/s_{ex})(s_{exb}\Delta L_{exb}/L_{exb}) \qquad (6)$$

where Σ_i sums across education groups and Σ_j sums across experience levels. Equation 6 demonstrates that white wages will fall with migrant entry into the group's own education level (term 2) and education-experience cell (term 3). As a counterweight, wages will rise with an increase in labor supply into skill cells that are complements in production (term 1).[35]

The effect of black migration on the wages of black workers in skill group e-x is expressed by equation 6 with an additional term capturing the potentially imperfect elasticity of substitution between men of different races in the same skill group:

$$\Delta w_{exb}/w_{exb} = \Delta w_{exw}/w_{exw} - 1/\sigma \; (\Delta L_{exb}/L_{exb}). \qquad (7)$$

In the case of perfect substitutability by race, σ is equal to ∞ and black migration will have an equal effect on black and white wages in the same skill group. If σ is less than ∞, the arrival of new black workers will have a larger negative effect on existing black workers.

Equations 6 and 7 demonstrate the effect of an increase in black labor supply on the wages of white and black men in a specific skill cell (e-x). The effect of black inflows on *average* black and white wages will be a weighted sum of these cell-specific effects. Black migration will have a larger effect on black wages than on white wages if: (1) the skill distributions of whites and blacks are sufficiently different, and/or (2) the elasticity of substitution by race within skill cell (σ) is low.

Obtaining an unbiased estimate of the elasticity of substitution by race (σ) is central to understanding the effect of black migration on relative black wage growth in the North. A simple expression for σ can be found by taking the ratio of black-to-white wages in a skill group e-x from equation 2:

$$\ln(w_{exb}/w_{exw}) = -1/\sigma \; \ln(L_{exb}/L_{exw}) + \ln(\theta_{exb}/\theta_{exw}). \qquad (8)$$

The wage gap between blacks and whites in skill group e-x is a function of the ratio of black-to-white labor supply in that group and the ratio of

---

[35] I assume that capital completely adjusts with the new labor supply, in which case we can ignore the impact of this inflow on the capital-labor ratio.

the race-specific productivity terms. If blacks and whites are perfect substitutes ($\sigma = \infty$), the wage ratio will be invariant to relative labor supply. A positive coefficient on the relative supply term implies that black and white workers in the same skill group are not used interchangeably in production ($\sigma \neq \infty$).

I estimate a version of equation 8 by pooling data from four Census years (1940–70):

$$\ln(w_{exbt}/w_{exwt}) = \beta \ln(L_{exbt}/L_{exwt}) + e + x + \tau$$
$$+ (e \cdot x) + (e \cdot \tau) + (x \cdot \tau) + \varepsilon_{exbt}/\varepsilon_{exwt}. \tag{9}$$

Relative labor supplies in each skill cell can be observed in the data, but the ratio of cell-specific productivity cannot be. I proxy for these productivity terms with a series of fixed effects for education levels (e), work experience (x), and Census year (τ) and all two-way interactions. The interactions ($e \cdot \tau$) and ($x \cdot \tau$) allow the returns to schooling and experience to change over time, and the interaction ($e \cdot x$) allows experience profiles to differ by education. A comparison of equations 8 and 9 reveals that the elasticity of substitution (σ) can be inferred from the expression $\sigma = -1/\beta$.

CHAPTER 4

Black Migration, White Flight

THE FIRST ACT of Bruce Norris's 2011 Pulitzer Prize–winning play *Clybourne Park* is set in 1959 in a white neighborhood of Chicago. The characters Russ and Bev are packing up to move to the suburbs. Russ boasts that after the move, the commute from their driveway to his suburban office will take only six and a half minutes. Drama enters this domestic scene in the form of their neighbor, Karl, who is upset because Russ and Bev sold their house to a black family. In Karl's vision of the neighborhood's future, "first one family will leave, then another and another, and each time they do, the values of these properties will decline . . . and *some* of us, you see, those who *don't* have the opportunity to simply pick up and move at the drop of a hat, then *those* folks are left holding the bag, and it's a fairly *worthless* bag, at that point" (Norris 2011, 80).

Flight is not an option for Karl and so he decides to "fight" for the racial character of his neighborhood instead. But Karl's pleas for Russ and Bev to stay in the neighborhood do not succeed. Neither does his offer to buy back the house from the prospective black neighbors on behalf of the Clybourne Park Improvement Association.[1] By the second act of *Clybourne Park*, set fifty years later, the neighborhood has been through a full cycle of decline and revival that started with the arrival of one black family and was followed by white departures, heightened crime and poverty, and finally a wave of gentrification.

Decades of suburban moves by white couples like Russ and Bev contributed to the extreme segregation that took root in northern areas by 1970. In 1940, half of white metropolitan residents in the North still lived in the central city. Northern black communities were small, representing only 4 percent of the typical city's population. As a result, majority-black neighborhoods were few in number, such that the aver-

---

[1] As it happens, these new neighbors are the Youngers, whose struggles were chronicled fifty years earlier by Lorraine Hansberry's classic play *A Raisin in the Sun* (1959).

age black resident lived in a neighborhood that was "only" 58 percent black. By 1970, after three decades of in-migration, the black population share in northern cities had quadrupled to 16 percent. Meanwhile, the share of white metropolitan residents remaining in the central city dwindled to 29 percent. As a result, in that year, the typical urban black resident in the North lived in a neighborhood that was 75 percent black.

White suburbanization was primarily motivated by economic forces, including rising incomes, new highway construction, and the falling cost of credit in the decades after World War II. But white departures from the city were also, in part, a reaction to black in-migration. I present new causal evidence on the relationship between black arrivals to cities and white departures, a trend that I refer to as "white flight."[2] The simultaneity of black in-migration from the South and white relocation to the suburbs, both of which peaked from 1940 to 1970, suggests that the two population flows may be related. Moving beyond this national time series, I use variation in the timing of black in-migration to the seventy largest cities in the North and West to distinguish white flight from other causes of suburbanization.

Documenting a correlation between black arrivals and white departures is not sufficient evidence of white flight. Black migrants to a city may have been attracted by the same underlying economic conditions that encouraged white suburbanization in the first place (such as industrial growth). Ideally, one would be able to observe the white response to a flow of black migrants who settled in northern cities for reasons unrelated to the area's current economic health. I approximate this strategy by using the estimates of out-migration from southern counties discussed in chapter 1 to predict out-migration from each southern state as a result of local factors. I then assign these predicted migrant flows to northern cities using established patterns of chain migration between particular southern areas and northern cities. This process generates an instrumental variable for changes in black population in a northern city. My estimates imply that each black arrival encouraged more than one white departure from the central city, leading to net population decline.

Existing white residents may have left the central city as black migrants arrived for many reasons. First, any population inflow to a city can raise housing prices and rents, prompting some residents to seek

---

[2] Unlike the colloquial usage of the term, which is often broadly applied to any form of white suburbanization, I use "white flight" to refer to those white departures from the central city that were in direct response to changing racial composition.

more affordable housing options elsewhere (the *housing market channel*). In addition, as historical case studies make clear, white households who lived near black enclaves left the city to avoid interactions with black neighbors (the *social interactions channel*). Yet, as the next chapter will show, the typical white household lived quite far from a black neighborhood in sections of the city that were at little risk of racial turnover. These distant households may have relocated to the suburbs as aspects of local city policy, including the property tax rate and spending priorities, changed in response to the growing black population (the *fiscal/political channel*).

PATTERNS OF RESIDENTIAL SEGREGATION IN NORTHERN CITIES, 1940–70

In 1940, the typical city outside of the South was only 4 percent black. The black population share quadrupled to 16 percent by 1970 and then increased again to 23 percent by 2000. As the black population in northern cities expanded, the number of majority-black neighborhoods also increased, as did black isolation from whites in metropolitan areas. However, despite large numbers of new black arrivals, white exposure to black neighbors did not increase at all in the North. Whites were able to achieve this remarkable isolation from blacks by moving from the diversifying city to the suburbs.

The racial pattern of residence in northern and western metropolitan areas changed considerably over the twentieth century. Table 4.1 presents a series of facts about neighborhood racial composition at three points: in 1940, as the largest decade of black migration got underway; in 1970, after thirty years of sustained migration to the North; and in the year 2000 for a contemporary comparison. Panel B of Table 4.1 divides city neighborhoods into four categories: uniformly white (0–1 percent black); predominantly white (1–5 percent black); integrated (5–50 percent black); and majority black. Neighborhoods are defined according to Census tracts, geographic units containing approximately 4,000 residents that are designed to reflect distinct local areas. Tract borders often follow natural or man-made boundaries such as rivers and large streets.

In 1940, the vast majority of Census tracts in northern cities were uniformly white (67 percent), and only 5 percent of city neighborhoods were majority black. Yet these majority-black areas housed nearly 60 percent of northern blacks. The remaining 40 percent of blacks lived in

Table 4.1: Neighborhood racial characteristics, northern and western
cities and metropolitan areas, 1940–2000

	1940	1970	2000
A. *Black population share, central city*	0.043	0.158	0.226
B. *Neighborhood type, % of central city*			
0–1 percent black	67.2	40.3	9.1
1–5 percent black	15.4	15.2	23.8
5–50 percent black	12.7	20.8	35.4
50+ percent black	4.7	23.7	31.8
Total	*100.0*	*100.0*	*100.0*
C. *Black isolation index*			
City	0.58	0.76	0.70
Suburb	–	0.56	0.43
Metropolitan area	–	0.72	0.62
D. *White isolation index*			
City	0.97	0.91	0.87
Suburb	–	0.97	0.94
Metropolitan area	–	0.95	0.91

Note: Panel A: Average black population share in the central city of the 70 metropolitan areas listed in Appendix Table 4.1. The central city is defined according to the 1940
boundaries in both 1940 and 1970; see note 36 in chapter 4 for details. The 2000 figure is
calculated from the actual city boundaries. Panels B–D: Figures for the 33 large northern
and western cities with available tract-level data in 1940 as listed in Appendix Table 4.1.
Neighborhoods are defined using Census tracts, and the central city is defined according
to the 1950 boundaries using data provided by Nathaniel Baum-Snow. The black isolation index in Panel C is a weighted average of the black population share in the Census
tracts of all black residents, and similarly for whites in Panel D. Suburban areas were not
divided into Census tracts in 1940 and so the isolation index cannot be calculated either
for the suburbs or for the metropolitan area as a whole in that year. Metropolitan areas
are defined according to the 1970 county definitions in both 1970 and 2000.

predominantly white or integrated neighborhoods, with roughly equal
proportion in each. However, many neighborhoods classified as integrated here were undergoing a process of racial transition. Ellen (2000)
documents that neighborhoods that were racially mixed in 1970 often
became majority black by 1990, and the same was likely true earlier in
the century.[3]

One summary indicator of residential segregation at the metropoli-

[3] By Ellen's count, only 56 percent of neighborhoods that were integrated in 1970
(defined as 10–50 percent black) remained so twenty years later; for comparison, more
than 80 percent of predominantly white and majority-black neighborhoods retained their
racial character during this period.

tan level is the isolation index, which measures the black population share in the typical black resident's neighborhood (or the equivalent for whites).[4] The higher the isolation index, the lower the probability that a black resident encounters a white neighbor in daily life and vice versa. Black isolation can increase either with growth in an area's black population or because a black population of a given size becomes more residentially concentrated.

In 1940, the black isolation index was 58 percent, which implies that the "typical" black resident of a northern city would encounter black and white neighbors in roughly equal measure (Table 4.1, Panel C). In this case, the isolation index provides a weighted average of the 60 percent of blacks who lived in majority-black neighborhoods and the 40 percent who lived in more integrated areas. In contrast, the typical white resident of a northern city in 1940 lived in a neighborhood that was 97 percent white, suggesting that white urban residents were easily able to avoid daily interaction with the small black communities living in their cities at the time (Panel D).[5]

After three decades of heavy black in-migration, the racial composition of city neighborhoods changed dramatically. The share of city neighborhoods that were uniformly white declined from 67 to 40 percent, mirrored by a large increase in majority-black neighborhoods (from 5 to 24 percent) and a smaller rise in integrated neighborhoods (from 28 to 36 percent). As in-migration continued, black isolation in the central city increased from 58 percent in 1940 to 76 percent in 1970, both because the typical black resident was more likely to live in a majority-black neighborhood in 1970 and because majority-black neighborhoods were themselves more likely to be "uniformly" black.[6] The intensification of black isolation during this period is consistent with trends in other common measures of residential segregation, including the dissimilarity index.[7]

[4] The isolation index is a weighted average of neighborhood-level black population share across all black residents. For an overview of different measures of segregation, see Massey and Denton 1993.

[5] As a point of comparison, in 1910, southern and eastern European immigrant groups (such as Italians and Russians) experienced isolation rates of around 12 percent (Cutler, Glaeser, and Vigdor 2008, 482). At the time, each group represented around 2 percent of the urban population. Blacks were twice as numerous in 1940, making up 4 percent of city population, but had isolation rates that were nearly five times as large.

[6] The share of metropolitan blacks living in a majority-black neighborhood increased from 59 to 69 percent during this period, while the black population share in majority-black neighborhoods increased from 79 to 84 percent.

[7] Cutler, Glaeser, and Vigdor (1999) track the dissimilarity index for sixty large cities

What is more remarkable is that black in-migration had *no effect* on white contact with blacks in northern metropolitan areas. White isolation at the metropolitan level remained stable during this period, falling only from 96 to 95 percent.[8] For whites who stayed in the central city, isolation did decline (from 97 percent in 1940 to 91 percent in 1970), although the extent of this drop was far smaller than if each neighborhood received a black inflow commensurate with the city total. However, despite falling isolation in cities, whites were able to maintain their high isolation levels overall by moving to predominantly white suburbs. Although the share of all-white neighborhoods declined in cities during this period (from 67 percent in 1940 to 40 percent in 1970), the share of all-white neighborhoods in metropolitan areas remained stable at around 60 percent because of the growth of the suburbs.

By 2000, thirty years after black migration to the North had tapered off and reversed, black isolation in the North and West had fallen considerably and even white isolation began to decline. From 1970 to 2000, black isolation in metropolitan areas fell from 72 to 62 percent. Declines in black isolation occurred both in cities (a drop from 76 to 70 percent) and in suburbs (from 56 to 43 percent). Despite reductions in black isolation, blacks remained the most residentially segregated group in U.S. metropolitan areas in 2010.[9]

ECONOMIC UNDERPINNINGS OF POSTWAR
WHITE SUBURBANIZATION

Black migrants arrived in northern cities in large numbers during World War II and the subsequent decades, a period in which existing white residents were departing for the suburban ring. White suburban-

---

nationwide from 1890 to 1990. From 1890 to 1940, as blacks first began moving to cities in large numbers, the dissimilarity index increased from 0.46 to 0.72. With the expansion of black ghettos during and after World War II, dissimilarity rose again, peaking at 0.79 in metropolitan areas in 1970.

[8] It is impossible to calculate isolation at the metropolitan level in 1940 because suburban areas were not divided into Census tracts. Instead, I estimate white isolation at the metropolitan level in 1940 by assuming that the few blacks who lived in the suburbs were evenly distributed throughout suburban neighborhoods. If, instead, at the other extreme, suburban blacks were entirely isolated in all-black suburban neighborhoods, the white isolation index would have been 98 percent (rather than 96 percent) in 1940. The truth probably lies somewhere in between.

[9] In 2010, black-white dissimilarity was 0.59, compared with lower index values for Hispanic-white dissimilarity (0.48) and Asian-white dissimilarity (0.41) (Logan and Stults 2011).

ization was primarily motivated by factors unrelated to racial diversity, including an expanding market for credit, rising incomes, and the construction of a new highway network that facilitated commuting to the city center.[10] Indeed, as pioneering sociologists Alma Taeuber and Karl Taeuber (1965, 7) noted in the 1960s, "to attribute the processes of racial transition [in central cities] primarily to . . . whites fleeing incoming Negro population is an exaggeration . . . given the prevalent tendency of high-status whites to seek newer housing on the periphery of the urbanized area." However, as I demonstrate later in the chapter, the phenomenon of "white flight," whereby white households moved to the suburbs in response to the changing racial composition of central cities, did accelerate the process of urban departures.

Residential moves to suburban areas were taking place steadily through the first two-thirds of the twentieth century. In 1900, 71 percent of metropolitan residents lived in a central city. This figure fell to 58 percent by 1940 before declining further to 39 percent by 1970. The growth of prewar suburbs initially occurred along streetcar lines and was later enhanced by the diffusion of the automobile in the 1910s and 1920s (Warner 1978; LeRoy and Sonstelie 1983). Suburbanization slowed during the Depression and early war years as new housing starts declined, first because of the economic downturn and then as a result of the allocation of available resources to the war effort (Jackson 1985; Hill 2013). The return to normal housing supply conditions coincided with an explosion in demand for housing after World War II, particularly for the detached single-family units characteristic of the suburban ring.

Returning veterans accounted for a portion of the heightened demand for housing. Some veterans took advantage of housing benefits that were provided in the GI Bill, including a mortgage program that allowed recipients to purchase a home with little or no down payment.[11] The Veterans' Administration assisted 2.1 million returning soldiers in purchasing homes between 1946 and 1950 alone (Bennett 1996, 24). In the process of becoming homeowners, many veterans chose to relocate

[10] For contemporary economic and demographic analysis of white suburbanization, see Bradford and Kelejian 1973; Guterbock 1976; Frey 1979; and Marshall 1979. This work is summarized in Mieszkowski and Mills 1993.

[11] Overall, 29 percent of World War II veterans made use of the loan guarantee provisions of the GI Bill (Mettler 2005, 101). Katznelson (2005, 121–28) argues that many black veterans were unable to take full advantage of these benefits because of discriminatory program officers.

to the suburbs where single-family homes were more prevalent (Mettler 2005, 100–104; Fetter 2013; Boustan and Shertzer 2013). The civilian market for credit also expanded in the 1930s and 1940s as the Federal Housing Administration (FHA) began insuring mortgages initiated by private lenders. Mortgage rates fell from around 6 percent in the 1920s to around 4 percent in the 1940s (Morton 1956; Jackson 1985, 205). It has become a truism that mortgage loans underwritten by the FHA were more readily available in the suburbs. Jackson's influential history of suburbanization, for example, unequivocally states that "FHA insurance went to new residential developments on the edges of metropolitan areas, to the neglect of core cities" (1985, 206). However, recent work by Glock (2013) demonstrates that in 1960, outstanding FHA insurance on loans for single-family housing was relatively evenly divided between central cities and suburbs at around one million units each. Forty-three percent of FHA mortgages for single-family homes were allocated to city properties in 1960, which nearly matches the share of single-family units in metropolitan areas that were located in central cities at the time (41 percent). Therefore, while the FHA likely contributed to the rise in homeownership, it is not clear that the availability of FHA loans specifically encouraged households to locate to the suburbs.

In addition to growing access to credit, postwar suburbanization was hastened by rising household incomes and new road-building programs. The construction of new highways would unambiguously encourage suburbanization by reducing the time cost of commuting. The effect of income on residential location is more complex. As incomes rise, households demand more of all normal goods, including larger housing units, better schools, and more open space, all of which are more readily available in the suburbs. However, as wages (and the opportunity cost of time) rise, households may prefer to locate downtown to minimize commuting time.[12]

Of course, in reality, households consider a variety of factors in addition to housing prices and commuting times when making a location decision. For households that were already deeply embedded in an urban neighborhood, an increase in income or a newly available highway may not have been a sufficient inducement to move to the suburbs. However, for a household that was on the fence between living in the

---

[12] Alonso (1964), Muth (1969), and Mills (1972) emphasize this trade-off in the canonical monocentric city model. Glaeser, Kahn, and Rappaport (2008) examine how empirical housing choices change as income rises.

city or the suburbs, a single change (e.g., a new highway) may have been enough to encourage the family to relocate. If the factor in question is important enough, it may be decisive for a large number of households, thereby encouraging population flows to the suburbs.

The twin roles of rising incomes and falling commuting costs in explaining suburban growth in the mid-twentieth century are borne out in the quantitative historical record. Margo (1992) examines the association between household income and suburban residence in Census microdata and demonstrates that rising income can explain around 40 percent of suburbanization from 1950 to 1980. Baum-Snow (2007, 800–801) concludes that another one-third of the change in city population can be explained by the construction of new highways as part of the federal Interstate Highway System. Highway construction also encouraged firms to relocate to the suburban ring (Baum-Snow 2010). In 1960, a few years after the federal highway program got underway, 59 percent of metropolitan residents still worked in a central city. By 2000, the share of metropolitan employment located in the city declined to 42 percent. The decentralization of employment was likely a further inducement to settle in the suburbs (Boustan and Margo 2009).[13]

Barriers to Black Suburbanization in the Mid-Twentieth Century

White residents of central cities moved to the suburbs in large numbers in the decades following World War II. But black suburbanization did not begin in earnest until after 1970. Less than 20 percent of metropolitan blacks lived in the suburbs in the years before 1970.[14] As a result of these divergent location patterns, the suburbs remained overwhelm-

---

[13] Given the importance of factors like federally funded highways in encouraging suburbanization, one common view is that the suburbs were an outgrowth of conscious— and intentionally exclusionary—social planning. Coates (2014) is perhaps the best-known proponent of this view; he argues that suburbanization was "a triumph of social engineering" rather than a "natural expression of [individual] preference." As I see it, suburbanization was both. Individual households make decisions in response to the available housing prices and neighborhood types, which are, in turn, a product of social-historical context, including deliberate government policy.

[14] Wiese (2005) narrates the often-forgotten history of the 20 percent of metropolitan black residents who lived in the suburbs in the years before 1970. Black suburbanites lived in neighborhoods on the outskirts of southern cities, as well as in working-class and middle-class enclaves in northern and western towns like New Rochelle, NY, Evanston, IL, and Pasadena, CA.

ingly white in the mid-twentieth century, while central cities became increasingly black. Black concentration in the central city cannot be attributed to racial differences in income alone or to the preferences of black migrants to live near other black households in centrally located black enclaves. Instead, the lack of opportunities for black suburbanization before 1970 was largely the product of a series of tactics that white residents used to bar black families from suburban areas.

Income differences between blacks and whites cannot explain the concentration of black residents in the central city. In this period, high-income black households were no more likely than their low-income counterparts to live in a suburban area. In 1960, for example, a 10 percent increase in income for metropolitan whites (around $4,000 in 2010 dollars) was associated with a 1.2 percentage point increase in the likelihood of living in the suburbs. In contrast, a 10 percent increase in income for metropolitan blacks raised the likelihood of living in the suburbs by less than 0.1 percentage points. Moreover, even if the strong relationship between income and suburbanization had been shared by black households, the actual racial gap in income would have only explained a third of the racial difference in suburbanization.

Furthermore, black concentration in the central city was not simply the product of migrants' preferences to cluster near friends and family in historic black enclaves.[15] Thernstrom and Thernstrom (1997) use responses to hypothetical neighborhood choices in the Multi-City Study on Urban Inequality to argue that blacks prefer plurality- or majority-black neighborhoods, two neighborhood types that are extremely uncommon in suburban areas. But when asked open-ended questions about *why* they preferred majority-black areas, many black respondents emphasized their concerns about being shunned or harassed by their white neighbors rather than their preference for living near other black households. In other words, there is a high cost to being a black pioneer in an all-white neighborhood, one that few families are willing to bear.[16] As Orin, a black eight-year-old who was interviewed by Robert Coles in *Children of Crisis* (1971, 87), explained, "My mother says that she'd like to get us out of here, into a better street. . . . The white people don't

---

[15] Of course, this explanation begs the question: why were historic black enclaves located in the central city in the first place? The answer is probably that black migrants to northern cities in the 1910s and 1920s settled near available factory work, which, at the time, was located downtown.

[16] For this alternative interpretation of the data in the Multi-City Study on Urban Inequality, see, for example, Farley et al. 1994 and Ihlanfeldt and Scafidi 2002.

like us moving out to where they live, though; so we may be here for a long time."

White residents used various tactics to exclude blacks from suburban areas. Historically, these forms of "collective action" included racially restrictive covenants on property, coordinated efforts by local real estate agents to limit black entry to suburban towns, and zoning regulations favoring large lots and single-family homes in suburban towns, which often priced out poorer black households. Blacks also faced barriers to the mortgage financing necessary to purchase single-family homes in suburban towns. Explicit violence against black neighbors, which has been documented in many cases, was a tactic more commonly used by white residents in the central city but was also present in some suburban areas. I will review each of these methods in turn.

Until the late 1940s, property owners could freely enter contracts, known as racially restrictive covenants, which obliged them not to sell or rent their property to members of various racial or religious groups.[17] The Supreme Court declared such covenants legally unenforceable in the 1948 *Shelley v. Kramer* decision. The prevalence of racial covenants in the metropolitan housing stock before the *Shelley* decision is hard to assess. Contemporary observers and historians have collected data on the coverage of racial covenants in a few metropolitan areas. Plotkin (1999) reports that 25 percent of neighborhoods in central-city Chicago made extensive use of these provisions. Dean (1947) similarly finds that 31 percent of new subdivisions in suburban New York City were covenanted, whereas Gotham (2002) documents that 75 percent of new subdivisions in suburban Kansas City were restricted by race. In general, covenants appear to have been more common in new suburban subdivisions than in existing urban neighborhoods. Most covenants required near unanimity among area property owners in order to go into effect (Philpott 1978, 193–94). Therefore, covenants were more difficult to apply retroactively to the existing urban housing stock proximate to central black enclaves.

Even if covenants were widespread in the suburbs, the lack of appreciable black suburbanization after the 1948 *Shelley* decision suggests either that covenants had never been effective or, more likely, that equally powerful substitutes could be used to hold the color line in the suburbs even after covenants were invalidated.[18] Often the desire on

[17] See Jones-Correa 2000 on how racially restrictive covenants were first instituted and how they diffused.

[18] Kucheva and Sander (2014) show that after the *Shelley* decision, blacks were able to

the part of individual sellers to avoid opprobrium from their neighbors was strong enough to enforce a high degree of segregation, particularly if sellers were staying in the same town, church, or school. Before the passage of the federal Fair Housing Act in 1968, individual homeowners in twenty-eight states could legally refuse to sell or rent their property to blacks.[19]

Actions of individual sellers in suburban areas were reinforced by real estate agents. Real estate agents had a strong motivation to maintain an area's existing racial character in order to preserve their reputation with the local community. As a result, a realtor would only represent a black family interested in buying or renting in a white area if the expected commission from this transaction outweighed the potential future loss of business from angry white neighbors.[20] In most suburban areas, then, real estate agents found it in their best interest to preserve the area's racial balance by preventing sales to pioneering black families.[21] However, in city neighborhoods close to black enclaves, expectations of "inevitable" racial transition lessened concerns about future reputation among white clients and prompted real estate agents to broker sales for black families. At the extreme, agents would hasten the process of racial transition using a tactic known as "block busting," whereby agents would sell one unit to a black family and then use the entry of the first black family to encourage other white owners to sell.[22]

---

move into formerly covenanted neighborhoods adjacent to black enclaves in Chicago and St. Louis. Thus the loss of restrictive covenants appears to have widened the set of housing options available to black families in central cities, even if it did not open access to the suburbs.

[19] Twenty-two states passed fair housing provisions before the 1968 federal law. However, Collins (2004) finds no evidence that states with strong fair housing laws experienced faster growth in black homeownership or in the quality of the black-owned or black-rented housing stock, perhaps because these laws suffered from weak enforcement.

[20] See Ouazad 2015 for a model of the economic incentives of realtors.

[21] Up until 1950, the National Association of Real Estate Boards' Code of Ethics required signatories to pledge "never [to] be instrumental in introducing into a neighborhood . . . members of any race or nationality . . . whose presence will be clearly detrimental to real estate values." Specific reference to race and religion was stripped from the code in 1950, but the remaining language in this section was retained until 1974 (Heller 2012).

[22] Sugrue (1996, 195) documents the practice of block busting in Detroit. Agents would sell "a house in an all-white block or neighborhood to a black family . . . [and then inundate] residents with leaflets and phone calls, informing them that 'Negros are "taking over" this block or area' and that they 'had best sell now while there is still a chance of obtaining a good price.'" See Gotham 2002, 103–19 on this form of panic selling in Kansas City.

Suburban towns also had the authority to restrict local land use through zoning ordinances and building codes. Many towns chose to exclude multifamily dwellings or to set minimum lot sizes, both of which effectively increase the price of entry into the suburbs, rendering suburban residence unaffordable to many poor households. These density restrictions may have been explicitly intended to exclude black households, given that blacks tended to be poorer than whites. However, in many cases, restrictive zoning laws may simply have been designed to preserve the local tax base rather than to target black households in particular (Henderson 1985; Wheaton 1993).[23] Even so, zoning may have limited black access to the suburbs. Pendall (2000) and Massey and Rothwell (2009) show that stricter zoning laws are correlated with lower black population share at the town level and with higher racial segregation at the metropolitan level.[24]

Limited access to mortgage financing created another institutional impediment that limited black entry into the suburbs. The vast majority of the suburban housing stock was owner-occupied, requiring a source of mortgage credit for purchase. Until the mid-1960s, black households had difficulty securing mortgages underwritten by the FHA (Jackson 1985, 208–15). Glock (2013) reports that in 1960, the FHA insured only 10 percent of mortgages on single-family homes occupied by non-white households, compared with 19 percent of such mortgages for white households; however, by 1970, this gap had almost entirely closed. As a result, black families often resorted to buying "on contract," engaging in a rent-to-own arrangement with the seller often at a high rate of interest and with little protection against repossession (Satter 2009).[25]

[23] It does not go without saying that the poor would necessarily want to live in a town with rich residents. In some models of jurisdiction choice, residents choose to locate near others with similar preferences about tax rates and public goods. In these models, the poor and the rich often self-segregate (Tiebout 1956; Ellickson 1971; Westhoff 1977; Epple and Romer 1991; Fernandez and Rogerson 1996).

[24] Lamb (2005) and Bonastia (2010) identify a crucial "path not taken" during the Nixon administration when the federal government flirted with, but ultimately rejected, the idea of providing incentives to localities to diversify their population by race and class, for example, by directly building low-income housing or by relaxing local zoning laws.

[25] The Home Owners Loan Corporation (HOLC) developed the now infamous maps of neighborhood risk in the 1930s, which built in a strong relationship between the presence of black population in a neighborhood and perceived default risk. High-risk areas were colored red, hence the term "redlining." In the 1930s and 1940s, the FHA made extensive use of the HOLC underwriting maps in evaluating loan applications. Hillier (2003) questions the role of HOLC maps in setting FHA policy, documenting that in Philadelphia, private mortgage companies were already less likely to provide loans in "red-

Black households had particular difficulty obtaining financing to purchase a home in white suburbs. In a survey of 241 savings and loans associations conducted in the 1960s, only one institution included in the survey reports having offered a mortgage to a black family buying a home in a white neighborhood (Hirsch 1983, 31). John Field, who worked for the Detroit Commission on Community Relations in the 1960s, noted that the FHA "regularly refused loans to black homebuilders while underwriting the construction of homes by whites of a similar economic status a few blocks away" (Sugrue 1996, 44).

Residents of some white suburbs used violence and intimidation to limit black entry, although these tactics were more common in city neighborhoods.[26] The bulk of documentary evidence on white violence against black neighbors is based on the history of central-city Chicago and Detroit. Between 1940 and 1965, white Detroiters started numerous neighborhood associations designed to protect local property values. These organizations advocated for better public services, such as new stop signs or street lighting, but also took an active role in policing the color line.[27] Neighborhood associations regularly coordinated or tacitly supported intimidation against prospective black neighbors; Sugrue (1996, 233) documents "over two hundred incidents [in Detroit] against blacks moving into formerly all-white neighborhoods, including harassment, mass demonstrations, picketing, effigy burning, window breaking, arson, vandalism, and physical attacks."

Similar levels of violence rocked neighborhoods in central-city Chicago during this period. Philpott (1978, 170) recounts that in the 1920s, "bombs were going off at the rate of two per month." By the 1940s, Hirsch (1983, 41) describes Chicago as beset by "chronic urban guerrilla warfare," with 1.5 "racially motivated bombing[s] or arson[s]" each month.[28] However, limited evidence from other cities indicates that the violent crescendo reached in Chicago and Detroit was an out-

---

lined" areas before the advent of the maps, presumably because race was being used as a proxy for default risk by the private market as well. FHA policies toward black borrowers began to shift in the late 1940s (Weise 2005, 138–40).

[26] Kefalas (2003, 6–7) notes wryly that the working-class whites who sought to defend urban neighborhoods using violence were often viewed as "little more than barbarians to the enlightened elements of middle-class Americans who could afford to flee."

[27] See Seligman 2005, 170–81 on similar forms of community organizing in Chicago.

[28] From 1945 to 1950, the Chicago Commission on Human Relations received 360 reports of racial "incidents" related to housing or residential property (a rate of six per month), suggesting that more extreme events like bombing and arson were the tip of the iceberg (Hirsch 1983, 52).

lier. Los Angeles, for example, experienced "only" six race-related bombings and four arsons during the 1950s (Sides 2003, 103; see also Meyer 2001, 117–32).[29]

DOCUMENTING WHITE FLIGHT

Black migrants who arrived in the North at midcentury settled in cities that were in the process of being abandoned by the existing white residents. Many black migrants were too poor to join the exodus to the suburbs. Yet even black households with the financial resources to move to and the interest in living in the suburban ring were often blocked by white homeowners, local realtors, and mortgage brokers. These dual population flows—black migration to central cities and white suburbanization—gave rise to the well-known pattern of "chocolate cities" and "vanilla suburbs."[30] Whites who sought to avoid interactions with black newcomers were thus able to do so by relocating from the city to the suburbs.

I argue here that above and beyond other causes of suburbanization, white departures for the suburbs were greater in cities experiencing large inflows of black migration ("white flight"). I begin by developing a simple model of a metropolitan area housing market that generates predictions about how many white residents can be expected to relocate to the suburbs in response to a given number of black arrivals. I then examine the association between black in-migration to a city and white suburbanization, and find that each black arrival is associated with more than two white departures. Black migrants may have been attracted to cities with robust economic conditions that were otherwise undergoing suburbanization. However, I continue to find a strong correlation between black arrivals and white departures when I use southern conditions to generate an instrumental variable for black in-migration to particular northern cities.

Conceptual Framework

Before analyzing the empirical association between black arrivals and white departures from central cities, I start with a conceptual frame-

[29] In theory, an historical index of racially motivated housing violence could be compiled from digital indices of local newspapers.

[30] The term "chocolate city" was coined by the funk band Parliament in their 1975 album of the same name and was first used in the academic literature by Farley et al. (1978).

work that lays out the expected relationship under various conditions. Consider a set of households in a metropolitan area that are choosing between locating in the central city and locating in the suburbs. Suppose that, initially, all residents of the metropolitan area are white and are differentiated only by their income level. Each household takes into account two factors in making their location decision: the rental price of housing in the city versus the suburbs and the available bundle of local amenities in each place.[31] Local amenities can take many forms, including distance to work, the quality of local public goods (especially schools), and proximity to shopping and restaurants. For simplicity, I assume that rents and amenities are uniform within the city but differentiated between the city and the suburbs to emphasize the choice between the two locations.

Each household's goal is to minimize the cost of housing for a given amenity level. Assume that the urban housing stock is constrained both because cities have fixed land areas and because they impose restrictions on new development (e.g., height limits). Therefore, when the city population increases, urban rents will rise. In contrast, construction in new suburban areas is imagined to be relatively flexible and responsive to demand conditions; when the suburban population increases, temporarily raising rents, the construction sector responds by building new units.[32] In the simplest case, new construction will continue until rents in the suburbs no longer exceed construction costs.

The key assumption in the model is that with free mobility between the city and the suburbs, no household living in the city should prefer to locate in the suburbs, given the prevailing rent, and vice versa. If, instead, some households living in the city could improve their welfare by moving to the suburbs (say, because they strictly prefer having access to suburban schools, even at a higher rental price), they would do so. As the first of these disgruntled households leaves the city, their departure would cause the rental price of housing units in the city to

[31] To avoid having to consider the trajectory of future housing price, which is likely important to prospective homebuyers, I assume that all households rent their housing unit. This simplification, while common in economic models, comes at a cost. For example, I will argue that the arrival of new migrants pushes up rents in the central city, thereby encouraging some existing residents to leave. However, it is not clear that existing homeowners who would benefit from the price appreciation would choose to leave the city when housing prices/rents rise.

[32] The suburbs contained substantial tracts of open land in 1940, which likely rendered their construction sector more responsive than that of the city in this period.

fall. At this lower rent, some of the city dwellers who had coveted the suburban schools would rethink their decision. Eventually, after a sufficient outflow and corresponding decline in urban rental prices, the metropolitan system would reach an equilibrium in which all households would (weakly) prefer to stay in their current location.

Now imagine that a number of white migrants move into the central city of this metropolitan area. These new arrivals would increase the rental price of urban housing, prompting some existing residents to move to the suburbs.[33] Despite this induced demand for suburban residence, housing construction in the suburbs would ensure that the rental price of suburban units remains constant (or, at least, does not rise by as much as the corresponding increase in the city). The outflow to the suburbs in response to the higher rental price in the central city would continue until the relative price of city and suburban housing units returned to its previous level, at which all residents weakly preferred their own location to the alternative.

This example illustrates that *any* migrant to a city, regardless of race or social position, can encourage some suburbanization because of his effect on urban rents (or what I call the *housing market channel*). If the suburban construction sector fully responds to new arrivals, equilibrium will be restored when each in-migrant to the city is matched by exactly one new departure from the city.[34] However, if the suburban construction sector is not perfectly responsive or if city developers add some new units downtown to accommodate new residents, the outflow from the city can be less than one-for-one. I take the one-for-one departure rate as an upper bound on how many suburban moves we would expect through the housing market channel alone.

Instead, imagine that the central city receives an inflow of southern black migrants rather than white migrants. These new arrivals will have two effects on the city; not only will they raise urban rents by in-

[33] Saiz (2007), for example, shows that an inflow of new immigrants to a city equivalent to a 1 percent increase in city population also increases average rents and housing values by around 1 percent.

[34] Boustan (2010) provides a more formal proof of this proposition. The intuition, though, is straightforward. Depending on the responsiveness of a city's construction sector (elasticity of housing supply), each migrant arrival will increase rents by some amount x. If one existing resident then leaves the city with each migrant arrival, urban rents will decline by precisely the same x. Relocation to the suburbs will not increase suburban housing prices under the assumption that the suburban construction sector immediately responds to changes in demand. Therefore, a one-for-one departure rate will restore equilibrium to the metropolitan system.

creasing housing demand in the central city, but they will also elevate the level of racial diversity in the city population.[35] If existing residents consider racial diversity to be a disamenity (either through the *social interactions channel* or through the *fiscal/political channel*), changes in the bundle of urban characteristics will prompt some additional out-migration to the suburbs.

Absent a distaste for diversity, black migrants will encourage white departures only insofar as their arrival increases city rents, prompting exactly one white departure (or less). If, however, whites exhibit some distaste for diversity, we would expect the number of whites leaving the city with every black arrival to be higher—perhaps even more than one-for-one. A white departure rate above one-for-one would also have long-term implications for urban housing prices. If each black arrival is associated with net population decline in the central city, we would expect urban rents to decline in the long run. Thus even if black in-migration initially increases city rents, we would expect rents to eventually fall.

Empirical Evidence of White Flight: Correlations

The central cities that experienced the largest increases in black population in the mid-twentieth century also lost the greatest number of white residents, often to the suburban ring. Figure 4.1 illustrates this relationship in the seventy largest metropolitan areas outside the South for the decade of the 1950s; Appendix Table 4.1 contains a list of cities included in the analysis. Each dot in the scatter plot represents population change in a central city after controlling for Census region and for decadal population growth in the metropolitan area. I define both central cities and metropolitan areas using constant boundaries throughout the period.[36]

[35] Although blacks and whites rarely lived in the same neighborhoods, population growth in black areas could still influence the rents paid in white areas. As black neighborhoods grew overcrowded, some black families moved to boundary areas between black and white neighborhoods, thereby outbidding existing white residents and "spreading" the rental effect of black in-migration from black neighborhoods to white ones.

[36] I measure city population as residents living inside the city's 1940 borders in every year from 1940 to 1970, even if the city borders expanded over time. To do so, I subtract Census Bureau counts of the number of residents added to the central city through annexation from the city's actual population and reassign this population to the suburbs (Bogue 1953; U.S. Bureau of the Census 1962, 1972). Furthermore, I retroactively apply the 1970 county-based definition of metropolitan areas to earlier years to account for expansion in metropolitan scope due to population growth. These adjustments have no effect

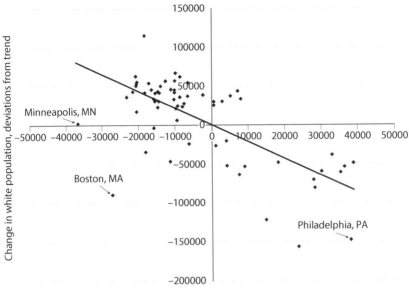

Figure 4.1. Changes in black and white populations in northern and western central cities, 1950–60. This figure is based on the set of 70 metropolitan areas in the North and West listed in Appendix Table 4.1. Each point in the scatter diagram represents the residual change in a city's black and white populations after controlling for region fixed effects and changes in the metropolitan area's population. The slope of a regression line through these points is –2.016 (s.e. = 0.291). The four largest cities—Chicago, Detroit, Los Angeles, and New York—are omitted for reasons of scale, but they fall close to the regression line.

The slope of the relationship in Figure 4.1 suggests that each black arrival was associated with more than two white departures in the 1950s (coefficient = –2.16). A similar relationship holds in every decade between 1940 and 1970. The simple model presented in the previous section suggests that if whites were only motivated by the relationship

---

on the share of the metropolitan population living in the suburbs in New England, where annexation was rare, but increase the suburban share of the metropolitan population by up to 10 percentage points in other regions. Dye (1964) and Jackson (1985, 138–56) discuss the historical patterns of annexation in the United States. Some annexation activity may have been correlated with black arrivals, either positively or negatively (Austin 1999; Alesina, Baqir, and Hoxby 2004). As it turns out, my estimates of white flight are similar whether using actual city population or annexation-corrected population.

between new migrant arrivals and rising rental prices, we would expect to find at most a one-for-one white departure rate. Instead, it appears that every black arrival is correlated with two white departures, which suggests that some of this white flight was motivated by additional concerns about racial diversity.

White response to black in-migration varied by region and over time. Table 4.2 explores heterogeneity in the estimates of white flight in cities with different characteristics. For comparison, the first row presents the coefficient estimates for the full sample; the underlying regression equation is presented in the appendix in this chapter. As in Figure 4.1, each black arrival was associated with around two white departures in the average decade from 1940 to 1970. White departure rates were around one-for-one in both the Northeast and Midwest but appear to be larger in the West (row 2).[37] However, the strong relationship in the West is entirely driven by the anomalous case of the San Francisco-Oakland metropolitan area.[38] Many western cities were physically sprawling, with pockets of single-family homes that offered good substitutes for suburban living.[39] Dropping western cities from the full sample reduces the coefficient from –2.11 to –1.31; this value can still be statistically distinguished from a one-for-one departure rate. White flight increased in intensity over time, starting with a one-for-one rate in the 1940s and growing to a two-for-one rate in the 1950s and 1960s (row 3). Moving to the suburbs was more difficult in the 1940s, given the war-related slowdown in housing construction in the first half of the decade.

In the median city, the black population increased by 18,000 residents from 1940 to 1970. According to the estimates of white flight in Table 4.2, 25,000 to 38,000 white residents would have left the central city in response.[40] As a result, the net urban population would have declined by somewhere between 4 to 11 percent, from a base of 182,000 residents in 1940. Baum-Snow (2007) reports that the average city lost 17 percent of its population from 1950 to 1990. My conservative esti-

---

[37] Note that the national estimates are larger than a weighted average of their regional counterparts because they are driven by both within- and between-region variation.

[38] The black population in San Francisco and Oakland increased at twice the rate of that of other western cities. At the same time, San Francisco and Oakland were the only cities in the West to lose white population during these decades.

[39] Schneider (2008, 996) describes Los Angeles as an "already sprawling city . . . coupled with relatively young housing stock and the existence of de facto segregation."

[40] These figures use the coefficient of –2.11 in the full sample and –1.31 in the sample without western cities, respectively.

Table 4.2: Estimated relationship between black arrivals and white departures from central cities by city type, 1940–70

Full sample		
OLS	*IV*	*Drop West*
–2.113	–2.643	–1.312
(0.544)	(0.793)	(0.134)
N = 280	*N = 212*	*N = 224*
	By region	
Northeast	*Midwest*	*West /// West without SF*
–1.119	–0.894	–2.414 / / / 0.086
(0.137)	(0.256)	(1.489) / / / (0.953)
N = 116	*N = 108*	*N = 56 /// 52*
	By time period	
1940s	*1950s*	*1960s*
–1.073	–2.166	–2.111
(0.634)	(0.829)	(0.478)
N = 140	*N = 140*	*N = 140*
	By initial city size	
Below median	*Above median*	*Drop top 10 destinations*
0.081	–2.088	–1.447
(1.139)	(0.561)	(0.413)
N = 140	*N = 140*	*N = 244*
	By initial black share	
Below 25th percentile	*25th–75th percentile*	*Above 75th percentile*
–1.638	–3.732	–1.283
(0.669)	(0.660)	(0.162)
N = 68	*N = 140*	*N = 72*
	By initial HS grad share	
Below 25th percentile	*25th–75th percentile*	*Above 75th percentile*
–1.199	–1.294	–2.809
(0.303)	(0.147)	(1.274)
N = 72	*N = 140*	*N = 68*

Note: Dependent variable = number of white residents in the central city. Coefficients on number of black residents in the central city. This table reports coefficient estimates on the number of black residents in the central city from Appendix Equation 1 for different subsamples of northern and western cities. The main sample (row 1) contains the 70 largest cities outside of the South; see Appendix Table 4.1 for a list of included cities. The IV analysis includes the 53 cities with published mobility counts by race in 1940 necessary for construction of the instrument. Row 2 presents results by Census region, and row 3 separates the sample by decade. The second estimate for the western region (row 2, column 3) drops San Francisco. Rows 4–6 divide the sample by initial city characteristics in 1940 including city size, black population share, and high school graduation share.

mate implies that without black in-migration to central cities after 1940, around one-quarter of urban population loss would have been forestalled (= 4/17).[41] Of course, ending the black migration entirely without replacement by an alternative set of workers is an extreme counterfactual. A more likely scenario is that black arrivals would have been replaced by white ethnics or Hispanic in-migration. But in this case, the housing market channel would have still been operative, suggesting that any new inflow of workers would have been counterbalanced by an equal flow out to the suburbs.

The remaining rows in Table 4.2 divide the sample by initial city characteristics. White residents of small cities exhibited no reaction to black arrivals; instead, the estimated effect of black in-migration is concentrated in the thirty-five cities of above-median size. However, the results are not driven by the ten largest cities in the sample alone; a strong relationship between black arrivals and white departures remains even after dropping these ten cities. Cities with a particularly high or low black population share in 1940 (such as Baltimore and St. Louis, which were already more than 10 percent black in 1940, or Duluth, Minnesota, and Salt Lake City, Utah, with essentially no black population in that year) were less responsive to black inflows than were cities with a black population share in the intermediate range. Cities with higher-income residents (as proxied by education levels in 1940) were more responsive to black inflows than were poorer cities, perhaps because higher-income residents were better able to afford a suburban residence.

Empirical Evidence of White Flight: Causal Relationships

The negative relationship between black arrivals and white departures from a city may reflect a process of "white flight," whereby white households seek to avoid the racial diversity of central cities by relocating to the suburbs. Alternatively, the observed relationship could arise if black migrants were attracted, either directly or indirectly, to cities that were already undergoing suburbanization. First, as whites relocated to the suburbs, they left behind an existing urban housing stock.

---

[41] My larger estimate can explain two-thirds of the observed decline in urban population. However, this pattern does not imply that "only" one-third of the decline in urban population could then be ascribed to economic factors like rising incomes and new highways. Rather, it is likely that, absent these factors, urban population would have actually *grown* after 1940, perhaps keeping pace with suburban population.

Falling demand for these urban units among whites would lower housing prices in the city, thereby potentially drawing in new migrants.[42] Second, rates of white suburbanization were higher in metropolitan areas with a strong local economy and rising incomes, factors that may have attracted new black job seekers to the area.

To determine the causal direction of this relationship, one would ideally be able to isolate a group of black migrants who settled in a city without regard for its current economic conditions—for example, by following family members who had already settled in the area. I approximate this experiment by considering migrants who left the South because of changes in the agricultural economy and then followed established settlement patterns from particular southern states to specific cities in the North. Consider, for example, the case of Chicago. Some black migrants were attracted to Chicago by the plentiful factory jobs available in the city, while others were motivated by low or erratic wages in Mississippi, a state that traditionally sent many of its black out-migrants to Chicago. A strong manufacturing sector in Chicago likely boosted white income in Chicago as well, thereby encouraging departures for the suburbs. However, wages in Mississippi should not otherwise influence the location decisions of white households in the Chicago metropolitan area *except* through their connection to black migration.

I extend this logic to the rest of the country using data on local economic conditions in the South and historical migration flows between southern states and northern cities. I highlight the key steps in this method here; the details are presented in Boustan 2010.

First, I determine the historical patterns of black migration from southern sending states to northern cities using the "Where did you live 5 years ago?" question from the 1940 Census. In particular, I calculate the share of black migrants from every southern sending state that settled in each northern destination between 1935 and 1940.[43]

Second, I predict how many blacks could be expected to leave each

---

[42] Gamm (1999), for example, argues that black migrants were attracted to the Dorchester and Roxbury neighborhoods of Boston by the decline in housing prices following a wave of Jewish suburbanization.

[43] I conduct this procedure for the fifty-three cities in my sample with published mobility tables available by race from the 1940 Census. The published data provide counts of the city and state of residence in 1935 for all residents of a given city in 1940 (U.S. Bureau of the Census 1943).

southern state by decade from 1940 to 1970 solely in response to local economic conditions. For this, I rely on the county-level analysis reported in chapter 1 that relates outflows of black migrants to factors like the share of land planted in cotton. I use these results to predict black out-migration from southern counties and then aggregate these totals to the state level.

Finally, I combine the predicted black migrant outflows by southern state with the information on chain migration patterns to northern cities to predict black inflows to each northern destination. These simulated changes in black in-migration serve as an "instrumental variable" for actual changes in the black population by central city.[44]

The idiosyncrasies of early settlement decisions ensure that there is enough variation to separately identify the timing of black in-migration into different northern cities. Take, for example, the case of Alabama and Mississippi, two neighboring, cotton-producing states in the Deep South. Despite their geographic proximity and cultural and economic similarity, migration from these two states followed substantially different paths to the North. Northward migrants from Mississippi overwhelmingly settled in Chicago and St. Louis, which together accounted for 62 percent of black Mississippians in the North in the 1940 Census. In contrast, Detroit was the top destination for black migrants leaving Alabama. Migration from Alabama was less concentrated, with the two top destinations (Detroit and Chicago) accounting for only 47 percent of the population in the North.

The distinct migration patterns of departure from these neighboring states are consistent with differences in their railroad connections to the North. The black population in Mississippi was clustered along the Mississippi River, a region served by only one interstate railroad (the Illinois Central), whose main hubs were St. Louis and Chicago. In contrast, the large cities in Alabama, Mobile and Birmingham, were each served by two major railroads: the Gulf, Mobile, and Ohio railroad, which connected to the Illinois Central network in St. Louis, and the Alabama Great Southern Railroad, which terminated in Chattanooga, Tennessee. In Chattanooga, riders could transfer to trains bound for Detroit and Cleveland; Cleveland was the third most popular northern destination for black migrants leaving Alabama.[45]

---

[44] There is an extensive literature in economics, beginning with Altonji and Card 1991, that uses aspects of chain migration to generate an instrumental variable for immigration to a metropolitan area. Card 2001 is closest in spirit to the method outlined here.

[45] Grossman (1989, 99) writes that "the first [migrant from Mississippi] to leave for

Original differences in destination choice were then cemented in place by subsequent chains of friends and family. As Wilkerson (2010, 243) observed, "a map of the crosscurrents of migration would link otherwise completely unrelated southern counties and towns with seemingly random northern cities that, other than the train lines and sometimes in spite of them, made little practical sense but nonetheless made sister cities of the unlikeliest of pairings. Palestine, Texas, and Syracuse, New York; Norfolk, Virginia, and Roxbury in Boston; Brookhaven, Mississippi, and Bloomington, Illinois." Stuart and Taylor (2014) quantify black chain migration, showing that every black migrant induced four additional movers to join them; chain migration was substantially weaker among white southerners.

The strength of chain migration in this context generates a tight relationship between predicted migrant inflow into a city and actual changes in black population. Figure 4.2 shows a positive association between predicted migrant flows into northern cities and actual changes in black population for the decade of the 1950s.[46] Cities like Baltimore that lie above the regression line experienced more black population growth than would be expected by predicted outflows from their typical sending states, perhaps owing to positive economic shocks that attracted arrivals from new source areas. The reverse is true of cities like St. Louis that fall below the regression line.

The first row of Table 4.2 reports results from a two-stage least squares analysis using the instrumental variable described here.[47] In this case, each black migrant is associated with around 2.5 white departures, suggesting that, if anything, the relationship between black arrivals and white departures intensifies after addressing causality. From this, I conclude that the correlation analyzed earlier was primarily driven by white response to black arrivals rather than by the location decisions of black migrants. Furthermore, a departure rate that is greater than one-to-one suggests that white flight was motivated in

---

Chicago probably chose the city because of its position at the head of the Illinois Central." See Grossman 1989, 66–119 and Gottlieb 1987, 39–62 for a broader discussion of the role of train routes and information networks in black migration. New work by Black et al. (2015) uses proximity of a black southerner's birthplace to a train line to predict out-migration.

[46] As for Figure 4.1, each point on the scatter plot here represents residual changes in black population after controlling for region fixed effects and overall metropolitan area growth. The relationship is equally strong in other decades.

[47] Boustan (2010) reports a series of alternative specifications for this instrumental variables analysis.

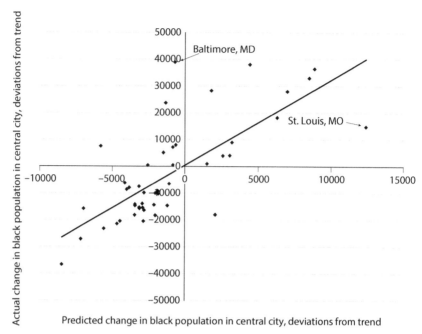

Figure 4.2. Predicted versus actual change in black population in northern and western cities, 1950–60. The sample includes the 53 metropolitan areas with available mobility counts by race in 1940. The predicted change in black population is calculated by assigning predicted migration flows from southern states to northern cities using 1935–40 settlement patterns. See text for detailed description of the instrument's construction. Each point in the scatter diagram represents the residual change in a city's actual and predicted black population after controlling for region fixed effects and changes in the metropolitan area's population. The slope of a regression line through these points is 3.187 (s.e. = 0.419). The four largest cities—Chicago, Detroit, Los Angeles and New York—are omitted for reasons of scale. Adding the four largest cities increases the slope somewhat (coeff. = 4.278, s.e. = 0.228).

part by distaste for racial diversity. White flight may have been driven by an aversion to black neighbors or by a preference for the bundle of taxes and local public goods available in racially homogeneous suburbs. I explore these factors in more detail in the next chapter.

The white flight documented here begs the question: what were the social and economic consequences of white suburbanization for residents who remained in the central city? A full answer to this question is beyond the scope of this book, but a partial understanding can be gleaned from the existing literature. First, white flight reduced white enrollment in city schools, which may have lowered black student achievement, at least to the extent that white and black students would have shared the same schools had white families stayed in place (Guryan 2004; Lutz 2011). Second, the loss of white residents reduced demand for city housing, leading to declines in urban housing prices. Lower housing prices allowed some black households to afford homeownership for the first time, which anchored some black communities and led to black wealth creation (Boustan and Margo 2013; Charles and Hurst 2002; Dietz and Haurin 2003).[48] On the other hand, lower housing prices reduced the assessed value of the residential property tax base, which may have put a strain on city budgets (Lutz 2008). Third, cities with a growing black population share were more likely to elect black mayors and city councilmen, who often expanded black employment in municipal positions (Eisinger 1982; Nye, Rainer, and Stratmann 2010). Fourth, white departures contributed to the rise of majority-black neighborhoods, many of which later became sites of concentrated poverty. Yet the association between residential segregation and poor black outcomes found in modern data only emerged in 1970, as the black middle class began to leave for the suburbs, and so should be considered, if anything, an indirect result of white flight (Wilson 1987; Collins and Margo 2000; Cutler and Glaeser 1997; Ananat 2011).[49] Overall, white flight appears to have had mixed consequences for remaining residents, lowering the quality of citywide institutions but offering a larger share of city resources to the black community.

[48] As whites left central cities, the rate of black homeownership increased from 19 percent in 1940 to 46 percent in 1980. Boustan and Margo (2013) estimate that for every 100 white household departures, 9 black households transitioned into homeownership. Hirsch (1983, 28) describes this process in Chicago: "As vacancies began to appear around established black communities in the late 1940s and 1950s, black 'pioneers,' eager to escape ghetto conditions and both willing and able to compete economically for the inner-city housing becoming available, moved into previously all-white neighborhoods."

[49] At midcentury, black enclaves were home to both poor and middle-class black families. Sugrue (1996, 183) writes that in Detroit, for instance, "virtually all of [the city's] blacks—regardless of class and education, occupation, age, or place of birth—shared the experience of discrimination in the city's housing market." Yet there was some class segregation within black neighborhoods. Trotter (1985, 180) describes this process in Milwaukee, noting that "black business and professional people, joined by a few better-paid and skilled workers, occupied the better housing within and on the edges of the black district."

CONCLUSION

From 1940 to 1970, the black population share in northern cities quadrupled as a result of new in-migration from the South and white departures for the suburban ring. Black newcomers who could afford to settle in the suburbs were often prevented from moving to a suburban town. Thus black residential isolation increased as whites left the city; by 1970, the average black resident of a northern city lived in a neighborhood that was 75 percent black. White suburbanization was driven, in large part, by rising incomes, new road construction, and expanded access to credit. Yet a portion of white suburbanization can be traced to responses to black arrivals in central cities ("white flight"). My best causal estimates suggest a more than two-for-one white departure rate. The next chapter explores the motivation of white households who moved to the suburbs in more detail.

APPENDIX TO CHAPTER 4

This appendix describes the estimating equation underlying the scatter plot in Figure 4.1 and the coefficient estimates reported in Table 4.2. I consider the relationship between the number of white residents (W_CITY) and the number of black residents (B_CITY) in the central cities of the seventy metropolitan areas (m). In particular, I estimate:

$$W\_CITY_{mrt} = \alpha_m + \beta_1(B\_CITY_{mrt}) + \gamma_1(POP\_METRO_{mrt})$$
$$+ \upsilon_{rt} + \varepsilon_{mrt} \tag{1}$$

where t and r indicate Census decades and regions, respectively. α_m denotes a vector of metropolitan area fixed effects, and υ_{rt} are Census region-by-decade fixed effects. β_1 is thus estimated from changes in black population within a city over time, compared with other cities in the region. I also control for the overall population of the metropolitan area (POP_METRO) because growing areas will attract a large flow of both black and white in-migrants. Table 4.2 reports a two-stage least squares estimate of this equation instrumenting for the black population in the central city with the predicted black population. The instrumental variable is generated using the procedure outlined in the text.

Appendix Table 4.1: Northern and western
metropolitan areas in the 70-city analysis

Metropolitan area	State	Tract data in 1940	Metropolitan area	State	Tract data in 1940
Akron	OH	Y	Minneapolis-St. Paul	MN	Y
Albany	NY		New Bedford	MA	
Albuquerque	NM		New York City	NY	Y
Allentown	PA		Omaha	NE	
Baltimore	MD	Y	Peoria	IL	
Binghamton	NY		Philadelphia	PA	Y
Boston	MA	Y	Phoenix	AZ	
Bridgeport	CT	Y	Pittsburgh	PA	Y
Buffalo	NY	Y	Portland	OR	Y
Canton	OH		Providence	RI	Y
Chicago	IL	Y	Reading	PA	
Cleveland	OH	Y	Riverside	CA	
Clifton-Paterson-Passaic	NJ	Y	Rochester	NY	Y
Columbus	OH	Y	Rockford	IL	
Davenport-Moline	IL		Rome	NY	
Dayton	OH	Y	Sacramento	CA	
Denver	CO	Y	Salt Lake City	UT	
Des Moines	IA	Y	San Diego	CA	
Detroit	MI	Y	San Francisco	CA	Y
Duluth-Superior	MN-WI	Y	San Jose	CA	
Lorain-Elyria	OH		Seattle	WA	Y
Erie	PA		South Bend	IN	
Flint	MI	Y	Spokane	WA	
Fort Wayne	IN		Springfield	MA	
Fresno	CA		St. Louis	MO	Y
Grand Rapids	MI		Stockton	CA	
Harrisburg	PA		Syracuse	NY	Y
Hartford	CT	Y	Tacoma	WA	
Indianapolis	IN	Y	Toledo	OH	Y
Johnstown	PA		Trenton	NJ	Y
Kansas City	MO-KS	Y	Wichita	KS	
Lancaster	PA		Wilmington	DE	
Los Angeles	CA	Y	Worcester	MA	
Madison	WI		York	PA	
Milwaukee	WI	Y	Youngstown	OH	

Note: The sample includes all non-southern Standard Metropolitan Statistical Areas (SMSAs) that
either: (1) were anchored by one or more of the hundred largest cities in 1940 or (2) had at least
250,000 residents by 1970. Only two SMSAs that meet the first criterion fall short of the later population benchmark (Bridgeport and New Bedford). The second criterion adds ten metropolitan areas
to the sample, including growing western cities (e.g., Phoenix) and smaller areas in Pennsylvania,
Ohio, and upstate New York (e.g., Harrisburg). A "Y" in columns 3 and 6 indicates the subset of
cities with available tract-level information in 1940. These 33 cities underlie the tract-level analyses
of neighborhood composition in Table 4.1 (as well as Table 5.1). Atlantic City, NJ is the one city
with available tract information in 1940 that did not meet the criteria for inclusion in the broader
sample.

CHAPTER 5

Motivations for White Flight: The Role of Fiscal/Political Interactions

THE MID-TWENTIETH CENTURY was a period of rapid suburbanization in U.S. metropolitan areas. I have argued that a portion of this mobility was a response of white urban residents to the arrival of black southern migrants ("white flight"). But *why* did white households choose to leave their homes and neighborhoods as black migrants arrived in central cities?

The existing literature focuses on the concern that black families would move into white neighborhoods. Yet given the high degree of residential segregation within central cities, only a portion of urban whites lived in neighborhoods that were at risk of racial transition during this period. Even by 1970, after three decades of heavy black in-migration from the South, more than half of white residents in northern and western cities still lived in a Census tract that was uniformly white (99 percent or more), and the average white household in a city lived more than three miles away from a majority-black enclave.

My estimates of white flight presented in the previous chapter are too large to be solely explained by the decisions of white households who lived close to expanding black neighborhoods. Instead, I suggest that white flight was also driven by the choices of white households living farther from black areas, some of whom moved to the suburbs to avoid *fiscal/political interactions* with black arrivals living across town. New black migrants shifted the racial and socioeconomic composition of the city electorate, which in turn influenced local spending priorities, property tax rates, and public schools. These concerns took many forms: in some cities, white neighborhoods maintained their own local elementary schools, but parents balked at sending their children to in-creasingly diverse high schools; in others, white residents feared that growing needs in black areas worsened the response time of city police and fire services. Furthermore, the changing composition of the urban electorate was often associated with a rise in black municipal employment and local officeholding.[1] Moving to the suburbs allowed white households to isolate themselves from the changing bundle of local public goods and fiscal obligations offered in the central city.

To document the role of these fiscal/political concerns, I compare the trajectory of housing prices in adjacent neighborhoods separated by a municipal border. In each of these pairs, one neighborhood is located within the city limits and the other is just across the border into the suburbs. The housing stock and local attributes of these neighborhoods were virtually identical, but residents on either side of the municipal border were assessed different property tax rates and had access to a different set of public goods. I show that the price premium associated with suburban units increased at the border as the black population share rose in the city from 1960 to 1980, even though the racial composition of the neighborhoods under consideration was little changed. This pattern suggests that the decline in the demand for city residence with black in-migration was, in part, due to fiscal/political changes at the citywide level.

The interpretation of these results rests on two assumptions: first, that one can use housing prices to study the demand for residence in a particular area, and second, that it is possible to find comparison neighborhoods that are almost indistinguishable from each other, except for the jurisdiction in which they are located (city or suburb). Following the literature on hedonic prices, I argue that housing prices provide useful information about the value of location-specific goods that are implicitly traded through the housing market rather than sold directly to consumers; local public goods are one such location-specific attribute. By this logic, features that command higher housing prices are those that the typical homeowner prefers, while those that command lower housing prices are those that the typical homeowner seeks to avoid. Detailed Census geography down to the block level allows me to focus on virtually identical areas that are separated only by a municipal border.[2]

---

[1] By 1980, black representation in municipal employment was commensurate with the black share of the population; blacks made up 24 percent of residents in non-southern central cities and 22 percent of workers in the Census industry "local public administration." Eisinger (1982, 380) argues that areas with larger black populations also had more black municipal employment, one "tangible benefit of black political power." On this point, see also Saltzstein 1989.

[2] Census blocks are roughly the size of a city block, containing around forty housing

124 · CHAPTER 5

I find that the housing price gap between cities and suburbs increased as black migrants arrived in the central city. However, at the border, housing prices responded more to changes in the average income level in a municipality rather than to changes in racial composition. Black migrants were poorer than existing residents and so their arrival was associated with a decline in the median income of city residents. I further show that the demand to leave cities as the income level of their residents fell stemmed from rising property tax rates, rising expenditures on public safety (to police "other people's" neighborhoods), and a falling share of residents with a college degree, which could be a proxy for the quality of peers in public school. Race itself began to matter more in the 1970s, when some cities in the sample fell under court order to desegregate their public schools. Before mandated desegregation, residential patterns ensured that the typical white student in the central city attended a predominantly white school; after desegregation plans were put in place, the exposure of white students in the city to black peers increased.

THE RACIAL GEOGRAPHY OF CENTRAL CITIES, 1940–2000

Despite black in-migration to central cities, the typical white resident of a northern city continued to live far from a black enclave throughout this period. Figure 5.1 illustrates this racial pattern for the city of Chicago. Census tracts are grouped into categories by distance to a majority-black area. Chicago's South Side and West Side were already majority black in 1940, and much of the city's central core was within one mile of these enclaves. But a large portion of the city was two to four miles away from a black enclave, and more than eighty Census tracts on the city's North Side were located more than four miles away from a black enclave.

The pattern observed in Chicago was present in many other cities in the North and West. Table 5.1 charts neighborhood patterns for thirty-three large cities with available tract-level data in 1940 by distance from a black enclave. I define a historic black enclave as any neighborhood that was majority black in 1940 (or, for cities without a majority-black neighborhood, as the neighborhood with the highest black population

units. Census blocks are fully nested into Census tracts, my measure of a city neighborhood. I focus on blocks that are themselves immediately adjacent to the city-suburban border.

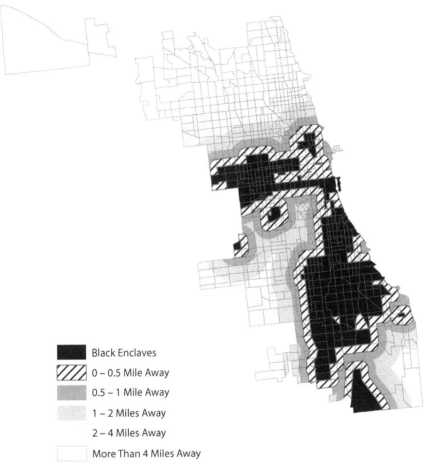

Black Enclaves

0 – 0.5 Mile Away

0.5 – 1 Mile Away

1 – 2 Miles Away

2 – 4 Miles Away

More Than 4 Miles Away

Figure 5.1. Central-city neighborhoods by distance from historic black enclaves, Chicago. Census tracts shaded in black were 50 percent black or more in 1940; I consider these to be "historic black enclaves." Remaining Census tracts are shaded according to their minimum distance from the tract centroids in the historic black enclave. Map was created using Census tract shape files available at the National Historical Geographic Information System (Minnesota Population Center 2011).

share in 1940). Panel A reports the black population share in concentric zones around the historic black enclave. In 1940, few neighborhoods outside of the black enclave had any black residents at all. Even within half a mile of a black enclave, only 8 percent of neighborhood residents were black; the black population share fell to 2 percent in neighbor-

Table 5.1: Neighborhood characteristics in central cities by
distance to historic black enclaves, 1940–2000

	Distance from 1940 black enclave					
	< 0.1 mile	0.1–0.5 mile	0.5–1 mile	1.0–2.0 miles	2.0–4.0 miles	> 4.0 miles
	A. Black population share in neighborhoods X miles from historic black enclave					
1940	0.72	0.08	0.06	0.03	0.02	0.01
1970	0.88	0.57	0.46	0.35	0.18	0.08
2000	0.83	0.59	0.55	0.45	0.32	0.19
	B. Share of white city population living within X miles of historic black enclave					
1940	0.02	0.06	0.10	0.21	0.32	0.29
1970	0.00	0.04	0.06	0.16	0.32	0.42
2000	0.00	0.04	0.05	0.13	0.29	0.49

Note: The sample underlying this table includes neighborhoods in the 33 large cities in the North and West with available tract-level data in 1940; see Appendix Table 4.1 for a list of cities. Historic black enclaves are defined as Census tracts that were 50 percent black or more in 1940. For cities in which no Census tracts reached the 50 percent black threshold in 1940, the historic enclave is instead defined as the tract with the highest black population share. Panel A reports the black population share of neighborhoods within X miles of a historic black enclave. Panel B indicates the share of white residents in the central city living in these neighborhoods. The distance between each Census tract and a historic black enclave is calculated using tract-level GIS shape files from the National Historical Geographic Information System (Minnesota Population Center 2011).

hoods more than two miles away. The racial composition of these outlying city neighborhoods was similar to that of the suburban population in 1940.

As black migrants settled in northern cities during the next few decades, the boundaries of these historic black enclaves expanded outward. The number of black residents in northern cities more than doubled from 1940 to 1970 and, as Philpott (1978, 185) observed for the case of Chicago, "there was no way, of course, to cram twice as many people into the old ghetto limits." Instead, "the Black Belt and its existing satellites . . . expand[ed] into contiguous territory" previously settled by whites. This process can readily be seen in the larger sample. The black population share of neighborhoods within half a mile of a historic black enclave increased from 8 percent in 1940 to 57 percent by 1970, while that of neighborhoods in the next half-mile band increased to 46 percent by 1970.

Even as proximate areas were going through racial transition, city neighborhoods that were at some distance from the historic black core experienced little racial change. Neighborhoods more than four miles from a historic black enclave shifted from 1 percent black in 1940 to 8 percent black in 1970, a pace of change hardly different from that of the neighboring suburbs.[3] Changes in racial composition were much greater in neighborhoods in the next zone (two to four miles from a historic black enclave). These areas shifted from 2 percent black in 1940 to 18 percent black by 1970, a change that was likely significant enough to trigger some white out-migration.

In 1940, before mass black in-migration, few urban whites lived close to a majority-black neighborhood. Panel B of Table 5.1 reports the share of white city residents living a given distance from a historic black enclave. Only 6 percent of white households lived within half a mile of a majority-black neighborhood in 1940. In contrast, 61 percent of white city residents lived at least two miles from a black enclave and 29 percent lived at least four miles away. The average white resident lived more than three miles from a majority-black neighborhood. In 1970, after three decades of white departures, particularly from central areas, 74 percent of white residents remaining in the central city lived more than two miles from a historic black enclave; this figure reached 78 percent by 2000.

By this count, nearly one-third of white city residents in 1940 lived in areas far from a black enclave (more than four miles away) that were shielded from racial change and therefore were unlikely to leave the city because of concerns about their local neighborhoods. However, we cannot reconstruct the mind-set of these households from the data alone. It is likely that many such residents understood the strong geographic pattern of racial change, whereby neighborhoods near the historic black core quickly became majority black even as more distant areas retained their racial character. Awareness of this process may have led some white households to feel buffered from local racial transition. Yet because fears about racial change were widespread, some households may have (mis)

[3] The most relevant suburban comparison here is inner-ring suburbs sharing borders with the central city. The average inner-ring suburb was 5 percent black in 1970 but had reached 10 percent black by 1980, keeping pace with peripheral neighborhoods in the city but with a slight delay. These statistics are taken from the border sample described in Appendix Table 5.1. In contrast, only 5 percent of all suburban residents in the North and West were black in 1980.

perceived the likelihood that their neighborhood would be swept up in the upheaval.[4]

WHY DID WHITES FLEE FROM RACIALLY SEGREGATED CITIES?

Some white households lived close to expanding black enclaves, while others lived farther away. Typically, white departures are ascribed to concerns about local interactions with black neighbors, stemming from households' own preferences for racial homogeneity or their apprehension about the effect of black arrivals on property values.[5] I will assess here whether the number of white households plausibly subject to these concerns was large enough to quantitatively account for the extent of white flight documented in the previous chapter.

For whites living in transitional neighborhoods, concerns about the arrival of new black neighbors were often paramount. Contemporary observers documented intense expressions of white fear about neighborhood racial change. In the late 1960s, Robert Coles (1971, 293) interviewed urban residents, both white and black, for his *Children of Crisis* series of books. One woman worried that black families "are going to try to move in here. They'll hop, skip and jump their way towards us, inch by inch they will. . . . I tell my husband: we should sell the house while we can get a good price, and then rent someplace." Moving to the suburbs, she believed, would be an effective strategy to avoid interactions with black neighbors, but it was financially out of their reach. "If we had more money," she griped, "and could afford to live way out there in one of those plush suburbs, we'd be all right. No colored person can afford to live with the rich."

In many cases, the first few black families to move into a neighborhood were tolerated, but fears accelerated when the black population share reached a certain threshold. Another white respondent in Coles's

---

[4] Sampson and Raudenbush (2004) show that residents can misperceive the level of "disorder" in their area (presence of litter, graffiti, loitering, and so on); Quillian and Pager (2001) find the same for crime.

[5] Dorn (2010) augments a classic Schelling segregation model with beliefs about the effect of black arrivals on local housing prices. Although it was commonly believed that black arrivals would lower property values, areas that faced high rates of black in-migration often experienced *rising* housing prices in the 1960s (Kain and Quigley 1972; King and Mieszkowski 1973). Freund (2007) cautions that white concerns about property values were not strictly speaking "economic" considerations but embodied a new form of racism.

book (1971, 298) claimed that he would greet one black neighbor, however warily, but that a large number of black arrivals would likely trigger panic. "If one Negro came in here," he asserts, "I'd say: let's see what he's like; and if he's an OK guy, and he hasn't got any crazy, way-out ideas in his head, then fine, let him stay. Now, if they started trying to mass on us, you know, and drive us out . . . then we'd have to get together and decide what we're going to do. Do we stick together and fight them? Do we go our separate ways and all lose out in the end? It's like a war, when you come to think about it."

Quantitative evidence confirms that many white households left neighborhoods that were undergoing racial change. Shertzer and Walsh (2014) track neighborhoods in ten cities from 1900 to 1930; they find that each black arrival into a neighborhood is associated with at least two white departures from the immediate area.[6] In the contemporary period, scholars use longitudinal surveys to follow household mobility over time. For example, Ellen (2000) matches individual-level data on mobility from the American Housing Survey to characteristics of Census tracts in 1980 and 1990. She finds that a 10 percentage point increase in a neighborhood's black population share is associated with a 3 percentage point increase in the likelihood that a white household left the area.[7] Emerson, Chai, and Yancey (2001) try to disentangle concerns about racial composition from rising crime and falling school quality. They show that the black population share of (hypothetical) neighborhoods matters even when the crime rate in an area is low and the school quality is high.[8]

A given inflow of black population can have different effects on white departures depending on the neighborhood's initial racial mix. Some models of "tipping points" emphasize that increases in black population share have little effect below a certain threshold but that beyond that threshold, neighborhood turnover is very rapid (Schelling 1971).[9] Card, Mas, and Rothstein (2008) and Blair (2014) provide em-

[6] Earlier work by Taeuber and Taeuber (1965) and Alba and Logan (1993) studied the racial composition of Census tracts in single cross sections.

[7] See South and Crowder 1997, 1998 for similar analyses using longitudinal data from the Panel Study of Income Dynamics. Crowder and South (2008) add measures of the black population share in adjacent neighborhoods to the model.

[8] Krysan et al. (2009) expand on this methodology by showing subjects video clips of actual neighborhoods populated by white or black actors posing as residents. One interpretation of these findings is that households directly seek to avoid black neighbors; another is that the presence of black residents changes perceived neighborhood quality.

[9] In theory, perfect segregation can arise in a Schelling model even if few residents

pirical support for the presence of tipping points, demonstrating that outflows of white population experience a discontinuous jump after a neighborhood reaches a certain threshold of black population share.

Were local neighborhood dynamics powerful enough to account for the extensive white flight documented in the previous chapter? Imagine that black arrivals influence the location decision of white residents only through their effect on neighborhood racial change. Shertzer and Walsh (2014) estimate that each black arrival to a neighborhood circa 1930 encouraged around two white departures. Some whites who left these neighborhoods settled elsewhere in the city, while others relocated to the suburbs. Census data from 1940 suggest that only 15 percent of white urban residents who moved between 1935 and 1940 left the central city; this figure increased to 50 percent for city residents who moved between 1975 and 1980. Using the midpoint of this interval as the likely share of white departures that left the central city, these estimates suggest that 0.65 white households would leave for the suburbs for each black arrival in a local neighborhood (2 white movers × 0.325 share to suburbs).

From the best causal estimates in the previous chapter, recall that each black arrival is estimated to result in 2.6 white departures from the city (see Table 4.2, row 1). If 0.65 of these departures are due to neighborhood considerations (using Shertzer and Walsh's estimate) and up to one white departure can be attributed to higher urban rents (according to the conceptual framework in chapter 4), then nearly one white departure is left over to be explained by fiscal/political considerations. By this metric, around one-third of total white flight is potentially driven by concerns about local policy (= 0.95/2.6). This figure closely matches the share of white residents living four or more miles from a black enclave in the typical city. I turn now to a closer examination of these fiscal/political factors.

FISCAL/POLITICAL INTERACTIONS CONTRIBUTED TO WHITE FLIGHT

The typical white resident of a northern or western central city lived three miles from a black enclave in 1940. These distant city neighborhoods remained resoundingly white during the next thirty years. Fur-

---

have extreme preferences for segregation. Yet Bruch and Mare (2006) demonstrate that extreme segregation is unlikely to occur in such models for a wide range of preferences.

thermore, generous estimates of responsiveness to local neighborhood change and rising housing prices can account for less than 70 percent of observed white flight. I argue here that the remainder of white flight can be explained by the desire to avoid fiscal/political interactions with distant black residents in the central city.

By 1970, blacks represented nearly a quarter of the populace in northern and western cities, a large enough share to have a meaningful effect on local politics. In addition, racial diversity may have decreased the willingness of white voters to support public services that they perceived to be going to support "other people's" children or neighborhoods (Luttmer 2001; Dahlberg, Edmark, and Lundqvist 2012).[10] Furthermore, black migrants were less well-off than were existing city residents. The classic Tiebout (1956) model would predict that rich residents will leave the city as the number of poor residents grows, opting instead to self-select into suburban towns populated by others of the same income level (see, e.g., Ellickson 1971; Westhoff 1977; Epple and Romer 1991; and Fernandez and Rogerson 1996).[11] Alesina, Baqir, and Easterly (1999) add that preferences over local policies can also directly differ by race; examples may include attitudes toward local policing or curriculum in public schools.

Using Housing Prices to Infer Demand for City Residence

If homeowners prefer to live in a predominantly white suburb for fiscal/political reasons, we would expect housing prices to be higher in suburban towns than in neighboring cities. Furthermore, we would expect the housing price gap between city and suburb to increase as the city becomes more racially diverse. The previous chapter used out-migration as a measure of demand based on the idea of "revealed preference." That is, if households are free to settle anywhere in the metropolitan area, and we observe a household leaving place A (the city) to move to place B (the suburbs), we can conclude that the household must prefer place B to place A by virtue of their "revealed" choice. Changes in housing prices follow directly from the out-migration of existing residents. As households leave place A (the city), demand

---

[10] Hopkins (2009) proposes that such opposition is especially likely following an influx of new migrants, which can heighten the awareness of differences.

[11] Epple and Platt (1998) consider a model in which individuals differ along two dimensions: income and preferences for public goods. In this case, sorting need not happen only along income lines; a poor household with strong preferences for public goods may select to live in a "rich" community.

for city units declines and housing prices in place A can be expected to fall.

In relying on housing prices as a measure of demand, I follow a long literature in economics, going back to Rosen 1974, on hedonic pricing.[12] This approach uses housing prices to elicit preferences for—or, as it is often called, "willingness to pay" for—attributes that are implicitly traded through the housing market rather than directly exchanged in separate marketplaces. One example of such a good is an ocean view. Some residents elect to pay higher prices for a housing unit with an ocean view, while others prefer the lower prices for units farther from the beach. The higher housing prices associated with ocean views can be considered the "market price" of beachside access. In this case, I argue that some residents are willing to pay a premium to enjoy the bundle of public goods and taxes associated with predominantly white suburbs.

As for any good, the value placed on suburban residence will vary throughout the population. The market price for suburban residence, or the "suburban premium," will reflect the *marginal* resident's willingness to pay for a suburban housing unit. The marginal resident is the individual or household who is just indifferent—or on the fence—between remaining in the diversifying city and moving to the homogeneous suburbs at the given prices. Imagine a city with ten residents arrayed from most to least concerned about racial composition. As the urban composition begins to change with black in-migration, the most concerned resident (Mr. 1) may leave, leading the price of urban housing to fall and the relative price of suburban residence to rise. At this new price, the next most-concerned city resident (Mr. 2) may be equally happy to either move to the suburbs or stay put in the city. In this way, the new (higher) suburban premium reflects Mr. 2's willingness to pay for suburban residence. Mr. 1 would have been willing to pay more (but did not have to do so), whereas Messrs. 3–10 were willing to pay less.

Isolating this demand for suburban public goods is an empirical challenge because housing units in the city and suburbs differ for other reasons, including the age and quality of the housing stock. Ideally, one would identify otherwise similar neighborhoods, one of which was lo-

---

[12] The literature that uses housing values to estimate household preferences for neighborhood and community attributes includes Black 1999; Harris 1999; Kane et al. 2003; Barrow and Rouse 2004; Figlio and Lucas 2004; Chay and Greenstone 2005; Reback 2005; Greenstone and Gallagher 2008; Machin and Salvanes 2016; and Gibbons, Machin, and Silva 2013.

cated within the racially diverse central city while the other was located within a predominantly white suburb. An approximation of this experiment can be achieved by focusing on neighborhoods on either side of city-suburban borders. These areas tend to be far from historic black enclaves and therefore face a low probability of black in-migration. Yet because they are separated by a municipal border, residents on one side have access to a different bundle of local public goods than do residents on the other.[13]

In many cases, neighborhoods on city borders were quite similar to their suburban counterparts, in that their housing stock was built in the same period on a comparable street plan and their residents were equally proximate to employment, public transit, and local amenities. Freund (2007, 27) describes the uniformity of border areas in Detroit, writing that "the division between the city's outermost residential neighborhoods, already dominated by single-family homes, and the new 'suburban' subdivisions that cropped up after 1945 was purely jurisdictional, and in most cases invisible to the human eye." Of the Bay Area, Self (2003, 96) writes that "driving south from Oakland into the adjacent suburban community of San Leandro, an observer in 1948 would have found it impossible to know when he or she had crossed from one city into the other. The tree-lined streets and 1920s-era bungalows common to both would have offered no clue. Even the industrial landscape would have struck the casual observer rolling past small machine shops and warehouses as a single piece."

It is important to note that the willingness to pay for suburban public goods estimated at the border may not be generalizable to the city as a whole. In particular, residents on the urban periphery were predominantly white and better-off than the typical city resident. In some cities, this particular selection may be due to residency requirements that compelled public employees to live within the city limits. Relative to the city average, this population may be particularly interested in suburban amenities and thus might overestimate the general willingness to pay to settle in the suburbs.[14]

---

[13] Harris (1999) finds that, within a municipality, housing prices in neighborhoods that are 0–10 percent black are 16 percent higher than prices in neighborhoods that are 10–60 percent black. However, this estimate is likely confounded by aspects of neighborhood quality that are correlated with racial composition. Indeed, Harris shows that the strong association between housing prices and black population share disappears after controlling for the share of residents in poverty or who are college graduates.

[14] Baum-Snow and Lutz (2011, Figures 4–6) demonstrate that the largest outflow in

Constructing a Block-Level Data Set

The border analysis combines block-level data on housing prices and rents from the Census of Housing with municipality-level information on racial composition and median income from the Census of Population. Details on spending on local public goods are available for cities and suburbs with more than 10,000 residents from the Census of Governments. I use Census maps to identify border areas for which block-level data are reported on both sides, excluding borders that are entirely obstructed by features like a railroad track, a body of water, or a large tract of industrial land.[15] Appendix Table 5.1 lists the 102 borders in 31 metropolitan areas that contribute to the sample in 1970 and 1980; details of the sample construction are available in Boustan 2012, 2013. Fifty-six of these borders can be extended back to 1960.

Along each sample border, I collected data on housing prices and rents for the first six blocks away from the border in each direction. The available block-level variables include mean housing values for owner-occupied units (PRICE), mean rents for rental units (RENT), and a limited set of housing quality measures, such as the number of units on the block, the average number of rooms per unit by tenure status, the share of units that are in single-family structures, and the share of residents on the block who are black. Other well-known Census variables like the age of the housing units and the median income of residents were not reported at the block level in these years.

Finally, I matched border areas to socioeconomic characteristics of the municipalities in which they are located, including the black population share and the town-level median income.[16] I also compiled data on property tax rates and municipal expenditures by category from the

response to school desegregation occurred in neighborhoods farthest from the city center.

[15] Ruling out obstructed areas improves the comparability of housing units on either side of the border. However, it also raises the question of endogenous border formation. Municipalities can erect bulwarks against unwanted populations by zoning for industrial use along their borders or constructing large roadways with limited options for pedestrian crossing. Cicero, IL, for example, was (in)famous for its ethnic and racial exclusivity in the 1950s and 1960s, although the town now has a large Hispanic population (Keating 1988). It may be no coincidence, then, that the Chicago/Cicero border is obstructed by industrial land. As a result, ruling out obstructed borders will favor jurisdictions that are the *least* hostile to the city population, thus working against finding a housing price effect at the border.

[16] Boustan (2013) also considers the relationship between housing prices and a jurisdiction's poverty rate and its estimated property tax base per resident.

Census of Governments, including spending on police, fire protection, road maintenance, and so on. Data on effective property tax rates were drawn from a special Census of Governments survey that compares the property tax bill to the market price of recent home sales; these data are only available in 1970. Another important aspect of local public goods is the quality of the public school system. I proxied for the quality of peers in local schools with the share of residents in the jurisdiction who hold a college degree.

Not surprisingly, the suburban towns in the sample had lower black population shares, higher median income, and a higher college graduation rate than did their neighboring cities. Appendix Table 5.2 presents summary statistics of the jurisdiction-level variables in the border area sample. In 1970, the black population share in the typical suburb was 15 percentage points lower than in the cross-border neighbor, and median income was $12,000 higher (in 2010 dollars). In addition to demographics and income, local policy also varied substantially across borders. Crossing the typical border into the central city was associated with a 0.7 percentage point increase in the property tax rate (on a base of 2.5 percent) and a $600–650 increase in local government expenditures per capita both for educational purposes (on a base of around $4,000) and for non-educational purposes (on a base of around $1,000). Higher levels of government spending could indicate higher levels of service or, more likely, could be a sign of the higher costs associated with providing services to a poorer population.

Although the cities and suburbs on either side of the border differed significantly, the neighborhoods adjacent to the border were quite similar to their cross-border pairs. Appendix Table 5.3 presents summary statistics of the block-level variables in the border area sample. On average, housing units in the border sample had attributes usually associated with the suburban housing stock. The typical block had around 40 housing units, 80 percent of which were single-family structures. The average unit had a little fewer than six rooms, which would include a living room, a dining room, a kitchen, and three bedrooms. The average value for units near the border was $130,000 in 2010 dollars in 1960 and 1970 and increased to $200,000 by 1980. In 1960, the black population share in the border sample (2.7 percent) matched that of the average inner-ring suburb. By 1980, the black population share along the border was twice as high as that of the typical suburb (12.4 percent). Yet after excluding the two borders undergoing racial transition, the black population share is closer to the suburban average (7.3 percent black in the border sample; 5.6 percent black in the suburbs).[17]

I report average differences in housing characteristics across city-suburban borders in 1970 in the last column of Appendix Table 5.3. The average owner-occupied home commands a $6,000 price premium on the suburban side of the border (relative to the mean price of $130,000), a fact that will be explored in more detail below. Yet it does not appear that this price gap can be attributed to differences in local housing characteristics. Suburban blocks are no denser, nor do they have larger housing units or more single-family homes. The black population share is somewhat lower on the suburban side of the border (1.3 percentage points), although this gap is not statistically significant and is driven primarily by the two borders undergoing racial transition. The similarity of the housing stock on either side of the border suggests that the observed housing price gap is not driven by differences in local zoning regulations. In general, stricter zoning rules tend to be associated with higher housing prices (Ihlanfeldt 2004; Turner, Haughwout, and Van der Klaauw 2014). Yet there is no evidence for the most common forms of zoning regulation, including limitations on multifamily dwellings or lot size requirements, which would reduce the number of housing units on the block.

Housing Prices at City-Suburban Borders

Homebuyers were willing to pay more for an otherwise identical house located in a racially homogeneous suburb. Figure 5.2 contrasts average housing prices on the city and suburban sides of the 102 sample borders; Appendix Equation 1 reports the underlying estimating equation. The figure designates blocks on the city side of the border with positive numbers and blocks on the suburban side with negative numbers. Price levels are presented relative to the first block on the city side (in percentage terms). Positive values mean that housing units on the block were more expensive, on average, than those on the first city block, while negative values mean that the housing units were less expensive.

If fiscal/political concerns mattered to households' location decisions, we would expect to find a discontinuous drop in housing prices between the last block in a white suburb and the first block in a racially diverse city. Indeed, housing prices just across the border on the subur-

---

[17] The two excluded borders, Inglewood and Westmont, CA, are both in the Los Angeles area.

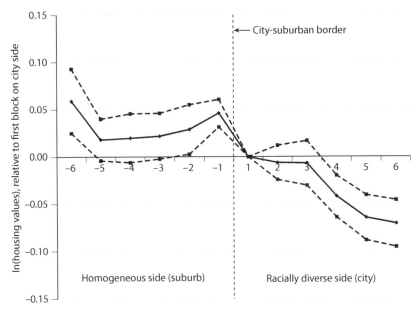

Figure 5.2. Housing values relative to the first block on the city side, by distance to city-suburban border, 1960–80. Each point is a coefficient from the regression presented in Appendix Equation 1 (N = 18,103). The dotted lines indicate 95 percent confidence intervals. Distance from the city-suburban border is indexed between 6 and –6, with positive numbers falling on the city side of the border and negative numbers falling on the suburban side. Higher numbers (in absolute value) indicate distances further from the border. Housing price estimates are relative to the first block tier on the city side.

ban side (block –1) are 5 percent higher than those of their cross-border neighbor (block –1); this difference is statistically significant. In contrast, comparing housing prices on two adjacent blocks in the suburbs or in the city does not yield a statistically significant difference (compare block 1 to block 2 or block –1 to block –2). The fact that moving one block *within* a jurisdiction has a negligible effect on housing prices suggests that the cross-border gap is not simply picking up a continuous change in housing quality on neighboring blocks located a given distance from the city center. Yet comparisons of more distant blocks (say, block 1 to block 6) reveal significant housing price declines over space, likely reflecting deterioration of housing or neighborhood quality closer to the urban core. This pattern reinforces the importance of generating conclusions from a comparison of neighboring blocks.

For simplicity, Figure 5.2 compares the average housing price on the city side of sample borders to the average housing price on the suburban side, given that cities tend to be more racially diverse. Figure 5.3 explores the data in more detail, relating the actual city-suburban difference in black population share to the observed gap in housing prices at the border. Details of the underlying estimation can be found in Appendix Equation 2. This approach leverages the substantial variation in racial gaps between cities and their neighboring suburbs. For example, in 1970, when the city of Chicago was 33 percent black, one of its suburbs (Evanston) was 16 percent black, while another (Oak Park) was less than 1 percent black.

The wider the gap in black population share between city and suburb, the larger the estimated difference in housing prices at the border. The first set of bars in Figure 5.3 considers housing units up to eight blocks away from the border on either side. In this broad sample, a 15 percentage point gap in black population share (the sample mean) is associated with a 5 percent decline in housing prices. The next set of bars narrows the sample to blocks along the border. In this more comparable sample, the typical cross-border racial gap is associated with a 3 percent decline in housing prices. Controlling for available block-level characteristics in the third column reduces the coefficient somewhat further.

The desire to avoid racially diverse cities could be driven by the correlation between race and income. In other words, at the municipality level, poor whites may have been just as unwelcome as poor blacks. The fourth column of Figure 5.3 assesses this possibility by jointly estimating the effect of municipal black population share and median income on housing prices.[18] I find *no effect* of black population share on housing prices after controlling for median income. In contrast, median income survives this test; the estimated coefficient suggests that a 20 percent increase in town-level median income (the sample average) was associated with a 5 percent increase in housing values and a 4 percent increase in rents at the border.[19] In fiscal/political terms, the most salient feature of black arrivals appears to have been their low income levels rather than race per se.

---

[18] Variation in median income can arise from the in-migration of the poor to central cities and from declining earnings of longstanding residents—for example, as a result of shocks to particular industries, like those of automobiles and steel, during this period.

[19] I do not find a significant effect of the interaction between black population share and median income on housing prices.

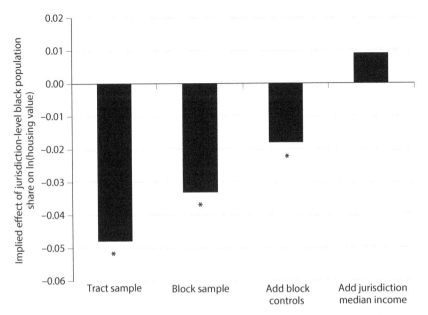

Figure 5.3. Implied effect of a 15 percentage point increase in city's black popu-lation share (the mean cross-border difference) on housing prices at city-suburban borders, 1960–80. The reported effects are based on the coefficients from Appendix Equation 2. A * indicates effects that are significantly different from zero at the 5 percent level. The first bar (marked "tract sample") contains blocks up to eight tiers away from the border on either side ($N = 20{,}352$), while the second bar (marked "block sample") only contains blocks adjacent to the border ($N = 6{,}326$). Block-level control variables in the third bar include: num-ber of housing units on block; share of units that are single-family structures; average number of rooms; and black population share at the block level. The fourth bar includes the logarithm of median income at the jurisdiction level as an additional regressor.

Local Public Goods and the Demand for Suburban Residence

Housing price patterns suggest that the marginal homebuyer was will-ing to pay more for an identical unit located in a higher-income suburb, even after controlling for neighborhood composition. This section con-siders a series of local policies that may account for this observed demand.

Historians have noted the role of local public goods in motivating suburban moves. For the case of Oakland, Self (2003, 130) argues that many white residents moved to suburbs in the East Bay to avoid "the greater proportion of social problems, and financial responsibility for them, [that] remained in the central city." Likewise, in Detroit, white residents were attracted to the fact that "each suburb had its own school district, recreation programs, libraries and public services, paid for by local taxes" (Sugrue 1996, 246). In general, local political institutions, including "tax authorities, zoning districts, school precincts and the like[. . . make] town lines attractive to movers" (Fischer et al. 2004, 53).

In order for variation in local public goods to explain the demand for living in a high-income town, it must be that (1) high-income towns offer a different bundle of tax rates and public services than their neighboring cities and (2) this bundle is attractive to the marginal resident. Data on local taxes and expenditures are available for 61 sample borders in 1970. I consider differences between poor cities and their better-off suburbs in the effective property tax rate; instructional spending in schools; the share of residents with a college degree (a proxy for the quality of peers in school); and expenditures on police services, fire protection, sewers, and local roads.

I identify three major differences between high-income towns and poorer cities in the data. First, high-income towns set lower property tax rates. An additional $12,000 of town-level median income in 2010 dollars (the average cross-border difference) is associated with a 0.6 percentage point reduction in the effective property tax rate on a base of 2.5 percent, which is equivalent to $900 in annual tax relief in 2010 dollars. Second, wealthy towns spent less than poor cities on non-educational functions, particularly on public safety, perhaps because they faced fewer social problems.[20] However, wealthy towns did not allocate more funds to educational expenditures per pupil overall; nor did they spend more on fire protection, parks, road maintenance, and sanitation. Finally, a larger share of residents in high-income towns held a college degree, a potential proxy for higher peer quality in local public schools. All three distinctive attributes of high-income towns—lower property tax rates, lower police expenditures, and a larger share of college-educated residents—were associated with higher housing prices.[21]

---

[20] Higher rates of police spending in the city may be a proxy for a higher crime rate. Cullen and Levitt (1999) show that more crime was associated with out-migration from central cities during this period (see also Ellen and O'Regan 2010; and Foote 2015). However, crime rates are unlikely to vary much in neighboring blocks directly across the municipal border.

[21] The results in the previous two paragraphs are presented in detail in Boustan 2013, Tables 6 and 7.

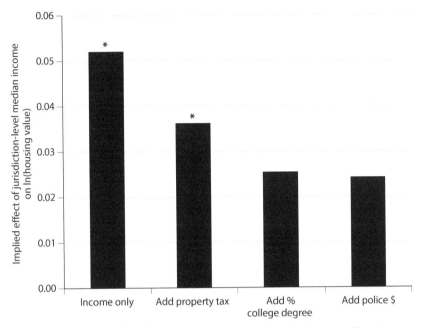

Figure 5.4. Implied effect of a 20 percent increase in suburban median income (the mean cross-border difference) on housing prices at city-suburban borders, 1970. The reported effects are based on the coefficients from (a modified version of) Appendix Equation 2. A * indicates effects that are significantly different from zero at the 5 percent level. The sample includes blocks adjacent to the 61 borders in 1970 with information on all local policy variables ($N = 1,631$). The regression underlying the first bar includes median income as the only jurisdiction-level regressor. The remaining columns add local policy variables in a cumulative fashion, starting with the effective property tax rate.

Differences in local policies can account for most of the estimated housing price premium associated with living in a wealthy suburb. I start in Figure 5.4 by reproducing the main relationship between municipality-level median income and housing prices using data from 1970, the year in which the full set of public goods measures is available. When the local property tax is added as a regressor in column 2, the estimated effect of median income on housing prices declines by 30 percent. Adding the share of the population with a college degree in column 3 generates an additional 30 percent decline and the coefficient is no longer statistically different from zero. Column 4 adds police expenditures, and the coefficient is little changed. It appears that two factors—lower property tax rates and higher-quality peers in public schools—can explain most of the willingness to pay to live in a town with wealthy co-residents.[22]

COURT-ORDERED DESEGREGATION
AND WHITE FLIGHT IN THE 1970S

As black migrants arrived in northern cities, fiscal/political concerns about citywide public goods prompted some white households to relocate to the suburbs. However, before 1970, many of these white urban households lived far from a black enclave and sent their children to local public schools with predominantly white classmates, particularly at the elementary level. During the 1970s, some central cities in the North and West were required to desegregate their public school systems by race. Desegregation orders exposed many urban students to cross-race peers for the first time, often by being reassigned to a school outside of their immediate neighborhood. I find that the marginal homebuyer was willing to pay 6 percent more for a housing unit located in a district unaffected by desegregation policy (around $8,000 in 2010 dollars). The housing price response to school desegregation is on par with the willingness to pay to be in a wealthy suburb.

In the 1950s and 1960s, most northern districts did not face desegregation litigation. Early cases focused on schools that were legally separated by race, a form of segregation that only existed in the South.[23] In the 1973 *Keyes v. Denver* decision, the Supreme Court ruled that school districts without de jure segregation could be legally required to desegregate if their school assignment procedures had contributed to de facto segregation (Clotfelter 2011). Under the *Keyes* decision, many northern and western school districts could be found liable for enacting policies that created or maintained racial separation.

The Chicago public school system offers one example of such de facto school segregation. With black in-migration, schools in Chicago's

---

[22] Given that school attendance is determined by local residence, elementary schools directly across the border may have had a similar set of peers. Junior high and high schools draw from a wider area and thus may have differed in quality substantially.

[23] *Brown v. Board of Education* (1954) declared racially separate school systems to be unconstitutional, and *Green v. County School Board* (1968) required accelerated compliance with *Brown*. Fifty percent of large southern districts that desegregated through the courts received their court order in or before 1970, compared with only 18 percent of northern and western districts (Guryan 2004).

historic Black Belt became severely overcrowded. Yet rather than reassign some black students to historically "white" schools, the district responded first by holding classes in any available space in the school buildings in black neighborhoods, including the gymnasium and the cafeteria; then by reducing school hours in order to use classrooms on double shifts; and finally by adding portable classrooms, nicknamed "Willis wagons" after then-superintendent Benjamin Willis (Seligman 2005, 129–30).[24] In a related strategy, Kansas City regularly shifted the boundaries of school attendance areas to achieve racially separate schools (Gotham 2002, 99–103). Overall, Lieberson (1980, 116) deemed such northern policies "hardly different" from those found in the South, "except for the crucial fact that they were [not] enforced by law."

Subsequent Supreme Court rulings exempted most suburban districts from legal scrutiny. The 1974 *Milliken v. Bradley* decision established stringent conditions for extending desegregation remedies across district lines (Orfield and Eaton 1996, xxii). Under the logic of *Milliken*, suburban districts could only be included in a desegregation plan if the district itself engaged in a policy of segregation or if an interdistrict plan was required to correct segregation arising from state-level education policy; de facto segregation between a central city and its suburbs could not be cause for court action. Furthermore, a district could only be considered segregated if the racial composition of individual schools were found to be out of balance with the district as a whole. Ironically, then, all-white suburbs would *never* be considered segregated given that each school would automatically reflect the demographics of the wider district.

As a result of the *Keyes* decision, some northern cities faced court-ordered desegregation during the 1970s, while the *Milliken* decision exempted their neighboring suburbs. Therefore, desegregation orders may have increased the demand for suburban residence among households seeking to avoid cross-race contact in schools.[25] I used the methods outlined earlier to compare the prices of housing units on either side of city-suburban borders before and after the city district fell under court order to desegregate its schools.[26] Twenty-nine borders in the

---

[24] These often flagrant tactics notwithstanding, Chicago did not face a mandate to desegregate until a 1980 consent decree following a threatened law suit by the U.S. Department of Health, Education and Welfare (Jackson 2010).

[25] A non-exhaustive list of the historical literature on white responses to desegregation includes Webb 2005; Sokol 2006; and Crespino 2007.

[26] Clotfelter (1975) uses housing prices to estimate willingness to pay to avoid school desegregation in Atlanta.

sample had one district under court order to desegregate during the 1970s, while 52 borders faced desegregation on both sides or not at all.[27] I collected data on desegregation court orders by school district from the *State of Public School Integration* website. Any district required by the court to take at least one action to address desegregation during the 1970s is considered to be under court order; such actions include redistricting school attendance areas, mandatory busing of students between schools, and creating magnet schools.[28]

Desegregation court orders were enforced (at least to some degree) in this sample, leading to notable changes in school-level racial composition. In 1970, the black enrollment share in the average white student's school in city districts that later fell under court order was 12 percent, nearly identical to the share in comparison districts. During the 1970s, average white exposure to black peers increased by 20 percentage points in cities under court order but only by 6 points in comparison cities. By 1980, the black enrollment share faced by the typical white student in a district under court order was nearly equivalent to the black share of the total student body in those areas, suggesting that desegregation plans managed to achieve "full integration," in the sense that each school reflected the demographics of the district as a whole.[29]

Given that desegregation plans were well enforced, it is reasonable to expect that court orders would have had effects on local housing prices. If residents did not like living in a racially integrated school system, either because of direct concerns about mixed-race classrooms or because the enforcement of desegregation plans often required that children be sent to non-neighborhood schools, we would expect housing prices in treated districts to fall relative to those of their neighboring suburbs. Figure 5.5 explores the effect of desegregation on the value of owner-occupied housing. The underlying estimating equations are explained in detail in Appendix Equations 3 and 4.

[27] Of these 52 borders, 7 contain 2 districts that were required to desegregate during the 1970s; 5 faced an early desegregation court order in the 1960s; and the remaining 40 avoided any court action during the 1970s. The remaining 21 borders in the full sample divide municipalities that share a school district and thus are not included in this analysis.
[28] I associate each plan with the date of the court order, even if the case was later appealed to a higher court. For example, the Denver plan is coded as being handed down in 1969, even though the Supreme Court ruled on the case in 1973.
[29] The findings reported in this paragraph are based on Boustan 2012, Table 4. Results in this sample are consistent with those of Reber (2005), who demonstrates that the average desegregation plan successfully increased white exposure to black peers nationwide.

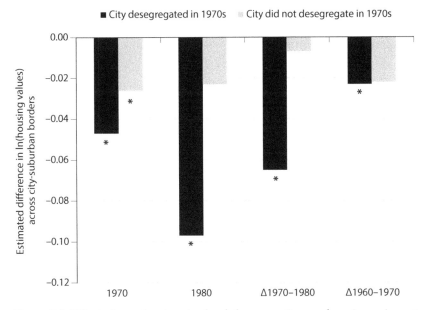

Figure 5.5. Effect of court-ordered school desegregation on housing prices at city-suburban borders. Columns report estimated differences in housing values across city-suburban borders for sample cities that did/did not face desegregation court orders in the 1970s. Columns 1 and 2 represent coefficients from Appendix Equation 3a (black bars) or Appendix Equation 4a (gray bars). Coefficients that are significantly different from zero at the 5 percent level are marked with a *. Column 1 includes data from 1970 before court-ordered desegregation. Column 2 includes data from 1980 after the "treatment" borders were placed under court order to desegregate. Column 3 reports coefficients from Appendix Equations 3b and 4b of changes in housing prices from 1970 to 1980 on the interaction between being in the central city and in the 1980 Census year ($N = 4,368$). Column 4 conducts the same regression for the previous decade (1960–70) ($N = 2,495$). Note that the coefficients in column 3 are not exactly equal to the difference between the coefficients in columns 1 and 2 because the regressions underlying column 3 also include additional fixed effects.

Passage of a desegregation court order doubled the housing price gap at city-suburban borders. The dark bars in Figure 5.5 represent the urban price penalty along the 29 borders whose central city faced a desegregation court order in this period. In 1970, the price for units on the city side of these borders was already 5 percent lower than those of their suburban neighbors, perhaps due to preexisting disparities in school quality (column 1). By 1980, after the imposition of court-ordered desegregation, the housing price gap across these borders doubled to 10 percent (column 2).[30] The third column represents the change in the city-suburban housing price gap from 1970 to 1980; as we would expect, the price gap grows by 5 percentage points.[31]

Other factors, such as fiscal mismanagement, may have led the fiscal/political value of living in a central city to decline in the 1970s period. I consider this possibility by measuring changes in the housing price gap along the 52 borders that avoided court supervision during this period. The gray bars indicate that this group did not experience a similar change in the urban price penalty during the 1970s. The city-suburban housing price gap of 2 percent measured along these borders in 1970 was still in place by 1980.

Central cities ordered to desegregate may have been on a downward trajectory during the 1970s for other reasons—for example, because of race-related rioting in the late 1960s.[32] In this case, we would expect to see larger housing price declines in these cities over the long run, both before desegregation (say, from 1960 to 1970) and afterward. The final set of columns in Figure 5.5 demonstrates that this was not the case: during the 1960s, the urban price penalty increased by 2 percentage points along both treatment and control borders. The difference between these two city groups is negligible. It is therefore unlikely that the estimated change in housing prices during the 1970s is simply picking up long-run trends in urban demand.[33]

Prices for city housing declined following court-ordered school desegregation, a strong indication of falling demand for urban residence. Objections to racially integrated schools may have been rooted in fears

---

[30] One might think it would also be interesting to see how housing prices responded to the news of a new court order in the year after the decision was handed down. However, residents closely watched the courts and were likely to be able to anticipate policy changes. Schneider (2008, 1007) summarizes this process in Los Angeles, noting that residents thought "desegregation was coming, it was going to be a problem, and it was not worth the risk to stick around and see how it would go."

[31] Column 3 pools data from 1970 and 1980 to estimate changes over time in the housing price gap at city-suburban borders. Because I am able to control for additional aspects of the neighborhood in this specification, the estimated price change is slightly larger than the difference between the estimates in columns 1 and 2 (6 percentage points rather than 5); see Appendix Equation 3b for details.

[32] Collins and Margo (2007) find that housing prices fell in cities that experienced a riot in the 1960s.

[33] The results in column 4 represent the fifty-six borders for which block-level data are available in 1960. Overall patterns are similar in this subsample.

about mixed-race classrooms and associated declines in student pre-paredness but may also reflect concerns about the loss of neighborhood schools. In order to comply with desegregation orders, school districts could no longer place all students in the nearest school but rather needed to assign some white students to distant schools in black neigh-borhoods and vice versa. I use estimates from the literature to assess the contribution of each factor to the overall aversion to desegregation.

Kane, Riegg, and Staiger (2006) use school assignment policy in Charlotte-Mecklenburg, North Carolina, to estimate the willingness to pay to avoid black peers, while controlling for distance to school. Ac-cording to their results, the 20 percent increase in black enrollment ex-perienced by the typical white student in my sample following school desegregation would have reduced housing prices by 4 percent. By this measure, two-thirds of the estimated housing price response to school desegregation at the city border can be attributed to worries about mixed-race classrooms (= 4 percent decline due to mixed-race class-rooms/6 percent decline overall).[34]

The remainder of the estimated price response is likely due to the loss of neighborhood schools. All students in court-ordered districts would experience some change in the racial composition of their peers. However, some students would have remained in their local school as new students arrive, while others would have been reassigned to more distant schools. To achieve racial balance, around 30 percent of the stu-dent body would have needed to be reassigned in the typical district. Bogart and Cromwell (2000) estimate that assignment to a non-neighborhood school reduces housing prices by 7.5 percent. If 30 per-cent of households faced this reassignment penalty, the loss of neigh-borhood schools can account for the remainder of the housing price response (2 percent = 30 percent reassigned × 7.5 percent housing price decline).

CONCLUSION

Around 2 white residents left northern cities for each black southern arrival in the mid-twentieth century. Yet many urban whites lived in

[34] Hanushek, Kain, and Rivkin (2009) find little effect of black enrollment share on the test scores of white students in Texas. If anything, higher black enrollment harms the performance of enrolled *black* students. Perhaps unaware of these patterns, white parents may have acted out of concern that their children's academic performance would have suffered in mixed-race classrooms.

predominantly white neighborhoods far from expanding black enclaves. These distant neighborhoods experienced little racial change,
suggesting that concerns about local social interactions with new black
neighbors cannot fully explain the phenomenon of white flight.

This chapter proposes that some white households left central cities
to avoid fiscal/political interactions with black arrivals through shared
municipal elections and public schools. I measured the role of local
public goods by comparing the trajectory of prices for adjacent housing
units along city-suburban borders as the city became more racially diverse. I found that homebuyers and renters were willing to pay more
for a similar unit located in a racially homogeneous suburb. But this
price gap can be entirely explained by differences in income levels between blacks and whites. Cities with a lower median income also had
higher property taxes and lower-quality schools, two factors that re-
pelled housing demand. After school desegregation plans were imple-
mented in the 1970s, race itself became more salient. The housing price
gap at city-suburban borders doubled during the 1970s in cities under
court order to desegregate their schools. The willingness to pay to avoid
school desegregation was due to a combination of aversion to mixed-
race classrooms and concerns about school reassignment.

APPENDIX TO CHAPTER 5

Housing Prices and Jurisdiction-Level Characteristics

Figure 5.2 compares prices of housing units up to six blocks away from
the 102 municipal borders in the sample, which are listed in Appendix
Table 5.1. Each border area consists of a pair of jurisdictions, in most
cases one city and one suburb.[35] The figure divides jurisdiction pairs
into the racially diverse jurisdiction (often the city) and the racially homogeneous jurisdiction (often the suburb). I then estimate:

$$\ln(PRICE_{ijbt}) = \Gamma'[distance\ from\ border_{ijt}] + \Psi' d_{bt} + \varepsilon_{ijbt} \tag{1}$$

where i indexes Census blocks, j jurisdictions, b border areas, and t Census years. The dependent variable $PRICE$ measures the average value
of owner-occupied units on block i. The key independent variables are
a vector of dummy variables indicating distance to the border. Distance

---

[35] To increase the 1960 sample, I include fifteen borders that divide two suburbs large
enough to have available block data on both sides (e.g., Cambridge-Somerville, MA).

varies between 6 and -6, with positive values located in the city and negative values in the suburbs. Estimates are relative to the first tier of city blocks (+1), which is the omitted category. Of particular interest is the magnitude of the coefficient estimate γ_{-1} (a component of the vector Γ), which indicates whether housing values on the first tier of suburban blocks are significantly different from those on the city side. Equation 1 also includes a vector of dummy variables (d_{bt}) for each border area b in Census year t so that estimation occurs within border areas, not across them. I will say more about the importance of this specification choice below.[36]

The regression equation underlying Figures 5.3 and 5.4 replaces the vector *distance to the border* with one or more jurisdiction-level characteristics that are common to all blocks on a given side of the border. For example, I estimate:

$$\ln(PRICE_{ijbt}) = \beta\ SHARE\ BLACK_{jt} + \Phi'block_{it} + \Psi'd_{bt} + \varepsilon_{ijbt} \qquad (2)$$

where *SHARE BLACK* measures the black population share in the jurisdiction j. Other specifications include the median income or the local property tax rate in the jurisdiction instead. Some regressions also add available block-level housing and neighborhood quality controls ($block_{it}$).

The vector of border area fixed effects (d_{bt}) captures unobserved neighborhood characteristics that are common to residents on both sides of the border—for example, the presence of a nearby park, bus line, or commercial strip. These fixed effects also control for common aspects of the housing stock, such as the age and architectural style of the units. The effects of jurisdiction-level variables are thus identified by comparing the prices of neighboring housing units located on either side of the border. A negative β implies that houses located in a racially diverse city command systematically lower prices than do their cross-border neighbors.[37]

---

[36] For all regressions in this chapter, standard errors are clustered by border area and observations are weighted by the number of owner-occupied (or rental) units on the block. Regressions for which the dependent variable is housing values (rents) are limited to blocks with at least five owner-occupied (rental) units, given Census reporting requirements.

[37] For a thorough discussion of a related econometric framework, see Turner, Haughwout, and Van der Klaauw 2014.

Housing Prices and School Desegregation

Figure 5.5 relates the presence of a court order to desegregate the local public schools to housing prices on the city and suburban sides of juris-diction borders. I estimate three equations, one for 1970, one for 1980, and the third pooling data from 1970 and 1980 together. I index the subsample of metropolitan areas whose central city was required to de-segregate in the 1970s with the subscript $_{PLAN}$.

$$\ln(\text{PRICE})_{isbt} = \beta_{PLAN}(\text{CITY}) + \Psi'd_{bt} + \varepsilon_{isbt}\text{in } t = 1970, 1980 \qquad \text{(3a)}$$

$$\ln(\text{PRICE})_{isbt} = \beta_{PLAN}(\text{CITY} \times \text{T}) + \Omega'd_{bs} + \text{T} + (d_{bt} \times \text{T}) + \varepsilon_{isbt} \qquad \text{(3b)}$$

As before, i indexes Census block, b indexes border area, and t indexes Census year. School districts are represented by s. CITY is an indicator for blocks on the city side of the border, the district that faced school desegregation during the 1970s. Border area fixed effects (d_{bt}) capture neighborhood attributes that are shared by houses on either side of the border. The coefficient of interest in equation 3a, β_{PLAN}, estimates the mean difference in housing prices between the city and suburban sides of these borders, either in 1970 (before desegregation) or in 1980 (afterward).

Equation 3b pools data from 1970 and 1980. This added variation al-lows the inclusion of side-of-the-border fixed effects (d_{bs}), which are calculated as interactions between border area b and school district s (either city or suburb). The vector d_{bs} absorbs longstanding differences in school quality or housing attributes across borders. I also include an interaction between the border area fixed effects and a dummy variable for the 1980 Census year ($d_{bt} \times \text{T}$), which allows a common neighbor-hood trend as the border area gentrifies or declines over time.

The variable of interest in equation 3b is the interaction between CITY and the 1980 Census year. Here the coefficient β_{PLAN} identifies how the difference in housing prices between the city and suburban sides of the typical border *changed* with the implementation of a deseg-regation plan. My hypothesis is that $\beta_{PLAN} < 0$, or that the price of city housing declined during the 1970s relative to its neighboring suburb as the city underwent a process of school desegregation.

For comparison, I estimate a set of corresponding equations for the portion of the sample in which the city did not undergo court-ordered desegregation during the 1970s (or, both the city and suburb under-went desegregation). These metropolitan areas are indexed with the subscript $_{NOPLAN}$.

Appendix Table 5.1: Metropolitan areas included
in the border sample, 1960–80

		Number of borders			
Region	Metropolitan area	In sample, 1960–80	Added to sample, 1970–80	Sample, total	Excluded borders
North	Allentown-Bethlehem, PA		2	2	
	Boston, MA	2	1	3	4
	Hartford, CT		3	3	2
	New York, NY-NJ†	10		10	3
	Pittsburgh, PA	3		3	
	Providence, RI	3	1	4	
	Scranton, PA		1	1	
	Springfield, MA		1	1	1
Midwest	Akron, OH		2	2	2
	Canton, OH		1	1	
	Chicago, IL†	5	2	7	6
	Cleveland, OH	2		2	
	Dayton, OH	1		1	
	Des Moines, IA		2	2	
	Detroit, MI	1	6	7	
	Grand Rapids, MI		4	4	
	Indianapolis, IN		1	1	3
	Kansas City, KS-MO	2	2	4	3
	Madison, WI		1	1	
	Minneapolis/St. Paul, MN	1	1	2	3
	Moline-Davenport, IL-IA	1	1	2	
	South Bend, IN		1	1	
	St. Louis, MO	1		1	4
West	Denver, CO	1	2	3	
	Las Vegas, NV		1	1	
	Los Angeles, CA†	17	5	22	7
	Phoenix, AZ		1	1	1
	Portland, OR		2	2	1
	San Bern.-Riverside, CA		1	1	3
	San Francisco, CA†	2	1	3	
	San Jose, CA	4		4	
	TOTAL:	56	46	102	44

Note: Metropolitan areas marked with † contained secondary central cities in 1960 that are now considered by the Census Bureau to anchor their own, independent metropolitan areas. These are: Newark, Jersey City, and Clifton, NJ (New York); Gary, IN (Chicago); Anaheim, CA (Los Angeles); and Oakland, CA (San Francisco). Excluded borders are those that otherwise meet sample criteria but are entirely obstructed by a body of water, industrial land, a railroad, or a four-lane highway.

Appendix Table 5.2: Summary statistics in border sample, jurisdiction-level variables

Mean (S.D.)	1970		1970–80
	All jurisdictions	Difference across borders (Absolute value)	Change in cross-border difference over time (Absolute value)
Median family income ($2010)	$63,474 ($12,988)	$12,606 ($11,325)	$3,657 ($2,769)
Share black	0.0863 (0.1422)	0.151 (0.145)	0.0554 (0.0683)
Share college graduate	0.123 (0.081)	0.068 (0.071)	0.027 (0.030)
Property tax rate, % of sale price	2.535 (1.115)	0.723 (0.482)	
In $2010: Instruction $ per pupil	$3,811 ($828)	$650 (601)	
Non-education $ per capita	$935 ($538)	$626 (547)	
Police $ per capita	$145 ($067)	$8.45 ($5.73)	

Note: Demographic and socioeconomic variables are available for all 102 city-suburban borders. Expenditure variables are available for 97 borders and property tax rates for 65 borders. Differences across borders in columns 2 and 3 are reported in absolute value. Median family income and share college graduate are substantially higher in the suburbs, while share black, property tax, rate and non-educational spending are substantially lower in the suburbs.

$$\ln(\text{PRICE})_{isbt} = \beta_{\text{NOPLAN}} (\text{CITY}) + \Psi' d_{bt} + \varepsilon_{isbt} \qquad \textbf{(4a)}$$

$$\ln(\text{PRICE})_{isbt} = \beta_{\text{NOPLAN}}(\text{CITY} \times T) + \Omega' d_{bs} + T + (d_{bt} \times T) + \varepsilon_{isbt}. \qquad \textbf{(4b)}$$

Although I do not have a strong prediction about the sign of β_{NOPLAN} in equation 4b, the coefficient will be less than zero if other policy changes or events reduced the value of central-city residence during the 1970s.

Appendix Table 5.3: Summary statistics in border sample, block-level variables

	1960	1970	1980	Difference across border, 1970
Average value (in $2010)	$129,135 (67,765)	$130,367 (52,735)	$200,266 (116,666)	−$6,160.60 (2,314.73)
Number of units	42.689 (43.783)	39.347 (39.122)	41.954 (58.118)	0.328 (3.216)
Average # rooms, owned	5.713 (0.933)	5.736 (1.083)	5.478 (1.022)	−0.006 (0.048)
Share single family	0.735 (0.227)	0.796 (0.265)	0.839 (0.229)	0.008 (0.017)
Share black	0.027 (0.112)	0.064 (0.201)	0.124 (0.287)	0.013 (0.009)
Average rent (in $2010)	$581.53 (181.90)	$659.30 (214.92)	$731.27 (233.39)	−$13.99 (10.85)
N (own)/ N (rent)	4433/3027	9617/6102	8113/4681	

Note: In columns 1–3, cells contain means and standard deviations of block-level variables in the border area sample. Means are reported for blocks that have at least five owner-occupied units, the threshold above which the Census Bureau reports data on housing prices. The one exception is average contract rent, which is reported for blocks with at least five rental units. Column 4 reports coefficients and standard errors from a regression of the block-level characteristic on a dummy variable for being in the city in 1970 for blocks adjacent to the border ($N = 2,575$; for last row, $N = 1,884$).

EPILOGUE

Black Migration, Northern Cities, and Labor Markets after 1970

THE CORE CHAPTERS in the book have focused on the decades between 1940 and 1970, a period of rapid black in-migration to industrial cities in the North and West. I end here by examining how the three trends at the heart of this story—black migration from the South, the earnings convergence between blacks and whites, and white departures from central cities—have evolved in recent decades.

By 1970, black migration from the South slowed, and since 1980 the direction of black migration has reversed course, with more migration flow from North to South than vice versa. Yet despite this reversal, black migration from the South at midcentury had enduring effects on the distribution of the American population. The share of the black population living in the South decreased from nearly 90 percent at the beginning of the century to less than 50 percent in 1970, before rising to 57 percent today. It is unlikely that the black share of the population in the South will ever return to its pre–Great Migration levels.

Even after the slowing of black in-migration, black and white earnings have not converged further in northern cities. Just as black migration to northern cities tapered off, a new migration of low-skilled workers from Latin America was getting underway. This new migration wave coincided with decreased demand for manufacturing workers in American cities as a result of technological change and globalization. Thus, in recent years, black workers in northern cities have faced new sources of labor market competition, compounded by falling demand for some low-skilled operative and clerical positions, leading wages to stagnate further.

The ending of black in-migration also did not draw white households back to central cities. Contrary to the often trumpeted idea of urban revival, outflows of white households from the central city have continued, with the share of white metropolitan residents living out-side the central city falling from 62 percent in 1940 to 33 percent in 1980 to 26 percent by 2010. Yet white households that moved to the suburbs to avoid racially diverse central cities have found their suburban exclu-sivity beginning to erode in recent years. By 2010, 47 percent of black metropolitan residents lived in the suburban ring as well, contributing to declining racial residential segregation.

Before discussing each of these trends in turn, I begin with a short summary of the main findings of the book.

Summary of Main Findings

In 1910, nearly fifty years after emancipation from slavery, 86 percent of African Americans still lived in the South. Starting with the cohorts born immediately after the Civil War, the geographic mobility of southern-born blacks began to rise, although most of these moves took place from one agricultural region of the South to another. By the birth cohort of 1880, southern-born blacks were more likely than their white southern counterparts to move between states. Yet despite high wages in northern industry, black migration to the North only began in large numbers around 1915. The advent of black migration to the North awaited a period of particularly strong labor demand, which arrived during World War I and coincided with a temporary cutoff of typical labor supply from Europe. Once black migration to the North got un-derway, early migrants facilitated later moves of friends and family; out-migration from the South accelerated rapidly, peaking in the 1940s and the 1950s.

Black migration was greatest from agricultural areas that specialized in cotton production and from counties that were characterized by seg-regationist attitudes. These departures were prompted by the mechani-zation of cotton planting and harvesting and by a disruption in tenancy arrangements in favor of wage labor. The migrants themselves were drawn from both the top and the bottom of the occupational distribu-tion. In particular, migrants were more likely than non-migrants to have a father who was a white-collar or skilled blue-collar worker but were also more likely to have a father who was a common laborer. The migration of the low skilled is consistent with economic models of mi-grant selection, which predict that low-skilled workers will be the most likely to leave areas like the South that offer high returns to skill. The differential migration of highly skilled blacks from the South may be instead explained by attraction to the social and political freedoms available in northern cities.

The large gateway cities of New York, Chicago, Detroit, Philadelphia, and Los Angeles absorbed 60 percent of the black migrant flow to the North, with the remainder being widely distributed throughout the region's other metropolitan areas. By 1940, southern blacks could more than double their earnings by moving to the North. This estimate holds both in the full population and in comparisons of brothers, one of whom moved to the North while the other remained in the South. Upon arrival in the North, black migrants did not suffer an earnings penalty relative to northern-born blacks, but neither did they out-earn their northern-born counterparts (as some have suggested).

Southern in-migration doubled the size of the black workforce in the North from 1940 to 1970. Competition with southern blacks generated larger wage losses for existing black workers in the North than for similarly skilled whites; migration produced economic winners and losers within the black community. The winners included southern migrants themselves, while black workers in the North lost ground. Perhaps as a result, the welcome that black migrants received from the existing black community was at times halfhearted. Although black earnings were substantially higher in the North than in the South in 1940, subsequent black earnings *growth* was slower in the North, both in absolute terms and relative to white earnings. Slower earnings growth in the North can be partially explained by labor market competition from southern black migrants.

Intense competition between existing black workers and new migrant arrivals arose because of a lack of substitutability between similarly skilled black and white workers in the northern economy. This lack of substitutability can be attributed to actual differences in productivity driven by racial disparities in school quality and to discrimination in job assignments. Black workers, particularly those who were educated in the segregated South, attended schools that offered shorter school years and fewer resources per pupil. As a result, black workers who reported a certain number of years of schooling had fewer actual days of instruction than did similarly skilled whites. Furthermore, the hiring practices of some northern employers prevented many blacks from holding jobs for which they were otherwise qualified, especially in skilled crafts, retail and clerical work, and supervisory positions.

Beyond the labor market, black migrant arrivals also had profound effects on northern cities. In 1940, black communities in the North were small, and majority-black neighborhoods were few in number. By 1970, the black population share in northern cities had quadrupled, and the typical black resident lived in a neighborhood that was 75 percent black. During this period, many white households left central cities for the suburban ring. White departures from the city were, in part, a reaction to black in-migration.

Using variation in the timing of black in-migration to the seventy largest cities in the North and West, I have been able to distinguish white flight from other causes of suburbanization. Correlations suggest that each black arrival was associated with more than two white departures from the central city, leading to net population decline. By my most conservative estimate, white flight in response to black in-migration from the South can explain a quarter of population loss from central cities in the mid-twentieth century. This relationship also holds when accounting for the potentially non-random locations of black migrants by using southern agricultural change to generate an instrumental variable for black in-migration to northern cities.

Whites left central cities in response to black in-migration for many reasons. Any population inflow to a city can raise housing prices and rents, prompting some residents to seek more affordable housing options elsewhere. At most, this housing market channel would generate a one-for-one departure rate. Other white departures can be explained by a desire to avoid interactions with black neighbors. Yet the typical white household lived more than three miles away from a black enclave in a neighborhood at little risk of racial turnover. These distant households relocated to the suburbs to escape changes in municipal policy, including rising property tax rates and shifting spending priorities, as the city electorate became poorer and more racially diverse over time.

To document the role of these fiscal/political concerns, I compared the trajectory of housing prices in adjacent neighborhoods separated by a municipal border. In each of these pairs, one neighborhood is located within the city limits and the other is just across the border in the suburbs. The housing stock and local attributes of these neighborhoods were virtually identical, but residents on either side of the municipal border had access to a different bundle of public goods. The price premium associated with suburban units increased at the border as the black population share rose in the city, primarily as a result of the lower income levels (rather than the racial identity) of these new arrivals. Race itself began to matter more in the 1970s when some cities in the sample fell under court order to desegregate their public schools. Be-fore mandated desegregation, residential patterns ensured that the typical white student in the central city attended a predominantly white school; after these plans were put in place, the exposure of white students in the city to black peers increased. These patterns suggest that a portion of the decline in the demand for city residence with black in-migration was due to fiscal/political changes at the citywide level.

TRENDS AFTER 1970
Black Migration after 1970

The decades of black out-migration from the South have been followed more recently by substantial black mobility to the South from the rest of the country. These new black migrants join a nationwide flow of mi-grants to Sunbelt cities, but the rate of black migration to the South outpaces the national average. By 2010, 21 percent of blacks born out-side the region lived in the South, compared with only 14 percent of northern-born whites. Many recent black migrants to the South were attracted to the Sunbelt for its employment opportunities and low housing costs (Glaeser and Tobio 2008). Others were drawn by a con-nection to southern culture that, despite the region's long history of racial oppression, also tended to embrace black contributions.[1] Today the South has a higher black population share and lower levels of racial residential segregation than the rest of the country. In 2010, 19 percent of the southern population was black, compared to 9 percent of the North and West. Of the nation's ten largest metropolitan areas, the five in the South, including Atlanta and Houston, were far less segregated than the five in the North, with an average dissimilarity index of 53 in the South and 63 in the North (Glaeser and Vigdor 2012).[2]

Many black families have been in northern cities for only a genera-tion or two. With weak ties to the North, the personal cost of moving back to the South may have been low. Yet the higher rates of black mi-gration to the South cannot be explained by black "return" to the south-ern homes of their parents or grandparents. Black newcomers to the South live in a very different set of states than did previous generations of southern black residents. For example, in 1940, the cotton states of

[1] In contrast, the North prided itself on being racially progressive but was often hos-tile to black arrivals (Sokol 2014).

[2] See Cutler, Glaeser, and Vigdor 1999, Table 1 for measures of the dissimilarity index by region throughout the twentieth century.

Mississippi and Alabama were home to 22 percent of the southern black population, compared to only 7 percent of black migrants living in the South in 2010. Instead, 28 percent of new black southerners live in the fast-growing states of Texas and Florida, particularly in the big cities of Houston, Dallas, and Orlando. Most new migrants to the South live in large cities; this was not the case for the black population earlier in the century. For example, 50 percent of new black migrants to Georgia and the Carolinas live in Atlanta and Charlotte today, cities that housed only 7 percent of the black population of these states in 1940.

Alongside shifts in regional migration patterns, the national black population has also been augmented by immigration from abroad. Following a relaxation of immigration quotas after 1965, the foreign-born share of the black population rose from 2 percent in 1970 to 9 percent in 2010.[3] Jamaica, Haiti, and Nigeria contribute the largest numbers of black immigrants. These new arrivals are particularly concentrated in New England and the mid-Atlantic states. Twenty-one percent of the black population in these regions was foreign born in 2010, compared with 1.7 percent in the Deep South and 3.3 percent in the Midwest.[4]

Black-White Earnings Convergence after 1970

Nationwide, a substantial amount of the earnings convergence between blacks and whites took place between 1940 and 1975. Yet the majority of the relative improvements in black earnings in this period occurred in the South or can be attributed to migration from the low-wage South to the higher-wage North. The North itself experienced little change in the black-to-white wage ratio in the mid-twentieth century. A portion of the stagnation in relative black earnings in the North after 1940 can be attributed to competition with southern migrant arrivals. Yet relative black earnings in the North did not rebound after black in-migration from the South tapered off in the 1970s. In fact, if anything, black men in the North fell further behind white men from 1975 to 1990, erasing whatever small gains they had achieved since 1940 (see Figure 3.3 on page 84).[5]

[3] The share of foreign born increased from 5 percent in 1970 to 14 percent in 2010 in the full population.

[4] I refer to states in the east south-central region as the Deep South and to states in the east north-central region as the Midwest.

[5] The period 1975–90 was also an era of earnings stagnation in the South, both for whites and for blacks, putting racial earnings convergence temporarily on hold (although not reversing any gains). Convergence in the South picked up again in the 1990s. Today, the earnings gap between blacks and whites is virtually identical in the North and the South.

If the only change in the northern labor market after 1975 had been the ending of black in-migration, we might have expected black earnings to recover the losses associated with stiff labor market competition. However, the years after 1970 were also characterized by severe declines in labor demand in manufacturing. The Midwest and parts of the mid-Atlantic were particularly hard hit by this manufacturing decline. Bound and Freeman (1992) show that black workers in the North were concentrated in manufacturing industries that experienced falling wages during this period. Even within these industries, blacks tended to hold occupations with low and declining pay.

The decline in manufacturing employment after 1975 was a global phenomenon, driven by forces far beyond race relations in northern cities. Yet the resulting wage stagnation for lower-skilled workers was stronger in the United States than in many other countries, suggesting that there may have been a "path not taken" of more government involvement in the retraining of the workforce or direct support of manufacturing. The political decision to let Rust Belt cities languish as industry left the North may have been different if the affected population had not been urban, working class, and often black.[6]

Other factors that are often invoked to explain poor black economic performance cannot account for the especially slow pace of black earnings growth in the North after 1975, either because they are national in scope (migration from Latin America, rising incarceration) or because they fail to match the timing of the earnings slowdown (declining skills, racism in the workplace). The rate of immigration to the United States accelerated after 1975, but immigrants moved in roughly equal proportion to the North and the South. In 2010, 14 percent of the northern population was foreign born, only slightly higher than the immigrant share in the South (11 percent).[7] Using the methods outlined in chapter 3, Borjas, Grogger, and Hanson (2010) estimate that immigrant arrivals can account for one-third of the decline in the wages of black high school dropouts from 1980 to 2000 at the *national* level.

A recent deceleration of racial convergence of cognitive skills does not match the timing of the widening earnings gap between blacks and

[6] On the role of race in shaping the American welfare state, see, for example, Alesina, Glaeser, and Sacerdote 2001.

[7] Some northern states had large concentrations of black immigrants from Africa and the Caribbean, who may have been particularly competitive with native-born black workers. Yet at the same time, black workers in the South had to contend with large reverse flows of black migrants from the North.

whites after 1975. The reading and math test scores of black and white students converged through the late 1980s (Neal 2006). Although this skill convergence stopped by 1990, students in these later cohorts would not have entered the labor force until 1995.[8] Furthermore, the striking rise in black single motherhood in the late 1960s may contribute to the slowing of black skill development today but cannot explain wage stagnation in the 1970s and 1980s (Ruggles 1997).

The rise in mass incarceration after 1975 better fits the timing of the growing wage gap between blacks and whites, but the number of incarcerated black men is not large enough to drive general wage trends. Black male incarceration increased sevenfold from 1975 to 2000 while the white incarceration rate held steady.[9] By 2000, 17 percent of black men between the ages of eighteen and sixty-five either were currently incarcerated or had spent some time in prison (Bonczar 2003; Pew Charitable Trusts 2010). Not surprisingly, spending time in prison is associated with weakened employment opportunities and lower wages (Pager 2003; Mueller-Smith 2015). Although there is a strong association between prison time and wages at the individual level, Western (2002) has shown in a wage decomposition that the share of the black population that has been incarcerated is too low to explain much of the current wage gap between blacks and whites.

Finally, it is unlikely that the growth in the earnings gap between 1975 and 1990 was due to a rise in labor market discrimination in the North; if anything, labor market discrimination has been falling over time (Darity and Mason 1998). However, enduring discrimination could certainly help explain why the racial earnings gap has yet to reach parity. Recent experimental studies suggest that otherwise identical black job seekers are less likely than white job seekers to receive callback interviews (Bertrand and Mullainathan 2004; Pager, Western, and Bonikowski 2009). Moss and Tilly (2001, 4) interviewed a series of employers in large labor markets and found that differences in employment opportunities by race are primarily driven by stereotypes associated with black workers rather than direct antipathy toward blacks. "Not one employer told us 'I don't like blacks,'" they write, "but many,

[8] Consistent with the regional patterns in earnings convergence, the narrowing of the black-white skill gap in the 1980s was concentrated in the South (Chay, Guryan, and Mazumder 2009).

[9] Annual black prison admissions rates increased from one per 1,000 individuals in 1975 to seven per 1,000 by the late 1990s (Oliver 2001).

many managers made statements like 'blacks are less reliable' or 'immigrants work harder.'"

Residential Patterns in Metropolitan Areas since 1970

The growth of the suburbs in the mid-twentieth century was augmented by white flight from black in-migration to central cities. Yet despite the ending of black in-migration to central cities, suburbanization continued after 1970, albeit at a slower pace. The share of the metropolitan population living in a suburb increased from 56 percent in 1970 to 68 percent in 2010.[10] The suburban housing stock, public schools, and other amenities built in the heyday of suburban expansion continue to draw people to the suburbs today.

Contrary to recent media reports, urban revival is only evident in a short list of coastal cities (like New York and San Francisco) with high-end industry and a well-educated population. Of the fifty-six large cities in the United States studied by Rappaport (2003), only twelve experienced a population turnaround in the 1980s or 1990s.[11] The redevelopment of downtown areas for residential use has also been slow, until very recently (Couture and Handbury, 2015). Birch (2002) studied forty-five downtown cores, only eleven of which had population growth of any note in the 1980s or 1990s. An even smaller number (five of the eleven) were Rust Belt cities where active attempts at revitalization may have facilitated a downtown revival.

Even if overall city population is stagnant, it is often reported that gentrifying city neighborhoods are attracting a new type of well-to-do resident. A common refrain in the media is that there are now more poor people living in suburbs than in cities.[12] However, this is hardly surprising given that the suburbs have grown so large that they now contain more of *everything* in a metropolitan area (including poor people). More relevant is the *share* of city and suburban residents who are

[10] Writing in *The Atlantic*, Leinberger (2008) declared that "for 60 years, Americans have pushed steadily into the suburbs . . . but today the pendulum is swinging back toward urban living." Ehrenhalt (2008) agreed in *The New Republic* but argued that "the crucial issue is not the number of people living downtown . . . [but rather] who they are" (i.e., rich, educated, and white).

[11] Although only 21 percent of cities experienced a rebound by this measure, 35 percent of *city residents* lived in one of these locations in 2010, suggesting that, on a population basis, the phenomenon of urban revival is more widespread. This figure is driven by New York City and Chicago, two of the nation's most populous cities.

[12] For examples, see Dreier 2004; McGirr 2012; Medina 2014; and Edsall 2015. All of these articles cite research from the Brookings Institution (e.g., Garr and Kneebone 2010).

in poverty, and, by this measure, there has been little change in the relative standing of cities over time. Cooke (2010) documents that city poverty held steady at 14 percent from 1989 to 2005, while suburban poverty in both the inner and outer rings remained stable at 6 percent.[13] The high urban poverty rate is, in part, due to continued departures of the non-poor.

Despite the continued suburbanization of the population, outflows from central cities in recent decades have not been associated with rising racial residential segregation. Instead, residential segregation in metropolitan areas peaked in 1970 and declined thereafter. Segregation at the metropolitan level, as measured by the dissimilarity between blacks and non-blacks, fell from an index value of 80 in 1970 to 55 in 2010 (Glaeser and Vigdor 2012; see also Logan and Stults 2011).[14] Today black households enjoy expanded access to the suburbs, with 47 percent of black metropolitan residents living in suburbs in 2010 (up from 20 percent in 1970).[15] This new avenue of black mobility has weakened the link between suburbanization and residential segregation.

CONCLUSION

In 1910, before the Great Black Migration to the North began, nearly the entire black population in the United States lived in the South, primarily in rural areas. The few blacks who lived in metropolitan areas were disproportionately concentrated in central cities. In 2010, after a century of black mobility, the distribution of the black population has shifted radically. More than 40 percent of the black population now lives outside of the South, and almost half of metropolitan blacks now live in the suburban ring.

When *An American Dilemma* was published in 1944, Gunnar Myrdal rightly pointed to the South as the main site of racial injustice in the United States and to migration from the South as one way to ameliorate

[13] Likewise, Madden (2003) shows that the gap in poverty rates between central cities and suburbs remained stable between 1970 and 1990.

[14] The figures are from Glaeser and Vigdor (2012), which emphasizes declines in segregation over time. Logan and Stults (2011) report similar numbers (a decline in average dissimilarity from 79 in 1970 to 59 in 2010) but instead emphasize that segregation levels remained high in 2010. The two reports differ somewhat in their details, including the definition of racial groups (black versus non-black, or black versus white); the number of urban areas included in the analysis; and the weighting of urban areas by population.

[15] Madden (2003) reports that from 1970 to 1990, black households moved both to inner-ring and outer-ring suburbs.

persistently low earnings in the black workforce. In 1940, prospective black migrants from the South could double their earnings by moving North; over the next three decades, more than four million southern blacks (40 percent of the 1940 population) chose to do so. Today the regional rankings are reversed. Racial disparities are widest in the Midwest, the area whose cities remain persistently segregated by race and which was hardest hit by the decline of American manufacturing. Migration has again emerged as a response to scant opportunity, only this time northern-born blacks are heading South in large numbers, reversing the path that their parents or grandparents blazed in the last century.

References

Aaronson, Daniel, and Bhashkar Mazumder. 2011. "The Impact of Rosenwald Schools on Black Achievement." *Journal of Political Economy* 119.5: 821–88.

Abramitzky, Ran, Leah Platt Boustan, and Katherine Eriksson. 2012. "Europe's Tired, Poor, Huddled Masses: Self-Selection and Economic Outcomes in the Age of Mass Migration." *American Economic Review* 102.5: 1832–56.

———. 2014. "A Nation of Immigrants: Assimilation and Economic Outcomes in the Age of Mass Migration." *Journal of Political Economy* 122.3: 467–506.

Alba, Richard D., and John R. Logan. 1993. "Minority Proximity to Whites in Suburbs: An Individual-Level Analysis of Segregation." *American Journal of Sociology* 98.6: 1388–1427.

Alesina, Alberto, Reza Baqir, and William Easterly. 1999. "Public Goods and Ethnic Divisions." *Quarterly Journal of Economics* 114.4: 1243–84.

Alesina, Alberto, Reza Baqir, and Caroline Hoxby. 2004. "Political Jurisdictions in Heterogeneous Communities." *Journal of Political Economy* 112.2: 348–96.

Alesina, Alberto, Edward Glaeser, and Bruce Sacerdote. 2001. "Why Doesn't the United States Have a European-Style Welfare State?" *Brookings Papers on Economic Activity* no. 2: 187–254.

Alexander, J. Trent. 1998. "The Great Migration in Comparative Perspective: Interpreting the Urban Origins of Southern Black Migrants to Depression-Era Pittsburgh." *Social Science History* 22.3: 349–76.

Alonso, William. 1964. *Location and Land Use: Toward a General Theory of Land Rent.* Cambridge, MA: Harvard University Press.

Alston, Lee J. 1981. "Tenure Choice in Southern Agriculture, 1930–1960." *Explorations in Economic History* 18.3: 211–32.

Alston, Lee J., and Joseph P. Ferrie. 1993. "Paternalism in Agricultural Labor Contracts in the US South: Implications for the Growth of the Welfare State." *American Economic Review* 83.4: 852–76.

———. 2005. "Time on the Ladder: Career Mobility in Agriculture, 1890–1938." *Journal of Economic History* 65.4: 1058–81.

Altonji, Joseph G., and Rebecca M. Blank. 1999. "Race and Gender in the Labor Market." In *Handbook of Labor Economics*, ed. Orley Ashenfelter and David Card, 3143–3259. Amsterdam: Elsevier.

Altonji, Joseph G., and David Card. 1991. "The Effects of Immigration on the Labor Market Outcomes of Less-Skilled Natives." In *Immigration, Trade and the Labor Market*, ed. John M. Abowd and Richard B. Freeman, 201–34. Chicago: University of Chicago Press.

Ananat, Elizabeth Oltmans. 2011. "The Wrong Side(s) of the Tracks: The Causal

Effects of Racial Segregation on Urban Poverty and Inequality." *American Economic Journal: Applied Economics* 3.2: 34–66.

Arrow, Kenneth J. 1971. "The Theory of Discrimination." Working Paper No. 403, Princeton University, Department of Economics, Industrial Relations Section.

Atack, Jeremy, Fred Bateman, and Mary Eschelbach Gregson. 1992. "'Matchmaker, Matchmaker, Make Me a Match': A General Personal Computer-Based Matching Program for Historical Research." *Historical Methods* 25.2: 53–65.

Austin, D. Andrew. 1999. "Politics vs. Economics: Evidence from Municipal Annexation." *Journal of Urban Economics* 45.3: 501–32.

Bailey, Amy Kate, Stewart E. Tolnay, E. M. Beck, and Jennifer D. Laird. 2011. "Targeting Lynch Victims Social Marginality or Status Transgressions?" *American Sociological Review* 76.3: 412–36.

Bailey, Martha J., and William J. Collins. 2006. "The Wage Gains of African-American Women in the 1940s." *Journal of Economic History* 66.3: 737–77.

Baldwin, Davarian L. 2007. *Chicago's New Negroes: Modernity, the Great Migration, and Black Urban Life*. Chapel Hill: University of North Carolina Press.

Bandiera, Oriana, Imran Rasul, and Martina Viarengo. 2013. "The Making of Modern America: Migratory Flows in the Age of Mass Migration." *Journal of Development Economics* 102.1: 23–47.

Barrow, Lisa, and Cecilia Elena Rouse. 2004. "Using Market Valuation to Assess Public School Spending." *Journal of Public Economics* 88.9: 1747–69.

Barry, John M. 2007. *Rising Tide: The Great Mississippi Flood of 1927 and How It Changed America*. New York: Simon and Schuster.

Baum-Snow, Nathaniel. 2007. "Did Highways Cause Suburbanization?" *Quarterly Journal of Economics* 122.2: 775–805.

———. 2010. "Changes in Transportation Infrastructure and Commuting Patterns in U.S. Metropolitan Areas, 1960–2000." *American Economic Review* 100.2: 378–82.

Baum-Snow, Nathaniel, and Byron F. Lutz. 2011. "School Desegregation, School Choice, and Changes in Residential Location Patterns by Race." *American Economic Review* 101.7: 3019–46.

Bazzi, Samuel, Arya Gaduh, Alexander Rothenberg, and Maisy Wong. 2014. "Skill Transferability, Migration and Development: Evidence from Population Resettlement in Indonesia." Manuscript.

Beaman, Lori A. 2012. "Social Networks and the Dynamics of Labour Market Outcomes: Evidence from Refugees Resettled in the U.S." *Review of Economic Studies* 79.1: 128–61.

Becker, Gary S. 1957. *The Economics of Discrimination*. Chicago: University of Chicago Press.

Bennett, Michael J. 1996. *When Dreams Came True: The GI Bill and the Making of Modern America*. Washington, DC: Brassey's.

Berlin, Ira. 2010. *The Making of African America: The Four Great Migrations*. New York: Penguin.

Berry, Chad. 2000. *Southern Migrants, Northern Exiles*. Champaign: University of Illinois Press.

Bertrand, Marianne, and Sendhil Mullainathan. 2004. "Are Emily and Greg More Employable than Lakisha and Jamal? A Field Experiment on Labor Market Discrimination." *American Economic Review* 94.4: 991–1013.

Birch, Eugenie Ladner. 2002. "Having a Longer View on Downtown Living." *Journal of the American Planning Association* 68.1: 5–21.

Black, Dan A., Seth G. Sanders, Evan J. Taylor, and Lowell J. Taylor. 2015. "The Impact of the Great Migration on Mortality of African Americans: Evidence from the Deep South." *American Economic Review* 105.2: 477–503.

Black, Sandra E. 1999. "Do Better Schools Matter? Parental Valuation of Elementary Education." *Quarterly Journal of Economics* 114.2: 577–99.

Black, Timuel D. 2003. *Bridges of Memory: Chicago's First Wave of Black Migration.* Vol. 1. Evanston, IL: Northwestern University Press.

Blackmon, Douglas A. 2008. *Slavery by Another Name: The Re-Enslavement of Black Americans from the Civil War to World War II.* New York: Doubleday.

Blair, Peter Q. 2014. "The Effect of Outside Options on Neighborhood Tipping Points." Manuscript.

Bodnar, John, Roger Simon, and Michael P. Weber. 1982. *Lives of Their Own: Blacks, Italians, and Poles in Pittsburgh, 1900–1960.* Champaign: University of Illinois Press.

Bogart, William T., and Brian A. Cromwell. 2000. "How Much Is a Neighborhood School Worth?" *Journal of Urban Economics* 47.2: 280–305.

Bogue, Donald Joseph. 1953. *Population Growth in Standard Metropolitan Areas, 1900–1950: With an Explanatory Analysis of Urbanized Areas.* Vol. 1. Housing and Home Finance Agency, Division of Housing Research. Washington, DC: U.S. GPO.

Bonastia, Christopher. 2010. *Knocking on the Door: The Federal Government's Attempt to Desegregate the Suburbs.* Princeton: Princeton University Press.

Bonczar, Thomas. 2003. "Prevalence of Imprisonment in the U.S. Population, 1974–2001." Bureau of Justice Statistics Special Report. NCJ 197976. Washington, DC: U.S. Department of Justice.

Borjas, George J. 1985. "Assimilation, Changes in Cohort Quality, and the Earnings of Immigrants." *Journal of Labor Economics* 3.4: 463–89.

———. 1987a. "Immigrants, Minorities, and Labor Market Competition." *Industrial and Labor Relations Review* 40.3: 382–92.

———. 1987b. "Self-Selection and the Earnings of Immigrants." *American Economic Review* 77.4: 531–53.

———. 2003. "The Labor Demand Curve *Is* Downward Sloping: Reexamining the Impact of Immigration on the Labor Market." *Quarterly Journal of Economics* 118.4: 1335–74.

Borjas, George, Jeffrey Grogger, and Gordon Hanson. 2008. "Imperfect Substitution between Immigrants and Natives: A Reappraisal." NBER Working Paper w13887.

———. 2010. "Immigration and the Economic Status of African-American Men." *Economica* 77: 255–82.

Bound, John, and Richard B. Freeman. 1992. "What Went Wrong? The Erosion of Relative Earnings and Employment among Black Men in the 1980s." *Quarterly Journal of Economics* 107.1: 201–32.

Boustan, Leah Platt. 2009. "Competition in the Promised Land: Black Migration and Northern Labor Markets, 1940–1970." *Journal of Economic History* 69.3: 756–83.

———. 2010. "Was Postwar Suburbanization 'White Flight'? Evidence from the Black Migration." *Quarterly Journal of Economics* 125.1: 417–43.

———. 2012. "School Desegregation and Urban Change: Evidence from City Boundaries." *American Economic Journal: Applied Economics* 4.1: 85–108.

———. 2013. "Local Public Goods and the Demand for High-Income Municipalities." *Journal of Urban Economics* 76: 71–82.

Boustan, Leah Platt, and William J. Collins. 2014. "The Origin and Persistence of Black-White Differences in Women's Labor Force Participation." In *Human Capital in History: The American Record*, ed. Leah Platt Boustan, Carola Frydman, and Robert A. Margo, 205–40. Chicago: University of Chicago Press.

Boustan, Leah Platt, and Robert A. Margo. 2009. "Job Decentralization and Postwar Suburbanization: Evidence from State Capitals." *Brookings-Wharton Papers on Urban Affairs* 1–20.

———. 2013. "A Silver Lining to White Flight? White Suburbanization and African-American Homeownership, 1940–80." *Journal of Urban Economics* 78: 71–80.

Boustan, Leah Platt, and Allison Shertzer. 2013. "Population Trends as a Counterweight to Central City Decline." *Demography* 50.1: 125–47.

Bowles, Gladys K., James D. Tarver, Calvin L. Beale, and Everett S. Lee. 1990. "Net Migration of the Population by Age, Sex, and Race, 1950–1970." ICPSR Study No. 8493. Ann Arbor, MI: Inter-University Consortium for Political and Social Research [computer file].

Bowles, Samuel. 1970. "Migration as Investment: Empirical Tests of the Human Investment Approach to Geographical Mobility." *Review of Economics and Statistics* 52.4: 356–62.

Boyd, Robert L. 1996. "Demographic Change and Entrepreneurial Occupations: African Americans in Northern Cities." *American Journal of Economics and Sociology* 55.2: 129–43.

———. 1998a. "The Storefront Church Ministry in African American Communities of the Urban North during the Great Migration: The Making of an Ethnic Niche." *Social Science Journal* 35.3: 319–32.

———. 1998b. "Residential Segregation by Race and the Black Merchants of Northern Cities during the Early Twentieth Century." *Sociological Forum* 13.4: 595–609.

Bradford, David F., and Harry H. Kelejian. 1973. "An Econometric Model of the Flight to the Suburbs." *Journal of Political Economy* 81.3: 566–89.

Broom, Leonard, and Norval D. Glenn. 1965. *Transformation of the Negro American*. New York: Harper and Row.

Brown, Claude. 1965. *Manchild in the Promised Land*. New York: Macmillan.

Bruch, Elizabeth E., and Robert D. Mare. 2006. "Neighborhood Choice and Neighborhood Change." *American Journal of Sociology* 112.3: 667–709.

Camic, Charles, and Yu Xie. 1994. "The Statistical Turn in American Social Science: Columbia University, 1890 to 1915." *American Sociological Review* 59.5: 773–805.

Campbell, Angus, and Howard Schuman. 1997. *Racial Attitudes in Fifteen American Cities, 1968.* ICPSR Study No. 3500-v2. Ann Arbor, MI: Inter-university Consortium for Political and Social Research [computer file].

Card, David. 2001. "Immigrant Inflows, Native Outflows, and the Local Market Impacts of Higher Immigration." *Journal of Labor Economics* 19.1: 22–64.

———. 2009. "Immigration and Inequality." *American Economic Review* 99.2: 1–21.

Card, David, and Alan Krueger. 1992. "School Quality and Black-White Relative Earnings: A Direct Assessment." *Quarterly Journal of Economics* 107.1: 151–200.

Card, David, and Thomas Lemieux. 1996. "Wage Dispersion, Returns to Skill, and Black-White Wage Differentials." *Journal of Econometrics* 74.2: 319–61.

———. 2001. "Can Falling Supply Explain the Rising Return to College for Younger Men? A Cohort-Based Analysis." *Quarterly Journal of Economics* 116.2: 705–46.

Card, David, Alexandre Mas, and Jesse Rothstein. 2008. "Tipping and the Dynamics of Segregation." *Quarterly Journal of Economics* 123.1: 177–218.

Carrington, William J., Enrica Detragiache, and Tara Vishwanath. 1996. "Migration with Endogenous Moving Costs." *American Economic Review* 86.4: 909–30.

Carruthers, Celeste K., and Marianne H. Wanamaker. 2014. "Separate and Unequal in the Labor Market: Human Capital and the Jim Crow Wage Gap." Manuscript.

Carter, Dan T. 2000. *The Politics of Rage: George Wallace, the Origins of the New Conservatism, and the Transformation of American Politics.* Baton Rouge: Louisiana State University Press.

Carter, Susan, and Matthew Sobek. 2006. "Employment, by Industry." In *Historical Statistics of the United States: Millennial Edition*, vol. 1, ed. Susan B. Carter, Scott Sigmund Gartner, Michael R. Haines, Alan L. Olmstead, Richard Sutch, and Gavin Wright, 489–94. New York: Cambridge University Press.

Cascio, Elizabeth, Nora Gordon, Ethan Lewis, and Sarah Reber. 2010. "Paying for Progress: Conditional Grants and the Desegregation of the South." *Quarterly Journal of Economics* 125.1: 445–82.

Chandra, Amitabh. 2003. "Is the Convergence in the Racial Wage Gap Illusory?" NBER Working Paper w9476.

Charles, Kerwin, and Erik Hurst. 2002. "The Transition to Home Ownership and the Black-White Wealth Gap." *Review of Economics and Statistics* 84.2: 281–97.

Chay, Kenneth Y. 1998. "The Impact of Federal Civil Rights Policy on Black Economic Progress: Evidence from the Equal Employment Opportunity Act of 1972." *Industrial and Labor Relations Review* 51.4: 608–32.

Chay, Kenneth Y., and Michael Greenstone. 2005. "Does Air Quality Matter?: Evidence from the Housing Market." *Journal of Political Economy* 113.2: 376–424.

Chay, Kenneth Y., Jonathan Guryan, and Bhashkar Mazumder. 2009. "Birth Cohort and the Black-White Achievement Gap: The Roles of Access and Health Soon after Birth." NBER Working Paper w15078.

Chay, Kenneth Y., and Kaivan Munshi. 2013. "Black Mobilization after Emancipation: Evidence from Reconstruction and the Great Migration." Manuscript.

Chicago Commission on Race. 1922. *The Negro in Chicago: A Study of Race Relations and a Race Riot*. Chicago: University of Chicago Press.

Chiswick, Barry. 1978. "The Effect of Americanization on the Earnings of Foreign-born Men." *Journal of Political Economy* 86.5: 897–921.

Christian, Cornelius. 2014. "Lynchings, Labour and Cotton in the US South." Manuscript.

Clotfelter, Charles T. 1975. "The Effect of School Desegregation on Housing Prices." *Review of Economics and Statistics* 57.4: 446–451.

———. 2011. *After Brown: The Rise and Retreat of School Desegregation*. Princeton: Princeton University Press.

Clubb, Jerome M., William H. Flanigan, and Nancy H. Zingale. 2006. "Electoral Data for Counties in the United States: Presidential and Congressional Races, 1840–1972." ICPSR Study No. 8611. Ann Arbor, MI: Inter-university Consortium for Political and Social Research [computer file].

Coates, Ta-Nehisi. 2014. "The Case for Reparations." *Atlantic Monthly*, June.

Cobb, James C. 1992. *The Most Southern Place on Earth: The Mississippi Delta and the Roots of Regional Identity*. New York: Oxford University Press, 1992.

Cohen, William. 1991. *At Freedom's Edge: Black Mobility and the Southern White Quest for Racial Control, 1861–1915*. Baton Rouge: Louisiana State University Press.

Coles, Robert. 1971. *Children of Crisis: The South Goes North*. Vol. 3. New York: Little, Brown.

Collins, William J. 1997. "When the Tide Turned: Immigration and the Delay of the Great Black Migration." *Journal of Economic History* 57.3: 607–32.

———. 2000. "African-American Economic Mobility in the 1940s: A Portrait from the Palmer Survey." *Journal of Economic History* 60.3: 756–81.

———. 2001. "Race, Roosevelt, and Wartime Production: Fair Employment in World War II Labor Markets." *American Economic Review* 91.1: 272–86.

———. 2003. "The Political Economy of State-Level Fair Employment Laws, 1940–1964." *Explorations in Economic History* 40.1: 24–51.

———. 2004. "The Housing Market Impact of State-Level Anti-Discrimination Laws, 1960–1970." *Journal of Urban Economics* 55.3: 534–64.

———. 2007. "Education, Migration, and Regional Wage Convergence in U.S. History." In *The New Comparative Economic History: Essays in Honor of Jeffrey G. Williamson*, ed. Timothy J. Hatton, Kevin H. O'Rourke, and Alan M. Taylor, 165–92. Cambridge, MA: MIT Press.

Collins, William J., and Robert A. Margo. 2000. "Residential Segregation and Socioeconomic Outcomes: When Did Ghettos Go Bad?" *Economics Letters* 69.2: 239–43.

———. 2003. "Race and the Value of Owner-Occupied Housing, 1940–1990." *Regional Science and Urban Economics* 33.3: 255–86.

———. 2006. "Historical Perspectives on Racial Differences in Schooling in the United States." In *Handbook of the Economics of Education Volume 1*, ed. Eric A. Hanushek and Finis Welch, 107–54. Amsterdam: Elsevier.

———. 2007. "The Economic Aftermath of the 1960s Riots: Evidence from Property Values." *Journal of Economic History* 67.4: 849–83.

———. 2011. "Race and Homeownership from the Civil War to the Present." *American Economic Review* 101.3: 355–59.

Collins, William J., and Marianne H. Wanamaker. 2014. "Selection and Economic Gains in the Great Migration of African Americans: New Evidence from Linked Census Data." *American Economic Journal: Applied Economics* 6.1: 220–252.

———. 2015a. "The Great Migration in Black and White: New Evidence on the Geographic Mobility of American Southerners." Manuscript.

———. 2015b. "Up from Slavery? Intergenerational Mobility in the Shadow of Jim Crow." Manuscript.

Cooke, Thomas J. 2010. "Residential Mobility of the Poor and the Growth of Poverty in Inner-Ring Suburbs." *Urban Geography* 31.2: 179–93.

Cortes, Patricia. 2008. "The Effect of Low-Skilled Immigration on U.S. Prices: Evidence from CPI Data." *Journal of Political Economy* 116.3: 381–422.

Costa, Dora L. 2004. "Race and Older Age Mortality: Evidence from Union Army Veterans." NBER Working Paper w10902.

Couture, Victor, and Jessie Handbury. 2015. "Urban Revival in America, 2000 to 2010." Manuscript.

Crespino, Joseph. 2007. *In Search of Another Country: Mississippi and the Conservative Counterrevolution*. Princeton: Princeton University Press.

Crowder, Kyle, and Scott J. South. 2008. "Spatial Dynamics of White Flight: The Effects of Local and Extralocal Racial Conditions on Neighborhood Out-Migration." *American Sociological Review* 73.5: 792–812.

Cullen, Julie Berry, and Steven D. Levitt. 1999. "Crime, Urban Flight, and the Consequences for Cities." *Review of Economics and Statistics* 81.2: 159–69.

Currie, Janet, and Joseph Ferrie. 2000. "The Law and Labor Strife in the United States, 1881–1894." *Journal of Economic History* 60.1: 42–66.

Cutler, David M., and Edward L. Glaeser. 1997. "Are Ghettos Good or Bad?" *Quarterly Journal of Economics* 112.3: 827–72.

Cutler, David M., Edward L. Glaeser, and Jacob Vigdor. 1999. "The Rise and Decline of the American Ghetto." *Journal of Political Economy* 107.3: 455–506.

———. 2008. "Is the Melting Pot Still Hot? Explaining the Resurgence of Immigrant Segregation." *Review of Economics and Statistics* 90.3: 478–97.

Dahlberg, Matz, Karin Edmark, and Heléne Lundqvist. 2012. "Ethnic Diversity and Preferences for Redistribution." *Journal of Political Economy* 120.1: 41–76.

Darity, William A., and Patrick L. Mason. 1998. "Evidence on Discrimination in Employment: Codes of Color, Codes of Gender." *Journal of Economic Perspectives* 12.2: 63–90.

Dean, John P. 1947. "Only Caucasian: A Study of Race Covenants." *Journal of Land & Public Utility Economics* 23.4: 428–32.

"Desegregation Court Cases and School Demographic Data." Brown University. http://www.s4.brown.edu/schoolsegregation/desegregationdata.htm.

Dietz, Robert D., and Donald R. Haurin. 2003. "The Social and Private Micro-level Consequences of Homeownership." *Journal of Urban Economics* 54.3: 401–50.

Donohue, John J., and James Heckman. 1991. "Continuous versus Episodic Change: The Impact of Civil Rights Policy on the Economic Status of Blacks." *Journal of Economic Literature* 29.4: 1603–43.

Dorn, David. 2010. "Price and Prejudice: The Interaction between Preferences and Incentives in the Dynamics of Racial Segregation." Manuscript.

Douglas, Paul. 1919. "Is the New Immigration More Unskilled than the Old?" *Quarterly Publications of the American Statistical Association* 16.126: 393–403.

Drake, St. Clair, and Horace R. Cayton. (1945) 1962. *Black Metropolis: A Study of Negro Life in a Northern City*. New York: Harper and Row.

Dreier, Peter. 2004. "Poverty in the Suburbs." *The Nation*, September 2.

Du Bois, William E. B. 1923. "The Hosts of Black Labor." *The Nation*, May 9.

Dye, Thomas R. 1964. "Urban Political Integration: Conditions Associated with Annexation in American Cities." *Midwest Journal of Political Science* 8.4: 430–46.

Edsall, Thomas B. 2015. "The Gentrification Effect." *New York Times*, February 25.

Ehrenhalt, Alan. 2008. "Trading Places." *New Republic*, August 13.

Eichenlaub, Suzanne C., Stewart E. Tolnay, and J. Trent Alexander. 2010. "Moving Out but Not Up: Economic Outcomes in the Great Migration." *American Sociological Review* 75.1: 101–25.

Eisinger, Peter K. 1982. "Black Employment in Municipal Jobs: The Impact of Black Political Power." *American Political Science Review* 76.2: 380–92.

Ellen, Ingrid Gould. 2000. *Sharing America's Neighborhoods*. Cambridge, MA: Harvard University Press.

Ellen, Ingrid Gould, and Katherine O'Regan. 2010. "Crime and Urban Flight Revisited: The Effect of the 1990s Drop in Crime on Cities." *Journal of Urban Economics* 68.3: 247–59.

Ellickson, Bryan. 1971. "Jurisdictional Fragmentation and Residential Choice." *American Economic Review* 61.2: 334–39.

Emerson, Michael O., Karen J. Chai, and George Yancey. 2001. "Does Race Matter in Residential Segregation? Exploring the Preferences of White Americans." *American Sociological Review* 66.6: 922–35.

Epple, Dennis, and Glenn J. Platt. 1998. "Equilibrium and Local Redistribution in an Urban Economy When Households Differ in Both Preferences and Incomes." *Journal of Urban Economics* 43.1: 23–51.

Epple, Dennis, and Thomas Romer. 1991. "Mobility and Redistribution." *Journal of Political Economy* 99.4: 828–58.

Epstein, Abraham. 1918. *The Negro Migrant in Pittsburgh*. Pittsburgh: University of Pittsburgh Press.

Eriksson, Katherine, and Gregory Niemesh. 2015. "The Impact of Migration on Infant Health: Evidence from the Great Migration." Manuscript.

Farley, Reynolds, Howard Schuman, Suzanne Bianchi, Diane Colasanto, and

Shirley Hatchett. 1978. "'Chocolate City, Vanilla Suburbs:' Will the Trend toward Racially Separate Communities Continue?" *Social Science Research* 7.4: 319–44.

Farley, Reynolds, Charlotte Steeh, Maria Krysan, Tara Jackson, and Keith Reeves. 1994. "Stereotypes and Segregation: Neighborhoods in the Detroit Area." *American Journal of Sociology* 100.3: 750–80.

Faulkner, Audrey Olsen, Marsel A. Heisel, Wendell Holbrook, and Shirley Geismar. 1982. *When I Was Comin' Up: An Oral History of Aged Blacks.* North Haven, CT: Archon Press.

Fernandez, Raquel, and Richard Rogerson. 1996. "Income Distribution, Communities, and the Quality of Public Education." *Quarterly Journal of Economics* 111.1: 135–64.

Ferrie, Joseph. 1996. "A New Sample of Males Linked from the Public Use Micro Sample of the 1850 U.S. Federal Census of Population to the 1860 U.S. Federal Census Manuscript Schedules." *Historical Methods* 29.4: 141–56.

———. 2006. "Internal Migration." In *Historical Statistics of the United States: Millennial Edition*, vol. 1, ed. Susan B. Carter, Scott Sigmund Gartner, Michael R. Haines, Alan L. Olmstead, Richard Sutch, and Gavin Wright, 489–94. New York: Cambridge University Press.

Ferrie, Joseph, and Jason Long. 2013. "Intergenerational Occupational Mobility in Great Britain and the United States since 1850." *American Economic Review* 103.4: 1109–37.

Fetter, Daniel K. 2013. "How Do Mortgage Subsidies Affect Home Ownership? Evidence from the Mid-Century GI Bills." *American Economic Journal: Economic Policy* 5.2: 111–47.

Figlio, David N., and Maurice E. Lucas. 2004. "What's in a Grade? School Report Cards and the Housing Market." *American Economic Review* 94.3: 591–604.

Fischer, Claude S., Gretchen Stockmayer, Jon Stiles, and Michael Hout. 2004. "Distinguishing the Geographic Levels and Social Dimensions of U.S. Metropolitan Segregation, 1960–2000." *Demography* 41.1: 37–59.

Fishback, Price V. 1984. "Segregation in Job Hierarchies: West Virginia Coal Mining, 1906–1932." *Journal of Economic History* 44.3: 755–74.

Fishback, Price V., William C. Horrace, and Shawn Kantor. 2006. "The Impact of New Deal Expenditures on Mobility during the Great Depression." *Explorations in Economic History* 43.2: 179–222.

Fligstein, Neil. 1981. *Going North: Migration of Blacks and Whites from the South, 1900–1950.* New York: Academic Press.

Freund, David M. P. 2007. *Colored Property: State Policy and White Racial Politics in Suburban America.* Chicago: University of Chicago Press.

Fogel, Robert W. 1994. *Without Consent or Contract: The Rise and Fall of American Slavery.* New York: W. W. Norton.

Foner, Nancy, and George M. Fredrickson, eds. 2004. *Not Just Black and White: Historical and Contemporary Perspectives on Immigration, Race, and Ethnicity in the US.* New York: Russell Sage Foundation.

Foote, Andrew D. 2015. "Decomposing the Effect of Crime on Population Changes." *Demography* 52.2: 705–28.

Foote, Christopher, Gavin Wright, and Warren Whatley. 2003. "Arbitraging a Discriminatory Labor Market: Black Workers at the Ford Motor Company, 1918–1947." *Journal of Labor Economics* 21.3: 493–532.

Frazier, E. Franklin. 1939. *The Negro Family in the United States*. Chicago: University of Chicago Press.

Frey, William H. 1979. "Central City White Flight: Racial and Nonracial Causes." *American Sociological Review* 44.3: 425–48.

Gamm, Gerald H. 1999. *Urban Exodus: Why the Jews Left Boston and the Catholics Stayed*. Cambridge, MA: Harvard University Press.

Gardner, John. 2013. "The Great Migration and Wages in the Northern United States." Manuscript.

Gardner, John, and William S. Cohen. 1971. *County-level Demographic Characteristics of the Population of the United States, 1930–1950*. ICPSR Study No. 20. Ann Arbor, MI: Inter-University Consortium for Political and Social Research [computer file].

Garr, Emily, and Elizabeth Kneebone. 2010. "The Suburbanization of Poverty: Trends in Metropolitan America, 2000 to 2008." Metropolitan Opportunity Series. Washington, DC: The Brookings Institution.

Gibbons, Stephen, Stephen Machin, and Olmo Silva. 2013. "Valuing School Quality Using Boundary Discontinuities." *Journal of Urban Economics* 75: 15–28.

Gill, Flora. 1979. *Economics and the Black Exodus: An Analysis of Negro Emigration from the Southern United States: 1910–1970*. New York: Garland Publishing.

Glaeser, Edward L., and Joseph Gyourko. 2005. "Urban Decline and Durable Housing." *Journal of Political Economy* 113.2: 345–75.

Glaeser, Edward L., Matthew E. Kahn, and Jordan Rappaport. 2008. "Why Do the Poor Live in Cities?" *Journal of Urban Economics* 63.1: 1–24.

Glaeser, Edward L., and Kristina Tobio. 2008. "The Rise of the Sunbelt." *Southern Economic Journal* 74.3: 610–43.

Glaeser, Edward L., and Jacob L. Vigdor. 2001. *Racial Segregation in the 2000 Census: Promising News*. Washington, DC: Brookings Institution.

———. 2012. *The End of the Segregated Century: Racial Separation in America's Neighborhoods, 1890–2010*. New York: Manhattan Institute for Policy Research.

Glock, Judge. 2013. "The Power of Urban Politics and the Federal Housing Administration, 1934–1960." Manuscript.

Goldin, Claudia. 1992. *Understanding the Gender Gap: An Economic History of American Women*. New York: Oxford University Press.

———. 2014. "A Pollution Theory of Discrimination: Male and Female Differences in Occupations and Earnings." In *Human Capital in History: The American Record*, ed. Leah Platt Boustan, Carola Frydman, and Robert A. Margo, 313–54. Chicago: University of Chicago Press.

Goldin, Claudia, and Robert A. Margo. 1992. "The Great Compression: The U.S. Wage Structure at Mid-Century." *Quarterly Journal of Economics* 107.1: 1–34.

Gotham, Kevin Fox. 2002. *Race, Real Estate, and Uneven Development: The Kansas City Experience, 1900–2000*. Albany: SUNY Press.

Gould, John D. 1980. "European Inter-continental Emigration. The Road Home:

Return Migration from the USA." *Journal of European Economic History* 9.1: 41–112.

Greenstone, Michael, and Justin Gallagher. 2008. "Does Hazardous Waste Matter? Evidence from the Housing Market and the Superfund Program." *Quarterly Journal of Economics* 123.3: 951–1003.

Gregory, James N. 2005. *The Southern Diaspora: How the Great Migrations of Black and White Southerners Transformed America.* Chapel Hill: University of North Carolina Press.

Griffin, Farah Jasmine. 1995. *"Who Set You Flowin'?": The African-American Migration Narrative.* New York: Oxford University Press.

Grogger, Jeffrey. 1996. "Does School Quality Explain the Recent Black/White Wage Trend?" *Journal of Labor Economics* 14.2: 231–53.

Grogger, Jeffrey, and Gordon H. Hanson. 2011. "Income Maximization and the Selection and Sorting of International Migrants." *Journal of Development Economics* 95.1: 42–57.

Grove, Wayne A., and Craig Heinicke. 2003. "Better Opportunities or Worse? The Demise of Cotton Harvest Labor, 1949–1964." *Journal of Economic History* 63.3: 736–67.

———. 2005. "Labor Markets, Regional Diversity, and Cotton Harvest Mechanization in the Post–World War II United States." *Social Science History* 29.2: 269–97.

Grossman, James R. 1989. *Land of Hope: Chicago, Black Southerners, and the Great Migration.* Chicago: University of Chicago Press.

Gottlieb, Peter. 1987. *Making Their Own Way: Southern Blacks' Migration to Pittsburgh: 1916–30.* Champaign: University of Illinois Press.

Guryan, Jonathan. 2004. "Desegregation and Black Dropout Rates." *American Economic Review* 94.4: 919–43.

Guterbock, Thomas M. 1976. "The Push Hypothesis: Minority Presence, Crime, and Urban Deconcentration." In *The Changing Face of the Suburbs*, ed. Barry Schwartz, 137–61. Chicago: University of Chicago Press.

Gutmann, Myron P. 1997. "Great Plains Population and Environment Data: Agricultural Data, 1870–1997." ICPSR Study No. 4254. Ann Arbor, MI: Interuniversity Consortium for Political and Social Research [computer file].

Hall, Patricia Kelley, and Steven Ruggles. 2004. "'Restless in the Midst of Their Prosperity': New Evidence on the Internal Migration of Americans, 1850–2000." *Journal of American History* 91.3: 829–46.

Hamermesh, Daniel S. 1996. *Labor Demand.* Princeton: Princeton University Press.

Hamilton, Horace C. 1959. "Educational Selection of Net Migration from the South." *Social Forces* 38.1: 33–42.

Handlin, Oscar. 1959. *The Newcomers: Negroes and Puerto Ricans in a Changing Metropolis.* Cambridge, MA: Harvard University Press.

Hansberry, Lorraine. (1959) 1994. *A Raisin in the Sun.* New York: Vintage Books.

Hanson, Gordon H. 2006. "Illegal Migration from Mexico to the United States." *Journal of Economic Literature* 44.4: 869–924.

Hanushek, Eric A. 1996. "School Resources and Student Performance." In *Does Money Matter? The Effect of School Resources on Student Achievement and Adult*

Success, ed. Gary T. Burtless, 43–73. Washington, DC: Brookings Institution Press.

————. 1999. "The Evidence on Class Size." In *Earning and Learning: How Schools Matter*, ed. Susan E. Mayer and Paul E. Peterson, 131–68. Washington, DC: Brookings Institution Press.

Hanushek, Eric A., John F. Kain, and Steven G. Rivkin. 2009. "New Evidence about *Brown v. Board of Education*: The Complex Effects of School Racial Composition on Achievement." *Journal of Labor Economics* 27.3: 349–83.

Harris, David R. 1999. "'Property Values Drop When Blacks Move in, Because . . .': Racial and Socioeconomic Determinants of Neighborhood Desirability." *American Sociological Review* 64.3: 461–79.

Hatton, Timothy J., and Jeffrey G. Williamson, eds. 1994. *Migration and the International Labor Market, 1850–1939*. London: Routledge.

————. 1998. *The Age of Mass Migration: Causes and Economic Impact*. New York: Oxford University Press.

————. 2006. "International Migration in the Long-Run: Positive Selection, Negative Selection and Policy." In *Labor Mobility and the World Economy*, ed. Federico Foders and Rolf J. Langhammer, 1–34. Berlin: Springer.

Heller, Frederik. 2012. "The Code Hits 100." *RealtorMag*. http://realtormag .realtor.org/law-and-ethics/ethics/article/2012/11/code-hits-100.

Henderson, J.Vernon. 1985. "The Impact of Zoning Policies Which Regulate Housing Quality." *Journal of Urban Economics* 18.3: 302–12.

Henri, Florette. 1975. *Black Migration: Movement North 1900–1920*. New York: Anchor Press.

Higgs, Robert. 1976. "The Boll Weevil, the Cotton Economy, and Black Migration, 1910–1930." *Agricultural History* 50.2: 335–50.

————. 1977a. "Firm-Specific Evidence on Racial Wage Differentials and Workforce Segregation." *American Economic Review* 67.2: 236–45.

————. 1977b. *Competition and Coercion: Blacks in the American Economy, 1865–1914*. Cambridge: Cambridge University Press.

Hill, Matthew J. 2013. "Homes and Husbands for All: Marriage, Housing, and the Baby Boom." Manuscript.

Hillier, Amy E. 2003. "Redlining and the Home Owners' Loan Corporation." *Journal of Urban History* 29.4: 394–420.

Hine, Darlene Clark. 1991. "Black Migration to the Urban Midwest: The Gender Dimension, 1915–1945." In *The Great Migration in Historical Perspective: New Dimensions of Race, Class, and Gender*, ed. Joe William Trotter Jr., 127–46. Bloomington: Indiana University Press.

Hirsch, Arnold R. 1983. *Making the Second Ghetto: Race and Housing in Chicago, 1940–1960*. Cambridge: Cambridge University Press.

Hopkins, Daniel J. 2009. "The Diversity Discount: When Increasing Ethnic and Racial Diversity Prevents Tax Increases." *Journal of Politics* 71.1: 160–77.

Hornbeck, Richard, and Suresh Naidu. 2014. "When the Levee Breaks: Black Migration and Economic Development in the American South." *American Economic Review* 104.3: 963–90.

Ihlanfeldt, Keith R. 2004. "Exclusionary Land-Use Regulations within Suburban Communities: A Review of the Evidence and Policy Prescriptions." *Urban Studies* 41.2: 261–83.

Ihlanfeldt, Keith R., and Benjamin Scafidi. 2002. "Black Self-Segregation as a Cause of Housing Segregation: Evidence from the Multi-City Study of Urban Inequality." *Journal of Urban Economics* 51.2: 366–90.

International Trade Administration. 2010. "The State of Manufacturing in the United States." http://trade.gov/manufactureamerica/facts/tg_mana _003019.asp.

Jackson, Kenneth T. 1985. *Crabgrass Frontier: The Suburbanization of the United States*. New York: Oxford University Press.

Jackson, Shawn L. 2010. "An Historical Analysis of the Chicago Public Schools Desegregation Consent Decree (1980–2006): Establishing Its Relationship with the *Brown v. Board* Case of 1954 and the Implications of Its Implementation on Educational Leadership." PhD diss., Loyola University Chicago.

Jasso, Guillermina, and Mark R. Rosenzweig. 1988. "How Well Do U.S. Immigrants Do? Vintage Effects, Emigration Selectivity, and Occupational Mobility." *Research in Population Economics* 6: 229–53.

Jaworski, Taylor. 2014. "World War II and the Industrialization of the American South." Manuscript.

Johnson, Daniel Milo, and Rex R. Campbell. 1981. *Black Migration in America: A Social Demographic History*. Durham, NC: Duke University Press.

Johnson, Kenneth M., Paul R. Voss, Roger B. Hammer, Glenn V. Fuguitt, and Scott McNiven. 2005. "Temporal and Spatial Variation in Age-Specific Net Migration in the United States." *Demography* 42.4: 791–812.

Jones, Jacqueline. 1985. *Labor of Love, Labor of Sorrow: Black Women, Work, and the Family, From Slavery to the Present*. New York: Basic Books.

Jones-Correa, Michael. 2000. "The Origins and Diffusion of Racial Restrictive Covenants." *Political Science Quarterly* 115.4: 541–68.

Kain, John F., and Joseph Persky. 1968. *The North's Stake in Southern Rural Poverty*. Cambridge, MA: Harvard University Press.

Kain, John F., and John M. Quigley. 1972. "Housing Market Discrimination, Home Ownership, and Savings Behavior." *American Economic Review* 62.3: 263–77.

Kane, Thomas J., Stephanie Riegg, and Douglas O. Staiger. 2006. "School Quality, Neighborhoods, and Housing Prices." *American Law and Economics Review* 8.2: 183–212.

Kane, Thomas J., Douglas O. Staiger, Gavin Samms, Edward W. Hill, and David L. Weimer. 2003. "School Accountability Ratings and Housing Values." *Brookings-Wharton Papers on Urban Affairs:* 83–138.

Katz, Lawrence F., and Kevin M. Murphy. 1992. "Changes in Relative Wages, 1963–1987: Supply and Demand Factors." *Quarterly Journal of Economics* 107.1: 35–78.

Katznelson, Ira. 2005. *When Affirmative Action Was White: An Untold History of Racial Inequality in Twentieth-Century America*. New York: W. W. Norton.

Keating, Ann Durkin. 1988. *Building Chicago: Suburban Developers and the Creation of a Divided Metropolis*. Columbus: Ohio State University Press.

Kefalas, Maria. 2003. *Working-Class Heroes: Protecting Home, Community, and Nation in a Chicago Neighborhood*. Berkeley: University of California Press.

Keil, Charles. 1966. *Urban Blues*. Chicago: University of Chicago Press.

Kennan, John, and James R. Walker. 2011. "The Effect of Expected Income on Individual Migration Decisions." *Econometrica* 79.1: 211–51.

Kerner Commission. 1968. Report of the National Advisory Commission on Civil Disorders. Washington, DC: U.S. GPO.

King, A. Thomas, and Peter Mieszkowski. 1973. "Racial Discrimination, Segregation, and the Price of Housing." *Journal of Political Economy* 81.3: 590–606.

Kirby, Jack Temple. 1983. "The Southern Exodus, 1910–1960: A Primer for Historians." *Journal of Southern History* 49.4: 585–600.

Kousser, J. Morgan. 1974. *The Shaping of Southern Politics: Suffrage Restriction and the Establishment of the One-Party South, 1880–1910*. New Haven: Yale University Press.

Krueger, Alan B., and Diane M. Whitmore. 2001. "The Effect of Attending a Small Class in the Early Grades on College-Test Taking and Middle School Test Results: Evidence from Project STAR." *Economic Journal* 111: 1–28.

Kruse, Kevin. 2005. *White Flight: Atlanta and the Making of Modern Conservatism*. Princeton: Princeton University Press.

Krysan, Maria, Mick P. Couper, Reynolds Farley, and Tyrone Forman. 2009. "Does Race Matter in Neighborhood Preferences? Results from a Video Experiment." *American Journal of Sociology* 115.2: 527–59.

Kucheva, Yana, and Richard Sander. 2014. "The Misunderstood Consequences of *Shelley v. Kraemer*." *Social Science History* 48: 212–33.

Kusmer, Kenneth L. 1976. *A Ghetto Takes Shape: Black Cleveland, 1870–1930*. Champaign: University of Illinois Press.

———. 1995. "African Americans in the City since World War II: From the Industrial to the Post-industrial Era." *Journal of Urban History* 21.4: 458–504.

Kuznets, Simon, and Dorothy Swaine Thomas, eds. 1957. *Population Redistribution and Economic Growth: United States, 1870–1950*. Vol. 1. Philadelphia: American Philosophical Society.

Lamb, Charles M. 2005. *Housing Segregation in Suburban America since 1960: Presidential and Judicial Politics*. New York: Cambridge University Press.

Lang, Kevin, and Jee-Yeon K. Lehmann. 2012. "Racial Discrimination in the Labor Market: Theory and Empirics." *Journal of Economic Literature* 50.4: 959–1006.

Lange, Fabian, Alan L. Olmstead, and Paul W. Rhode. 2009. "The Impact of the Boll Weevil, 1892–1932." *Journal of Economic History* 69.3: 685–718.

Lebergott, Stanley. 1964. *Manpower in Economic Growth: The American Record since 1800*. New York: McGraw-Hill.

Leinberger, Christopher B. 2008. "The Next Slum?" *Atlantic Monthly*, March.

Lemann, Nicholas. 1991. *The Promised Land: The Great Black Migration and How It Changed America*. New York: Alfred A. Knopf.

LeRoy, Stephen F., and Jon Sonstelie. 1983. "Paradise Lost and Regained: Transportation Innovation, Income and Residential Location." *Journal of Urban Economics* 13.1: 67–89.

Lewis, Edward E. (1931) 1968. *The Mobility of the Negro: A Study in the American Labor Supply*. New York: AMS Press.

Lieberson, Stanley. 1978. "A Reconsideration of the Income Differences Found between Migrants and Northern-Born Blacks." *American Journal of Sociology* 83.4: 940–66.

———. 1980. *A Piece of the Pie: Blacks and White Immigrants since 1880*. Berkeley: University of California Press.

Lieberson, Stanley, and Christy A. Wilkinson. 1976. "A Comparison between Northern and Southern Blacks Residing in the North." *Demography* 13.2: 199–224.

Logan, John R., and Brian J. Stults. 2011. "The Persistence of Segregation in the Metropolis: New Findings from the 2010 Census." Census Brief prepared for Project US2010. http://www.s4.brown.edu/us2010.

Logan, Trevon D. 2009. "Health, Human Capital, and African-American Migration Before 1910." *Explorations in Economic History* 46.2: 169–185.

Long, Larry H. 1974. "Poverty Status and Receipt of Welfare among Migrants and Non-Migrants in Large Cities." *American Sociological Review* 39.1: 46–56.

Long, Larry H., and Kristin A. Hansen. 1975. "Trends in Return Migration to the South." *Demography* 12.4: 601–14.

Long, Larry H., and Lynne R. Heltman. 1975. "Migration and Income Differences between Black and White Men in the North." *American Journal of Sociology* 80.6: 1391–1409.

Lubotsky, Darren. 2007. "Chutes or Ladders? A Longitudinal Analysis of Immigrant Earnings." *Journal of Political Economy* 115.5: 820–67.

Luttmer, Erzo F. P. 2001. "Group Loyalty and the Taste for Redistribution." *Journal of Political Economy* 109.3: 500–528.

Lutz, Byron F. 2008. "The Connection Between House Price Appreciation and Property Tax Revenues." *National Tax Journal* 61.3: 555–72.

———. 2011. "The End of Court-Ordered Desegregation." *American Economic Journal: Economic Policy* 3.2: 130–68.

MacDonald, John S., and Leatrice D. MacDonald. 1964. "Chain Migration, Ethnic Neighborhood Formation and Social Networks." *Milbank Memorial Fund Quarterly* 42.1: 82–97.

Machin, Stephen, and Kjell G. Salvanes. 2016. "Valuing School Quality via a School Choice Reform." *Scandinavian Journal of Economics* 118.1: 3–24.

Madden, Janice Fanning. 2003. "The Changing Spatial Concentration of Income and Poverty among Suburbs of Large US Metropolitan Areas." *Urban Studies* 40.3: 481–503.

Maloney, Thomas N. 1994. "Wage Compression and Wage Inequality Between Black and White Males in the United States, 1940–1960." *Journal of Economic History* 54.2: 358–81.

———. 2001. "Migration and Economic Opportunity in the 1910s: New Evidence on African-American Occupational Mobility in the North." *Explorations in Economic History* 38.1: 147–65.

Maloney, Thomas N., and Warren C. Whatley. 1995. "Making the Effort: The

Contours of Racial Discrimination in Detroit's Labor Markets, 1920–1940." *Journal of Economic History* 55.3: 465–93.

Margo, Robert A. 1986. "Race, Educational Attainment, and the 1940 Census." *Journal of Economic History* 46.1: 189–98.

———. 1988. "Schooling and the Great Migration." NBER Working Paper w2697.

———. 1990. *Race and Schooling in the South, 1880–1950: An Economic History.* Chicago: University of Chicago Press.

———. 1992. "Explaining the Postwar Suburbanization of Population in the United States: The Role of Income." *Journal of Urban Economics* 31.3: 301–10.

———. 1995. "Explaining Black-White Wage Convergence, 1940–1950." *Industrial and Labor Relations Review* 48.3: 470–81.

———. 2004. "The North-South Wage Gap, Before and After the Civil War." In *Slavery in the Development of the Americas*, ed. David Eltis, Frank D. Lewis, and Kenneth L. Sokoloff, 324–52. New York: Cambridge University Press.

Marks, Carole. 1989. *Farewell—We're Good and Gone: The Great Black Migration.* Bloomington: University of Indiana Press.

Marshall, Harvey. 1979. "White Movement to the Suburbs: A Comparison of Explanations." *American Sociological Review* 44.6: 975–94.

Martin, Douglas. 1987. "Fence Is Not Neighborly in a Suburb of Cleveland." *New York Times*, June 27.

Massey, Douglas S., and Nancy A. Denton. 1993. *American Apartheid: Segregation and the Making of the Underclass.* Cambridge, MA: Harvard University Press.

Massey, Douglas S., and Jonathan Rothwell. 2009. "The Effect of Density Zoning on Racial Segregation in U.S. Urban Areas." *Urban Affairs Review* 44.6: 779–806.

Masters, Stanley H. 1972. "Are Black Migrants from the South to the Northern Cities Worse Off than Blacks Already There?" *Journal of Human Resources* 7.4: 411–23.

McCabe, Kristen. 2011. "Caribbean Immigrants in the United States." Migration Policy Institute. http://www.migrationpolicy.org/article/caribbean-immigrants-united-states#2.

McGirr, Lisa. 2012. "The New Suburban Poverty." *New York Times*, March 19.

Medina, Jennifer. 2014. "Hardship Makes a New Home in the Suburbs." *New York Times*, May 9.

Mettler, Suzanne. 2005. *Soldiers to Citizens: The GI Bill and the Making of the Greatest Generation.* New York: Oxford University Press.

Meyer, Stephen Grant. 2001. *As Long As They Don't Move Next Door: Segregation and Racial Conflict in American Neighborhoods.* New York: Rowman and Littlefield.

Mieszkowski, Peter, and Edwin S. Mills. 1993. "The Causes of Metropolitan Suburbanization." *Journal of Economic Perspectives* 7.3: 135–47.

Mills, Edwin S. 1972. *Studies in the Structure of the Urban Economy.* Baltimore: Johns Hopkins Press.

Minnesota Population Center. 2011. *National Historical Geographic Information System: Version 2.0.* Minneapolis: University of Minnesota Press [machine-readable database].

Modell, John, Marc Goulden, and Sigurdur Magnusson. 1989. "World War II in the Lives of Black Americans: Some Findings and an Interpretation." *Journal of American History* 76.3: 838–48.

Montgomery, James D. 1991. "Social Networks and Labor Market Outcomes: Toward an Economic Analysis." *American Economic Review* 81.5: 1408–18.

Morton, J. E. 1956. *Urban Mortgage Lending: Comparative Markets and Experience.* Princeton: Princeton University Press.

Moss, Philip, and Chris Tilly. 2001. *Stories Employers Tell: Race, Skill, and Hiring in America.* New York: Russell Sage Foundation.

Mueller-Smith, Michael. 2015. "The Criminal and Labor Market Impacts of Incarceration." Manuscript.

Munshi, Kaivan. 2003. "Networks in the Modern Economy: Mexican Migrants in the U.S. Labor Market." *Quarterly Journal of Economics* 118.2: 549–99.

Muth, Richard F. 1969. *Cities and Housing: The Spatial Pattern of Urban Residential Land Use.* Chicago: University of Chicago Press.

Myrdal, Gunnar. (1944) 1962. *An American Dilemma, Volume 2: The Negro Problem and Modern Democracy.* New York: Harper and Row.

Naidu, Suresh. 2010. "Recruitment Restrictions and Labor Markets: Evidence from the Postbellum U.S. South." *Journal of Labor Economics* 28.2: 413–45.

Nall, Hiram. 2001. "From Down South to Up South: An Examination of Geography in the Blues." *Midwest Quarterly* 42.3: 306–19.

Neal, Derek A. 2006. "Why Has Black-White Skill Convergence Stopped?" In *Handbook of Economics of Education Volume 1*, ed. Eric A. Hanushek and Finis Welch, 511–76. Amsterdam: Elsevier.

Neal, Derek A., and William R. Johnson. 1996. "The Role of Pre-Market Factors in Black-White Wage Differences." *Journal of Political Economy* 104.5: 869–95.

Nelson, Bruce. 2001. *Divided We Stand: American Workers and the Struggle for Black Equality.* Princeton: Princeton University Press.

Norris, Bruce. 2011. *Clybourne Park.* New York: Faber and Faber.

Nye, John V. C., Ilia Rainer, and Thomas Stratmann. 2010. "Do Black Mayors Improve Black Employment Outcomes? Evidence from Large U.S. Cities." Manuscript.

Oliver, Pamela E. 2001. "Racial Disparities in Imprisonment: Some Basic Information." *Focus: Newsletter of the Institute for Research on Poverty at the University of Wisconsin-Madison* 21.3: 28–31.

Olmstead, Alan L., and Paul W. Rhode. 2008. *Creating Abundance: Biological Innovation and American Agricultural Development.* New York: Cambridge University Press.

Orfield, Gary, and Susan Eaton. 1996. *Dismantling Desegregation: The Quiet Reversal of Brown v. Board of Education.* New York: The New Press.

Osofsky, Gilbert. (1966) 1996. *Harlem, The Making of a Ghetto: Negro New York, 1890–1930.* Chicago: Ivan R. Dee.

Ottaviano, Gianmarco, and Giovanni Peri. 2012. "Rethinking the Effect of Immigration on Wages." *Journal of the European Economic Association* 10.1: 152–97.

Ouazad, Amine. 2015. "Brokers and the Dynamics of Segregation." *Journal of Economic Theory* 157: 811–41.

Pager, Devah. 2003. "The Mark of a Criminal Record." *American Journal of Sociology* 108.5: 937–75.

Pager, Devah, Bruce Western, and Bart Bonikowski. 2009. "Discrimination in a Low-Wage Labor Market: A Field Experiment." *American Sociological Review* 74.5: 777–99.

Painter, Nell Irvin. 1976. *Exodusters: Black Migration to Kansas after Reconstruction.* New York: Alfred A. Knopf.

Park, Robert Ezra, and Herbert Adolphus Miller. 1921. *Old World Traits Transplanted.* New York: Harper and Brothers.

Pendall, Rolf. 2000. "Local Land Use Regulation and the Chain of Exclusion." *Journal of the American Planning Association* 66.2: 125–42.

Peri, Giovanni, and Chad Sparber. 2009. "Task Specialization, Immigration, and Wages." *American Economic Journal: Applied Economics* 1.3: 135–69.

Pew Charitable Trusts. 2010. *Collateral Costs: Incarceration's Effect on Economic Mobility.* Washington, DC: Pew Charitable Trusts.

Phelps, Edmund S. 1972. "The Statistical Theory of Racism and Sexism." *American Economic Review* 62.4: 659–661.

Phillips, Kimberley L. 1999. *AlabamaNorth: African-American Migrants, Community, and Working Class Activism in Cleveland, 1915–45.* Champaign: University of Illinois Press.

Philpott, Thomas Lee. 1978. *The Slum and the Ghetto: Neighborhood Deterioration and Middle-Class Reform, Chicago, 1880–1930.* New York: Oxford University Press.

Plotkin, Wendy. 1999. "Deeds of Mistrust: Racial Restrictive Covenants in Chicago, 1900–1953." PhD diss., University of Illinois, Chicago.

Potepan, Michael. 1994. "Inter-Metropolitan Migration and Housing Prices: Simultaneously Determined?" *Journal of Housing Economics* 3.2: 77–91.

Quillian, Lincoln, and Devah Pager. 2001. "Black Neighbors, Higher Crime? The Role of Racial Stereotypes in Evaluations of Neighborhood Crime." *American Journal of Sociology* 107.3: 717–67.

Ramirez, Francisco O., and John Boli. 1987. "The Political Construction of Mass Schooling: European Origins and Worldwide Institutionalization." *Sociology of Education* 60.1: 2–17.

Ransom, Roger L., and Richard Sutch. 1977. *One Kind of Freedom: The Economic Consequences of Emancipation.* Cambridge: Cambridge University Press.

Rappaport, Jordan. 2003. "U.S. Urban Decline and Growth, 1950–2000." *Federal Reserve Bank of Kansas City Economic Review* 29.3: 15–44.

Reback, Randall. 2005. "House Prices and the Provision of Local Public Services: Capitalization Under School Choice Programs." *Journal of Urban Economics* 57.2: 275–301.

Reber, Sarah J. 2005. "Court-Ordered Desegregation: Successes and Failures in Integration since Brown." *Journal of Human Resources* 40.3: 559–90.

Roediger, David. 1991. *The Wages of Whiteness: Race and the Making the American Working Class.* London: Verso.

Rosen, Sherwin. 1974. "Hedonic Prices and Implicit Markets: Product Differentiation in Pure Competition." *Journal of Political Economy* 82.1: 34–55.

Rosenbloom, Joshua L. and William A. Sundstrom. 2004. "The Decline and Rise of Interstate Migration in the United States: Evidence from the IPUMS, 1850–1990." *Research in Economic History* 22: 289–325.

Roy, Andrew D. 1951. "Some Thoughts on the Distribution of Earnings." *Oxford Economic Papers* 3.2: 135–46.

Royster, Deirdre A. 2003. *Race and the Invisible Hand: How White Networks Exclude Black Men from Blue-Collar Jobs*. Berkeley: University of California Press.

Ruggles, Steven. 1997. "The Effects of AFDC on American Family Structure, 1940–1990." *Journal of Family History* 22.3: 307–25.

Ruggles, Steven, Matthew Sobek, Trent Alexander, Catherine A. Fitch, Ronald Goeken, Patricia Kelly Hall, Miriam King, and Chad Ronnander. 2008. "Integrated Public Use Microdata Series: Version 4.0" Minneapolis: Minnesota Population Center [machine-readable database].

Saiz, Albert. 2003. "Room in the Kitchen for the Melting Pot: Immigration and Rental Prices." *Review of Economics and Statistics* 85.3: 502–521.

———. 2007. "Immigration and Housing Rents in American Cities." *Journal of Urban Economics* 61.2: 345–71.

Saiz, Albert, and Susan Wachter. 2011. "Immigration and the Neighborhood." *American Economic Journal: Economic Policy* 3.2: 169–88.

Saltzstein, Grace Hall. 1989. "Black Mayors and Police Policies." *The Journal of Politics* 51.3: 525–44.

Sampson, Robert J., and Stephen W. Raudenbush. 2004. "Seeing Disorder: Neighborhood Stigma and the Social Construction of 'Broken Windows.'" *Social Psychology Quarterly* 67.4: 319–42.

Satter, Beryl. 2009. *Family Properties: Race, Real Estate, and the Exploitation of Black Urban America*. New York: Picador.

Schelling, Thomas C. 1971. "Dynamic Models of Segregation." *Journal of Mathematical Sociology* 1.2:143–86.

Schneider, Jack. 2008. "Escape from Los Angeles: White Flight from Los Angeles and Its Schools, 1960–80." *Journal of Urban History* 34.6: 995–1012.

Schulman, Bruce J. 1994. *From Cotton Belt to Sunbelt: Federal Policy, Economic Development, and the Transformation of the South, 1938–1980*. Durham, NC: Duke University Press.

Scott, Emmett J. 1919a. "Letters of Negro Migrants of 1916–1918." *Journal of Negro History* 4.3: 290–340.

———. 1919b. "More Letters of Negro Migrants of 1916–1918." *Journal of Negro History* 4.4: 412–65.

Self, Robert O. 2003. *American Babylon: Race and the Struggle for Postwar Oakland*. Princeton: Princeton University Press.

Seligman, Amanda I. 2005. *Block by Block: Neighborhoods and Public Policy on Chicago's West Side*. Chicago: University of Chicago Press.

Shertzer, Allison, and Randall P. Walsh. 2014. "The Dynamics of White Flight and Segregation in Urbanizing America." Manuscript.

Sides, Josh. 2003. *LA City Limits: African American Los Angeles from the Great Depression to the Present*. Berkeley: University of California Press.

Sjaastad, Larry A. 1962. "The Costs and Returns of Human Migration." *Journal of Political Economy* 70.5: 80–93.

Smith, James P. 1984. "Race and Human Capital." *American Economic Review* 74.4: 685–98.

Smith, James P., and Finis Welch. 1989. "Black Economic Progress after Myrdal." *Journal of Economic Literature* 27.2: 519–64.

Sokol, Jason. 2006. *There Goes My Everything: White Southerners in the Age of Civil Rights.* New York: Alfred A. Knopf.

———. 2014. *All Eyes Are Upon Us: Race and Politics from Boston to Brooklyn.* New York: Basic Books.

South, Scott J., and Kyle D. Crowder. 1997. "Escaping Distressed Neighborhoods: Individual, Community and Metropolitan Areas." *American Journal of Sociology* 103.4: 1040–84.

———. 1998. "Leaving the 'Hood: Residential Mobility between Black, White and Integrated Neighborhoods." *American Sociological Review* 104.1: 17–26.

Spear, Allan H. 1967. *Black Chicago: The Making of a Negro Ghetto, 1890–1920.* Chicago: University of Chicago Press.

Spencer, Jon Michael. 1992. "The Diminishing Rural Residue of Folklore in City and Urban Blues, Chicago 1915–1950." *Black Music Research Journal* 12.1: 25–41.

Spero, Sterling Denhard, and Abram Lincoln Harris. 1931. *The Black Worker: The Negro and the Labor Movement.* New York: Columbia University Press.

Steckel, Richard H. 1983. "The Economic Foundations of East-West Migration during the Nineteenth Century." *Explorations in Economic History* 20.1: 14–36.

Stuart, Bryan A., and Evan J. Taylor. 2014. "Social Interactions and Location Decisions: Evidence from U.S. Mass Migration." Manuscript.

Sugrue, Thomas J. 1996. *The Origins of the Urban Crisis: Race and Inequality in Postwar Detroit.* Princeton: Princeton University Press.

———. 2008. *Sweet Land of Liberty: The Forgotten Struggle for Civil Rights in the North.* New York: Random House.

Sundstrom, William A. 1994. "The Color Line: Racial Norms and Discrimination in Urban Labor Markets, 1910–1950." *Journal of Economic History* 54.2: 382–96.

———. 2000. "From Servants to Secretaries: The Occupations of African-American Women, 1940–80." Manuscript.

———. 2007. "The Geography of Wage Discrimination in the Pre–Civil Rights South." *Journal of Economic History* 67.2: 410–44.

Taeuber, Konrad E., and Alma F. Taeuber. 1965. *Negros in Cities: Residential Segregation and Neighborhood Change.* Chicago: Aldine Publishing Company.

Thernstrom, Stephan, and Abigail Thernstrom. 1997. *America in Black and White: One Nation, Indivisible.* New York: Simon and Schuster.

Tiebout, Charles M. 1956. "A Pure Theory of Local Expenditures." *Journal of Political Economy* 64.5: 416–24.

Tolnay, Stewart E. 1998. "Educational Selection in the Migration of Southern Blacks, 1880–1990." *Social Forces* 77.2: 487–514.

———. 2001. "The Great Migration Gets Underway: A Comparison of Black Southern Migrants and Nonmigrants in the North, 1920." *Social Science Quarterly* 82.2: 235–52.

———. 2003. "The African American 'Great Migration' and Beyond." *Annual Review of Sociology* 29: 209–33.

Tolnay, Stewart E., and E. M. Beck. 1995. *A Festival of Violence: An Analysis of Southern Lynchings, 1882–1930.* Champaign: University of Illinois Press.

Trotter Jr., Joe William. 1985. *Black Milwaukee: The Making of an Industrial Proletariat, 1915–1945.* Champaign: University of Illinois Press.

Turner, Matthew A., Andrew Haughwout, and Wilbert van der Klaauw. 2014. "Land Use Regulation and Welfare." *Econometrica* 82.4: 1341–1403.

U.S. Bureau of the Census. 1943. "16th Census of the United States: 1940, Internal Migration, 1935–40." Washington, DC: GPO.

———. 1962. "18th Census of the United States: 1960 Geographic Mobility for Metropolitan Areas." Washington, DC: GPO.

———. 1962, 1972. "18th and 19th Census of Housing: 1960, 1970. Various cities by census tracts and blocks." Washington, DC: GPO.

———. 1972a. "Census of Governments, 1972." Washington., DC: GPO.

———. 1972b. "19th Census of the United States: 1970 Geographic Mobility for Metropolitan Areas." Washington, DC: GPO.

———. 2012. "County and City Data Book Consolidated File: County Data, 1947–1977." ICPSR Study No. 7736. Ann Arbor, MI: Inter-university Consortium for Political and Social Research [computer file].

U.S. Department of Agriculture. 2005. "National Agricultural Statistical Service." http://www.nass.usda.gov/Data_and_Statistics/index.asp.

U.S. Department of Education. 2003. "Elementary and Secondary General Information System (ELSEGIS): Public Elementary-Secondary School Systems—Finances, Various Years." Ann Arbor, MI: Inter-university Consortium for Political and, Social Research [computer file].

Van Leeuwen, Marco H. D., and Ineke Maas. 2005. "A Short Note on HISCLASS." http://historyofwork. iisg. nl/docs/hisclass-brief.doc.

Vickery, William Edward. 1977. *The Economics of the Negro Migration: 1900–1960.* New York: Arno Press.

Vigdor, Jacob L. 2002. "The Pursuit of Opportunity: Explaining Selective Black Migration." *Journal of Urban Economics* 51.3: 391–417.

———. 2006. "The New Promised Land: Black-White Convergence in the American South, 1960–2000." NBER Working Paper w12143.

Warner, Sam Bass. 1978. *Streetcar Suburbs: The Process of Growth in Boston, 1870–1900.* Cambridge, MA: Harvard University Press.

Webb, Clive. 2005. *Massive Resistance: Southern Opposition to the Second Reconstruction.* New York: Oxford University Press.

Welch, Finis. 1979. "Effects of Cohort Size on Earnings: The Baby Boom Babies' Financial Bust." *Journal of Political Economy* 87.5: S65–S97.

Welch, Finis, and Audrey Light. 1987. *New Evidence on School Desegregation.* Washington, DC: U.S. Commission on Civil Rights.

Western, Bruce. 2002. "The Impact of Incarceration on Wage Mobility and Inequality." *American Sociological Review* 67.4: 526–46.

Westhoff, Frank. 1977. "Existence of Equilibria in Economies with a Local Public Good." *Journal of Economic Theory* 14.1: 84–112.

Whatley, Warren C. 1983. "Labor for the Picking: The New Deal in the South." *Journal of Economic History* 43.4: 905–929.

———. 1990. "Getting a Foot in the Door: Learning, State Dependence, and the Racial Integration of Firms." *Journal of Economic History* 50.1: 43–66.

Wheaton, William C. 1993. "Land Capitalization, Tiebout Mobility, and the Role of Zoning Regulations." *Journal of Urban Economics* 34.2: 102–17.

White, Katherine J. Curtis. 2005. "Women in the Great Migration: Economic Activity of Black and White Southern-Born Female Migrants in 1920, 1940 and 1970." *Social Science History* 29.3: 413–55.

White, Katherine J. Curtis, Kyle Crowder, Stewart E. Tolnay, and Robert M. Adelman. 2005. "Race, Gender, and Marriage: Destination Selection during the Great Migration." *Demography* 42.2: 215–41.

Whitman, David. 1991. "The Great Sharecropper Success Story." *Public Interest* 104: 3–19.

Wiese, Andrew. 2005. *Places of Their Own: African American Suburbanization in the Twentieth Century*. Chicago: University of Chicago Press.

Wilkerson, Isabel. 2010. *The Warmth of Other Suns: The Epic Story of America's Great Migration*. New York: Random House.

Wilson, August. 1991. *Three Plays*. Pittsburgh: University of Pittsburgh Press.

Wilson, William Julius. 1987. *The Truly Disadvantaged*. Chicago: University of Chicago Press.

Woodson, Carter G. (1918) 1970. *A Century of Negro Migration*. New York: AMS Press.

Woodson, Jacqueline. 2014. *Brown Girl Dreaming*. New York: Nancy Paulsen Books.

Woodward, C. Vann. (1955) 1981. *Origins of the New South, 1877–1913: A History of the South*. Baton Rouge: Louisiana State University Press.

Wright, Gavin. 1978. *The Political Economy of the Cotton South: Households, Markets, and Wealth in the Nineteenth Century*. New York: W.W. Norton & Co.

———. 1986. *Old South, New South: Revolutions in the Southern Economy Since the Civil War*. New York: Basic Books.

———. 2013. *Sharing the Prize: The Economics of the Civil Rights Revolution in the American South*. Cambridge, MA: Harvard University Press.

Yockelson, Mitchell. 1998. "They Answered the Call: Military Service in the United States Army during World War I, 1917–1919." *Prologue: Quarterly of the National Archives* 30.3: 228–34.

Index

schools); statistical, 71, 73–74; veteran
benefits and, 99n11; violence and, 27;
voting and, 27
disenfranchisement, 1
dissimilarity index, 97, 98n9, 158, 163
dropouts, 160
Du Bois, W. E. B., 11

earnings penalty, 41, 43, 55, 60, 156
Easterly, William, 131
education: birth cohorts and, 79–80;
Brown v. Board of Education and,
142n23; Census data and, 45–46, 56;
coastal cities and, 162; cognitive skills
and, 160–61; college, 79, 124, 133n13,
135, 140–41, *152*; competition and, 67–
68, 76; dropouts and, 160; GI Bill and,
25n32, 99; high schools, 28n38, 54, 56–
59, 64, 68, 74–76, 79, *113*, 122, 142n22,
160; *Keyes v. Denver* and, 142; labor
and, 3–4, 12, 35, 58, 66–71, 74–76, 79–
80, 88–92; migrant selection and, 40;
migration and, 46, 48, 59; mobility
and, 20n16; North and, 9, 28n38, 41,
45–46, 48, 57, 59, 67–68, 76; rising levels of, 2; schools and, 46 (*see also*
schools); social values and, 48; South
and, 40–41, 44n5, 45, 55, 61; wages
and, 42–43; white flight and, 114,
119n49, 135, 140, 143
Eichenlaub, Suzanne C., 50–51
elasticity of substitution, 76–80, 89–92
Ellen, Ingrid Gould, 96, 129
emancipation, 8–9, 14, 18, 155
Emerson, Michael O., 129
enrollment, *44*, *78*, *83*, 119, 144, 147
Epple, Dennis, 131n11
equality, 2, 20, 30, 43, 73n10
Eriksson, Katherine, 4n7, 49, 55n23, 60n29,
62
estimation bias, 41, 49, 55–62, 87n32, 91
Exoduster movement, 24n27

federal expenditures, 26n34, 27–28, 30, 37,
80, 124, 131, 134–35, 140–42, *152*
Federal Housing Administration (FHA),
100, 105–6

Fences (Wilson), 14
Ferrie, Joseph P., 19–20, 26, 62
fiscal/political channel, 95, 110
fiscal/political interactions: black enclaves
and, 5, 95, 102–4, 119n49, 122, 124–33,
142, 148, 157; block-level data set for,
123, 134–39, 146n33, 149, *153*; court-
ordered desegregation and, 142–47; effects of, 130–42; housing prices and,
131–33, 136–39, 148–50; local public
goods and, 139–42; motivations for
leaving racially segregated cities and,
128–30; racial geography of central cities and, 124–28; white flight and, 122–
50, *151–53*
Fisher Body, 70
floods, 27, 30–32
Florida, 33n51, 159
Fogel, Robert W., 18
Ford Motor Company, 70
Frazier, E. Franklin, 12
Freeman, Richard B., 160
Freund, David M. P., 133

Gardner, John, 87n30
gender, 13, 42, 45
General Motors Company, 70
Georgia, 33n51, 158–59
ghettos, 13, 97n7, 119n45, 126
GI Bill, 25n32, 99
Gill, Flora, 27n37
Gini coefficient, 43, *44*
globalization, 4, 154, 160
Glock, Judge, 100
Goldin, Claudia, 73n12
Gotham, Kevin Fox, 103
Goulden, Marc, 25
graffiti, 128n4
Great Depression, 19n11, 25, 52, 99
Great Migration, 3, 6, 15, 19, 20n16, 27,
28n38, 36, 39n1, 50, 154
Green v. County School Board, 142
Gregory, James N., *22*, 23, 60
Griffin, Farah Jasmine, 30
Grogger, Jeffrey, 43n4, 160
Grossman, James, 3, 28n38, 70, 116n45

Milton Keynes UK
Ingram Content Group UK Ltd.
UKHW011220150624
444218UK00003B/155